THREADS

BY JOHANNA CORNELIA BOONSTRA

Sanibel, FL

"Dear God: The person who prays to you is just a little girl who makes mistakes and has to learn still so much. Please forgive me my sins and teach me to become a better person. Thank you so much for everything You gave me.   Amen."

Note for Librarians: A cataloguing record for this book is available from Library and Archives Canada at www.collectionscanada.ca/amicus/index-e.html
ISBN 1-4120-6929-7

Printed in Victoria, BC, Canada. Printed on paper with minimum 30% recycled fibre. Trafford's print shop runs on "green energy" from solar, wind and other environmentally-friendly power sources.

Offices in Canada, USA, Ireland and UK
This book was published on-demand in cooperation with Trafford Publishing. On-demand publishing is a unique process and service of making a book available for retail sale to the public taking advantage of on-demand manufacturing and Internet marketing. On-demand publishing includes promotions, retail sales, manufacturing, order fulfilment, accounting and collecting royalties on behalf of the author.

Book sales for North America and international:
Trafford Publishing, 6E–2333 Government St.,
Victoria, BC v8t 4p4 CANADA
phone 250 383 6864 (toll-free 1 888 232 4444)
fax 250 383 6804; email to orders@trafford.com
Book sales in Europe:
Trafford Publishing (uk) Limited, 9 Park End Street, 2nd Floor
Oxford, UK 0x1 1нн UNITED KINGDOM
phone 44 (0)1865 722 113 (local rate 0845 230 9601)
facsimile 44 (0)1865 722 868; info.uk@trafford.com
Order online at:
trafford.com/05-1840

10 9 8 7 6 5 4

TABLE OF CONTENTS

Reflections 7

PART 1: CHILDHOOD IN INDONESIA

Forefathers 11
My Parents 15
Meester Cornelis To Fort De Coq 19
Padang Pandjang And Padang 27
First Trip To Holland 1921 33
Magalang And Bandoeng 37
Kota Radja 1925 41
Boeloe Blanc Ara 1926 45
Lhogna 61
Second Trip To Holland: 1927 71
Life In Holland: 1927 77
Father Comes Home: 1930 87
Vacation In Switzerland: 1932 91
Back To The Indies: 1932 Bandoeng 95
A Wild Party 107
Friends In Bandoeng 1931-1933 111
Malang 117
Court Martial 129

PART 2: HOLLAND AND WORLD WAR II

Back To Holland 1936 .135
Bloemendaal. 141
The Invasion Begins. .147
Final Exams. 165
My New Friend Bram .169
My First Job. 175
Enemy Confrontation .181
Hiding And Hunger In 1942 189
Razzia 1943 197
The Wood Stove Adventure 1943 201
My Sister Meta 207
The Last Winter Of Misery 1944 to 1945 215
Liberation And Marriage. 229
Delft 1946. 237
Ingrid: August 4, 1948 243

PART 3: NEW LIFE IN AMERICA

A New Life In America. 253
Eric: February 5, 1952. 261
Our First Home In Sharon 1952 265
The New House 1955 .279
The Joy Of All God's Creatures 285
Amber. 301
Health Or Else 1962 305
Teaching My Love Of Art. 309
Growing With Children. 323
Mrs. Sullivan 331
Ingrid's Wedding: June 15, 1974. 339
Eric Graduates Colby: May 1974 342
Bram Retires, Eric Starts Working, August 1977. 343
Our First Grandchild, Michelle 345

Trouble Comes In Bunches 347
Settling In Sanibel 1981 367
Indonesian Deja Vue 1981 369
Back In Sanibel 373
One More Time To Indonesia 1984 377
Eric's Wedding: September 29, 1984 379
Moving Again! 383
Accident Prone In 1987 387
At Home In Sanibel 391
Keeping A Stiff Upper Lip 395
Notes About My Sister 401
Bram's Illness 405
Memorial Service For Bram B. Boonstra 413
Life Goes On 417
The Fire And Flood: June 2000 419
New Millenium 425
My Philosophy 427
Postlude For Johanna Cornelia Boonstra 431
Mom's Memorial Celebration of Life: April 8, 2006 435

Acknowledgment 444
Forefathers Table 445

THREADS

BY JOHANNA CORNELIA BOONSTRA

REFLECTIONS

The dawn greets me once again with the gentle whisper of the cool morning breeze. Australian pines sway in response and make a soothing sound. Birds cry out, herons, gulls, crows, ospreys and cranes as Sanibel wakes to a new day. My sweet coffee steams up in the humid air. I remember many mornings such as this as I peer into the half-light. I remember from long ago, and I think I hear the chatter of the monkeys high up in the trees, but that was a place far away and long ago. I was born and raised in Indonesia, eighty-nine years ago now. I want to tell you about the chattering monkeys, and about those mornings long ago, and about Indonesia, about the war in Holland, and about coming to America. I want to tell my children and their children, and my friends, while I still can. I want to tell you what my life was like, about what I have learned and experienced. It was all so different then, it seems all so far away now, and yet all is still so fresh in my memory.

PART 1: CHILDHOOD IN INDONESIA

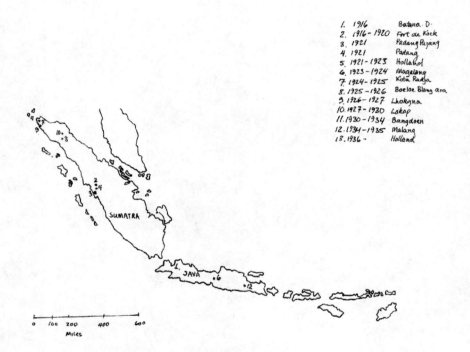

1. 1916   Batavia. D.
2. 1916 - 1920   Fort de Kock
3. 1921   Padang Pajang
4. 1921   Padang
5. 1921 - 1923   Hollahol
6. 1923 - 1924   Magelang
7. 1924 - 1925   Kota Radja
8. 1925 - 1926   Boeloe Blang ara
9. 1926 - 1927   Lhoksna
10. 1927 - 1930 Lokop
11. 1930 - 1934 Bangdoen
12. 1934 - 1935 Malang
13. 1936 -   Holland

FOREFATHERS

Grandmother Johanna was a beautiful woman with long thick blonde hair, which she wore in a braid, accentuating her bright blue eyes and distinguished straight nose. My mother was the image of her, except her hair was dark and her eyes were brown with dark brown specks. I barely remember this grandmother because I only saw her for a short time when I was five years old.

My mother, whose name was Cornelia Johanna, known as "Cor" to us, was born in Maasthuis, a province of south Holland. Her parents were Johanna Cornelia van Rees-Kooreman, and Koenraad Willem (Leo) Kooreman. This was the second marriage for Leo, who had lost his first wife in childbirth. Now he was left raising his surviving son, Jilles, whom we called "Jil", for short. Leo married grandmother when Jilles was five years old.

My maternal grandmother told me that her grandfather was very sick. He owned five farms, but he gambled away his farms somewhere along the way, and ended up having to work as a laborer on one of his own farms. This was such a scandal that his family never forgave him.

My maternal grandfather was a building engineer, well known for constructing bridges and the famous locks of Ymuiden. Queen Wilhelmmina rewarded him with a ribbon, the "Ridder van de Orde van Oranje Nassau". (Knight of the Order of Oranje-Nassau), which was quite an honor. He also taught at the Technical University in

Holland, where he was well thought of and renowned in his own right. I was very proud of him when I knew him better in later years. He had a great sense of humor and was kind and patient. Grandpa, or Opa as we called him, was "Dike Reeve" and always active. I still remembered how he looked in his storm-coat and wide storm hood when he went out to check a dike to see if it was not leaking. You see that same outfit in old Dutch paintings. Even when "Opa" was retired he still would leave the house in a storm to check the dikes. Dutch builders are famous all over the world as builders of water projects. After his retirement he puttered around the house and garden, repairing, making furniture, and tending roses when the weather permitted. I remember the beautiful drawings my grandfather showed me of the bridges he had built. After his death in 1935, at age 78, the drawings disappeared.

His family had come from Spain originally, and in those days when the Spanish occupied our country many Dutch girls married the handsome young Spaniards. In the province of "Zeeland" there are still many people with dark Spanish features. Mother remembered him as being a very kind and gentle brother, whose resemblance was a mirror image of his father. Nobody told him that he had a different birth mother, so he always thought that his stepmother was his own mother. When he was in his early twenties, an aunt told him by accident, the truth about the situation, leaving him in shock. He loved his stepmother so much that he really didn't care that she wasn't his real mother. He became an architect, married, and was sent to Indonesia where he lived and worked for many years.

Mothers two younger brothers were opposites. The older one got in trouble often. For instance, he found a stray dog on a street, brought it home and hid it in the tool shed. When his Mother found the howling dog, she was angry, but felt sorry for it, and let him keep the dog. Soon thereafter, the flower beds and vegetable garden were demolished by the animal, upsetting my Grandmother greatly.

The last brother, the youngest of the five children, was the opposite. He was gentle and his parents were worried that he was "too sweet" for a boy. He was always helping and defending the "underdogs". Once he saw several boys kicking the horse of the vegetable man, who would come to people's homes to sell his produce. My Uncle John could not stand to watch the boys being so cruel. A fight ensued even though he was much smaller than the other boys, and in the end, he was beaten quite badly, coming home with a black eye and a lot of other bruises. At the time Grandmother was not very happy about this son, but later she was proud of his ethics.

In later years John became very religious, always trying to bring peace to the world. Everybody liked him. He was an officer in the Dutch navy, but later he left the navy and started a travel bureau in America. He started this travel business in New York City, and this business prospered for several years. In 1928 he moved his travel business to Chicago, renting a small office on LaSalle, just inside the Loop. He believed that travel should be a personal, and life changing experience, and would only arrange trips for people after he got to know them better. When times were tough, he lived in this office. After marrying at age 93, he passed on when he was 98 years of age.

Mother's sister, Ploon, was one year younger than she, and they were close all their lives.

The Leeksma's, my paternal grandparents, had a happy marriage, but they were also very strict with their children, and the young ones had no say in their future. They were also very strict with Father's sister Louise, which caused her a lot of unhappiness. She fell in love with a young man but her parents told her she was too young to marry, and that she would not be allowed to see her intended for a whole year. Then if she was still in love at that time, permission would be given for them to marry. On the very day the year was up, she received a letter from her beau, telling her that he was going to marry someone else. For many years she lived a sad and secluded life and finally died tragically.

I knew my paternal grandfather only a short time. He was a typical teacher, a kind man who helped me with my schoolwork when I was thirteen. He had been the principal of a school and he knew exactly how to explain to me how to deal with my school problems when I was later teaching art.

I knew my paternal grandmother better, when I came back to Holland from Indonesia. She was a zestful person, very smart and full of life. She loved people and had many friends. She was also very religious which helped give me faith at times. Both my grandmother and mother were accomplished skaters, and once, when they were skating late in 1912, my mother noticed a handsome young man in his military uniform. My Father was impressed as well with the talented twenty three year old. After a short courtship, they were married. My mother was 25, my father 23 years old. On January 1, 1913, they boarded a ship to Indonesia. The whole family was happy for them, but sad about their leaving so suddenly.

MY PARENTS

My mother was the first born of grandfather's second marriage. More children followed, two boys and two girls. Mother told me that she was born after a very difficult delivery. The midwife thought she was stillborn so she put the new baby in a corner of the room and treated my grandmother, who was in critical condition. Just when my grandmother started feeling better, a loud cry was heard from the corner of the room, and the baby, who was thought to be dead, let everyone know she was alive and kicking.

Mother's was always telling me stories about her youth, how wonderful her parents were and how proud she was of them, how handsome they looked. All the children got along well. Mother's sister, was 18 months younger, and the two took full advantage of their beauty in their twenties. In later years, they told me of their trysts. They were close all their lives.

When mother was in her teens the family moved from "Den Helder" to Kampen, near a large river called the "Ysel". In wintertime it was fun when the Ysel river froze over. Everybody went skating. This scene is depicted in the landscape of many an "old Dutch Master" painting. Young and old alike push chairs in front of them to learn to skate. Dogs run back and forth, and men with long handled brooms, push the snow off the ice, into piles, alongside the skating area.

There was one problem though, that plagued my mothers family. Her grandmother suffered migraines, and had to stay in bed for days at a time. In addition, she had very high blood pressure and in those days medical science could not do much about it.

When mother was fourteen, something happened which had quite an impact on her. One evening her Father asked her to put a letter in the mailbox for him. It was early evening in what was considered to be a safe neighborhood. Mother went down the street, mailed the letter, and was running back when suddenly, a man came out of the shadows and jumped her. He pulled her down and tried to rip off her pants. She was petrified. She screamed and kicked at her assailant. Luckily she managed to free herself and run home, shocked and ashamed. She never told her parents, which was, of course, quite stupid. Later she found out that the man who had attacked her was the hired hand of a farmer who lived nearby. After that, she was very careful not to go out alone at night, and for the rest of her life she insisted that her home be locked up before dark. When we stayed in a hotel, without my Father, she would put a chair in front of the door.

Most of my mothers youth was spent in "Den Helders", which was near the sea in the province of North Holland. When storms were raging, especially in the wintertime, my Grandfather would put on his storm coat and hat, leaving his house for many hours at a time to inspect the dikes. When he discovered a crack or weak spot, he would summon men to help put sandbags where the trouble was, to hold back the stormy sea.

The winter of 1912 was very cold. The skating conditions were superb. Mother and her family went skating on the Ysel one nice afternoon and were having a lot of fun. Many of their friends were there, and when they tired, they would buy hot chocolate from the small booth on the ice, sipping the warming beverage as they rested at the river's edge. Several young cadets from the nearby military academy were there also, skating while keeping an eye on the girls around them. When they mustered up enough courage, they would ask a girl to skate with them, and that's how my parents met. They were a handsome pair. Soon afterwards they started dating, became engaged, and were married three months later.

Soon after my Father's graduation, he joined the infantry division of the Dutch East Indies army, and it soon became clear that they would be transferred to Indonesia. Their marriage took place in January of 1913, and my grandparents were quite sad because they knew that soldiers only got a furlough to come home every six years. That meant they wouldn't be seeing each other for a long time. Soon afterward, mothers sister also married an army man, and she also moved to Indonesia, leaving my grandparents even more distraught.

Before I describe my parents' life together, I must tell you of my Father's life before he met my mother Cornelia. Father was born in 1891 and had one sister and one brother. His father was the principal of a school, a good man, who was liked by his students and colleagues alike. His wife was one of ten children and her father owned a large farm. Eight of the children died before they reached adulthood, mostly from tuberculosis. Only two survived, but they were made of strong stock, and, remarkably, both lived to age ninety-six.

Father was the youngest child in his family. He had a sister Louise, six years older and a brother Henk, three years older, but Leo had a brilliant mind, and was the smartest of the three. He was such a talented musician, his uncle, his mothers brother, offered to pay his way through the conservatory, but his parents negated this, as it couldn't afford him a stable living. They also ignored the fact that he wanted to become a doctor. They allowed his older brother to study medicine instead because there was only enough money for one child to go to college. In those days, it was the custom that the first-born son inherited everything from the parents, and the younger sons had to fend for themselves. This is why Father was pushed into the army, against his will at age 15. It was not until many years later that Father told me that he never really wanted to be a military man. It seemed cruel of my grandparents to have forced him into this, although they meant well. That was how the system worked in those days.

MEESTER CORNELIS TO FORT DE COQ

While serving as a second lieutenant in the Dutch East army, my father's first army post was in Meester Cornelis, a suburb of Batavia (called Jakarta in later years). The climate was hot and humid and quite an adjustment for the lady from Holland, but she loved the large house and the servants. She made friends among the army families who worked through their homesickness together. In 1915 she became pregnant, and in April, 1916, I was born.

Mother had to learn the Indonesian-Malayan language, which was spoken by most of the Indonesian people, although there were many different dialects spoken on the various islands. Mother learned the most common, so that she could communicate with our household help, as well as with people in other parts of the community. As for the Dutch East Army, melding the Dutch soldiers with Indonesian, with such varied backgrounds, meant hard work for my father. This wasn't going to be an easy assignment.

Many battles were fought between the Dutch and Indonesian people, and it took a long time before the Dutch were able to rule the Indies effectively. We lived in Sumatra, the largest of the Indonesion Islands, in the twenties, and there were still problems with the Atjeh people. For that reason, Mother had a Luger pistol, and knew how to use it. When Father left to go on patrol, she never knew whether he would come back alive.

Health problems plagued us from the beginning. We collectively, contracted dysentery, and for the first half year of my life in Meester Cornelis, I struggled to stay alive. Because I could not hold my food down, mother was advised by the doctor to tie me up on an upright board to help keep the milk from being spilled. But after several months I was so emaciated that the doctor feared the worst. There was only one alternative, according to him, and that was for us to transfer to a colder climate. Luckily, Father got permission later in 1916 to move to Fort de Cock, a military base on a high plateau in Sumatra. Within a few months I started to perk up and regained the health of a normal baby. Of course, I don't remember this, but old photographs show the difference between my looks when I was a few months old and when I was two years.

Several earthquakes hit us when we lived in Fort de Cock. Everyone knows of the famous Krakatoa volcano, about ninety-five miles southwest of Jakarta, that erupted in 1883, killing some 35,000 people. Well, we were surrounded by highly active volcanic mountains in our area too, so we were not surprised to experience quakes now and then.

I especially remember one earthquake. I was about four, when early one morning, it happened! Most of the time people knew a quake was coming because everything in nature seemed to hold its breath. Animals became quiet, leaving moments of total silence. Then a distant roar was heard, breaking the silence. Closer and closer it came, so violent that when it reached us everything started to shake. The floor shifted, making it difficult to keep our balance. When it hit I held onto a table for dear life, as the table slid in all directions, pulling me with it. Mother screamed for me to hold on while she tried to reach me, but she lost her balance, and fell. Everything around us started to fall. Pictures, lamps, dishes, and even the furniture came crashing down around us. Our servants ran outside, falling and stumbling, screaming in terror. I was so frightened, I couldn't utter a sound, and finally after what seemed like an eternity, the quake subsided. Unbelievably, the house was still standing. It took me a while before I was able to let go of the table. We were lucky because the whole row of military houses was still standing, while destruction was evident all around us. In later years, I experienced several more earthquakes, but I never forgot that first one.

We were stationed at Fort de Cock for four years, and the year after we left, another quake hit the same area. This time, all the houses were destroyed. The officer, who lived in the house we just left, was killed instantly when the roof collapsed on him.

Mother always told me that the happiest years were the ones spent at Fort de Cock. The climate was cool with lots of sunshine. At night we needed blankets because it would get quite chilly. The surroundings were absolutely beautiful, with mountains, valleys and the famous "Karbouwen gat" (buffalo-hole), a deep canyon resembling the Grand Canyon in America, but on a smaller scale. It had been shaped by an earthquake long ago. Steep dirt roads lead to the bottom of the canyon, where rice fields are cultivated. Water buffaloes help turn the soil before the rice-plants are planted hence the name of the canyon.

My parents and I, often went on hikes, down the canyon roads, crossing small rivers (called Kalis), and passing small villages. Numerous children played in their Adam and Eve costumes, every-where. They were beautiful children with brown skin, fine features and black hair and eyes. They often had pets with them, like a baby goat or a piglet or a parrot, and sometimes they let me hold one. The native children were well cared for in their first years. But when they were older and reached the age of ten, they had to help their parents in the rice fields, at home or in their tiny shops (warongs).

One of my favorite places was a pond next to a Mosque, where huge carps in multiple colors swam. The carp were considered holy by the Muslims and nobody was allowed to harm or steal them. Some of them were more than fifty years old. As soon as we approached the pond, the fish swam towards us, begging for food. Most of the time we had some bread with us, and soon the fish took it right out of our hands. To me they looked like creatures straight from heaven, so perfect and beautiful.

Often Mom would go out in the morning and hike the surrounding area with me and her "baboe" (maid). Often she was joined by a neighbor, the Keuskamp's, who had an infant son. They became close friends and remained so until mom's death, forty-five years later.

Life in the army wasn't always easy, and mother told me many stories of the difficulties she encountered. She had to deal with a primitive life, domineering military wives, and with learning a new language. One time, when she first came to Indonesia and was still learning the language, she called a houseboy over to have him open a big window. She told the houseboy: "Boeka chelana!", to which he looked alarmed and shook his head saying "Tida mouw" (I don't want to) in refusal. My mother repeated "Boeka chelana!" a little louder, and the houseboy refused a second time, and ran out of the room. When my father heard the complaint from my mother that the houseboy had become insolent at a simple request to open the window, my father asked my mother exactly what she had said. When she responded, Father started laughing out loud with glee, he had a great sense of humor. It turns out that "Boeka chelana" means "drop your pants". What Mother meant to say was : Boeka yen dala". It took a little explaining with the houseboy to straighten that one out.

Scorpions and snakes fascinated me and I loved to play with them when I was little, giving my mother one heart attack after another. Many of the snakes were poisonous, as were the scorpions. My mother still yelled at me when I then started to play with the cockroaches.

My mother was an accomplished seamstress and was always embroidering and making our clothes. Among the small fish-bowl society of military women there were some women who were jealous of these skills and who made life difficult for my mother, mistreating her socially. She was also a beautiful women and many of the military men who came to our home would flirt with her, making Mother extremely uncomfortable. Father never noticed Mother's uncomfortableness and he really never appreciated her beauty until many years later.

In 1917, my father, then a second lieutenant, was one of the youngest officers in the infantry. Most officers were higher ranking and older with wives that liked to brag about their husbands, and gossip as they sipped their tea. One afternoon, my mother, her best friend, and several other women were having a good time when one of the women started to tease my mother. She was a proud and aloof woman, and in her station felt no qualms about commenting to my mother that "It must be difficult for you right now, because your husband is still so young and has to learn so much before he will be a mature military man". "Not at all", mother retorted, "you have to start somewhere, and after all, we still have most of our lives ahead of us".

The woman then turned to mother's friend, whose husband ranked between Father and her husband. "My dear", she said, "tell me what your father did for a living. Was he a military man and is he still living?" Mother's friend looked at her angrily, asking "Why do you want to know about my father, after all, it's none of your concern." The commanders wife pushed, "you don't have to tell me if you don't want to, or do you have a reason you don't want to talk about it? I just asked you a simple question, no harm done". The other women were looking at these two, mouths gaping, wondering how their conversation would end. One of the other women tried to direct the conversation in another direction. At first, she succeeded and everyone breathed a sigh of relief, but later, the unpleasant woman started to nag Moms friend again. Mom couldn't stand it any longer. She got up and asked her friend to come with her.

She did not know anything about her friend's father, nor did she care. All she knew was that she loved her and would be supportive. Just when they started to leave, mother's friend turned on her tormentor angrily and said, "Well, since you insist on knowing who and what my father is, I will tell you. He's the Governor General of the whole army, answering only to the Queen. I did not want you to know this because I wanted you to like me for myself, and I didn't want the position of my Father to be of any influence on my life and my friends." This episode strengthened their friendship, because mother had loved this woman for herself.

Here's another story of human behavior that happened on the army post in those days. Mother became friendly with a neighbor because they both had daughters about the same age. At first she seemed friendly enough, and she knew that mother made all my clothes for me, complete with embellishments of embroidery and smocking. She admired this work, until my mother offered to teach her how, then the woman's demeanor changed, claiming "this was too much work." My mother felt as if the woman resented her talents, not only in sewing, but also in the beautiful gardens she created wherever they settled.

Mother's love of gardening has been passed down to me. In my mother's gardens there were always geraniums, and all sorts of tropical flowers and orchids. Their beauty has always inspired me.

Mother had bought six teacups at a small store nearby called a "warong". She showed her purchase to all of us because she was so pleased with her choice. But then she decided to go back to the "warong" the next day to buy some more cups. The "warong" was closed, and the next door neighbor told mom that the owner had died the night before of the black plague, which the Dutch called "the pest". Mother came home immediately, and went straight to the army doctor to see if she might have contracted the dreadful disease. The doctor told her that he couldn't help her because there was no cure for it, and that she should put herself in isolation and wait to see if she would be lucky enough to get past the incubation period without any problem.

There were many cases of the plague at that time, and we saw funeral wagons passing our house nearly every day. We didn't dare leave the house every day for quite a while. Our gardener, "Kebon", was given strict orders to watch for rats, who had fleas, which were the host for the dreaded virus. Rats were rampant everywhere in those days, especially in the "kampongs", or native villages. The army was given orders to kill rats wherever they could find them. We were lucky, but there were many dangerous diseases in that area, so we got regular inoculations for typhus, cholera, and small-pox. Life on the outposts was quite primitive, and not without hidden dangers. Death appeared often, sometimes from snakebites or from bites from a scorpion. People died of tetanus, often being infected by manure. We had no telephone, limited mail, and often messages were sent within a town via a houseboy carrying a slate upon which a message had been written in chalk. We used outhouses and these were often placed above a river. To take a shower, the houseboy would bring in buckets of water, and we would use a dip pan to pour water over ourselves as we washed. We took this "shower" in the corner of a square concrete wash basin about 3 feet on either side and about 1-1/2 feet deep. It had a drain and a plug, just like a bathtub. Dysentery was a common disease, my mother had it once for a week. It made her very sick with blood in her stool I remember being worried she would die. My mother told me that in her years in Indonesia, she had dysentery five times. My father suffered from Malaria, as did many Dutch and Indonesian people. When my father had a malaria attack he would be terribly sick for days, and then he would regain his strength and continue in his duties.

PADANG PANDJANG AND PADANG

After Fort de Cock, we moved to a small outpost called Padang Pandjang not far from Fort de Cock. This was also a nice spot to live in but we stayed there only quite a short time. Soon afterwards Father was transferred yet again, this time to Padang, which is a seaport, West of Sumatra. The climate here was not half so nice as we had before.

For the move to Padan Pandjang, my parents decided to get rid of most of their furniture and some of our other belongings. The custom was to sell what you had to sell at an auction called "Lellang" or "Vendutie". Since there was little entertainment on most of the posts, these auctions were widely attended. Mother didn't have many luxuries. Father's salary was 75 guilders a month, which did not allow for much more than the necessities, but she did have a collection of tuberous begonias, which she had cultivated herself, the kind that look like can-can girls at the Follies Bergere in Paris. They sported great colored flounces of red, yellow, pink, and salmon, flung over their heads. She was very proud of them, and found them harder than anything else to part with, especially knowing they were at their flowering peak during the auction.

The evening before the auction she went outside once more to inspect her precious flowers, which were planted in two large white flowerpots. She hoped they would bring in some extra money for her. Mother always managed to save a few guilders each month and she was really proud of her small bankbook.

Early the next morning, when people started to gather, there was one man in particular, who had come just for the begonias, but when mother took him outside to show off her begonias, she discovered to her horror, that all of them had been cut and were scattered on the ground in many pieces. At first mother thought that maybe some animal had destroyed the flowers, although she had thought that they wouldn't be able to reach into the pots, which had been placed on tall posts. She called our houseboy and asked him if he knew what had happened, but he denied any knowledge of it, and mother believed him. She was heartbroken, but she accepted her bad luck.

A few days later, our houseboy told her he had found out what had happened to the begonias. The cook of the neighbor had told him that the neighbor's houseboy had been ordered to destroy the flowers in the middle of the night. My parents couldn't do anything about it because they knew the neighbors would deny everything, and it would end up being one persons word against another. Mom wondered how anyone could be so vicious out of resentment and jealousy.

After we moved to Padang Pandjang (translated, Long Padang), I was old enough to remember quite a few things. We used to walk a lot, nearly every morning when the air was cool. All around us, nature was fascinating. The menagerie of animals were pursuing their day all around us; wild pigs rutting, monkeys swinging through the trees, large frogs with their throaty voices, large tortoises, and every colorful species of bird you could possibly imagine. There wasn't a day that I didn't discover something new to admire. I would watch my mother as she painted beautiful patterns on pure silk, Batik style. The interior of my parents home was always very tasteful. The pillows and curtains in our house were all personally constructed by mother, and to my mind, it was all perfection. She performed miracles with small pieces of material. She would make our clothes because you could not buy European style clothes where we lived.

Only the native, "sarong or habaja" were available, and most of the women wore these occasionally, but when we went to a dinner party or some kind of celebration, everyone wore European clothing.

When we entertained, I would help mother. She would go out to the garden, picking beautiful bouquets of flowers which were placed in vases all over the house, making what was a modest home seem very elegant indeed. Even at an early age I was enchanted by the merchants near our house, who sold colorful parasols. It looked to me like a picture out of a coloring book. I kept myself very busy constructing small gardens with sticks and flowers and then I would draw my creations and surroundings on paper.

I learned how to swim in a pool nearby, where large carp kept us company. Once in a while I managed to grab the tail of these beautiful fish for a moment, which was a lot of fun, but I had to be very quick. In later years I found out that I was swimming like a dog, with arms and legs stretched out at the same time. But it worked for me and it kept me afloat and moving. What surprised me was that nobody, even my Father, ever tried to correct my swimming style.

I had my fifth birthday in Padang. This was the first time I realized that I was getting older and that it was wonderful to have a birthday party with other kids my age. I remember especially a present I got which I enjoyed very much. It was a small box with glass beads in bright colors. I learned to string them and make bracelets and necklaces out of them. This was the first time I discovered how handy I was at making things with my hands.

When I was about five years old, something happened to me that disturbed me for years to come. One sunny afternoon, I was playing on our front lawn with a kitten mother had given me not long before. I loved this pet, and took it with me everywhere I went. I strolled over to a small rock wall which divided our yard from the busy street. It was a street with a lot of bustling people, mostly natives, passing by with their carts, horse buggies, called "sados", and bicycles. Coolies carried their wares in baskets protruding at the end of bamboo poles which were balanced across their shoulders, swaying back and forth in rhythmic cadence. It was fun to watch them because it looked like they were dancing. When I reached the top of the rockery, nestling the kitten in my lap, something caught my eye.

On the street in front of me, I saw a man pushing a cart with very large wheels. I watched him and noticed an old rug partially hanging off the end of the cart, covering something I couldn't quite see, although I could tell that it was a very odd shape. When the cart passed about a yard from where I sat, the rug fell to the street. Unfurling it exposed a horrible sight. The rug contained the naked, decapitated corpse of a man, now lying on his stomach, blood seeping from his body. I stared at this spectacle for a few seconds, a feeling of terror growing inside me, then I started to scream. Unconsciously squeezing the kitten, it scratched my arms, which added to my hysteria. In the meantime, the man who was pushing the cart called "crobak", had stopped to pick up the rug from the street, trying to cover up the corpse. I ran to my house for help, screaming and holding my bleeding arm. Mother came running petrified that something might have happened to me. At first she thought I was yelling because of the scratches, but when I told her what I had seen, she was horrified. It was several nights and days before I calmed down, and for years after I would have nightmares in which I saw that corpse over and over again.

When my Father found what had happened, I was told another story to try to help me cope. According to my parents, there had been an accident. The man had stayed too long in a swimming pool that was being cleaned and his head was sucked in through the drainage hole. I often wondered in later years how my parents could have invented such a crazy story, but I wanted to believe the story and it made me very careful about being near the pool when it was being cleaned. The real story was that two men had fought over a woman, and one of them managed to hack off the head of the other with a large knife called a klewang.

Life in Indonesia could be very cruel as when friends of our family lost a son. My parents had some close friends, the Kamp family. He was a lawyer and they had two sons, the oldest boy, was one year older than I, and the other son was only two. I used to play with them, but then one day something horrible happened to their family. The younger son, Hank, became violently ill and died the next day. The autopsy showed that the young boys intestines were torn by bamboo splinters. The Kamps talked to the cook who had prepared cereal for Hank the day before his death, and she remembered that a vendor had come into the yard, near the kitchen, about that time. She had left the vendor alone for a moment to ask Mrs. Kamp if she wanted to see the vendors wares. The Kamps asked the police if they would find the vendor because he seemed to be the only person who had a chance to put something in Hank's food. After all, somebody must have done it and the cook was above suspicion because she had been a faithful servant for years. The police found the vendor, a criminal who had been paroled a short time before, after having served a long prison term.

It turned out that he was known to have hated Mr. Kamp, who had prosecuted him, and the criminal had sworn he would get even. Somehow he would take his revenge when he got out of prison. Placing bamboo slivers in someone's food was the local method used to eliminate people the Indonesian's wanted killed. The court decided that this man had gotten his revenge on Mr. Kamp, but nothing could be done to punish the culprit without proof or an eye witness, so they had to give him his freedom.

The Kamp's decided to go back to Holland. Mrs. Kamp, especially, felt the lifestyle of Indonesia was not something she wanted to deal with anymore. We kept in touch, so the Kamps were our friends until their deaths many years later. Unfortunately, they never got over their son's murder, even after another son was born to them. Mrs. Kamp always wore a small necklace which her son Hank had played with as a baby.

FIRST TRIP TO HOLLAND 1921

Our stay in Padang was not that long. Father was offered a chance to go back to Holland for a while to study engineering for the army. My parents were delighted for this chance because it would mean a promotion and a larger salary. That salary was still not very large so my parents had to be thrifty. We did not have much in material things, but I learned to be happy with what I got. When we left Padang, we traveled to Holland on a large ship which took five weeks altogether. This was the first time I realized there were different countries outside of Indonesia. The different harbors were especially fascinating to me, like Colombo, Port Said in Egypt and Marseille in France. Because my mother was often seasick, my parents decided to leave the ship in Marseille, and take a train to Holland. I remember a fellow passenger we had on the train. He was a priest just back from Africa, where he was working with the primitive African people. He told us many stories about his life there, and even though I was young at the time, I still remember this wonderful man.

When we arrived in Holland I met my maternal grandparents for the first time. They were delighted to see their first granddaughter, and I fell in love with them right away. We stayed with my grandparents for a while, their home was very neat and cozy. It was a typical patrician row house, with three floors and a small cellar. This house was heated only by one small coal stove, so in the winter it was colder the further away from the stove you got. In the sleeping rooms it was so cold that often frost would form on the covers. And the toilet seat felt especially cold in the winter. When you looked out through a front window, you could enjoy the most beautiful view because in front of the house was a small street next to a beautiful park, and next to this park was a large river called the Ijssel River. The river was always fascinating. A lot of traffic passed by and alongside the river there always were a lot of fishermen. On sunny days I went out in the park and played with neighborhood kids. Sometimes I asked my grandmother if she would give me a pail with water. I had befriended a fisherman who once in a while gave me a fish he had caught. I was so happy watching the fish swimming in my bucket, and when I managed to catch a frog to join the fish, my joy was complete.

One morning something happened which made my grand-mother scream with laughter. I had been playing in her yard, and a while later I came running in her house. "Oma", I said, "You have to come with me outside, because I have seen the most beautiful creatures you can imagine!". Grandmother joined me in the garden and she was speechless when I pointed out to her what kind of creatures I had admired so much. Then she burst out laughing because the creatures were aphids on her roses. Later on she told my mother that I never would be bored in my life, because I really enjoyed being on this beautiful planet.

Fall season arrived soon afterward and I was amazed about all the fall colors in nature, especially the chestnuts from the chestnut trees caught my eyes. I had not seen more beautiful nuts in my life. When the first snow arrived, I could not believe that the rain could turn into white fluffy pieces. Later on I helped some kids to build a snowman. I learned many new things and enjoyed my stay with my grand-parents so much.

My paternal grandparents came to visit a bit later. They came from Purmerend, a small city in the north of Holland where they lived. They took me for a weekend to their home. I felt so lucky to have four grandparents! Especially because I loved them all.

Unfortunately, this happy time was not meant to last. My Father came down with severe malaria. I felt so sorry for him when I saw how much he suffered. Because of his illness, he had to end his study of engineering, and he was ordered to return to Indonesia and resume his military career. In 1923 our family left Holland and returned to Indonesia. We settled in Magelang, my father's next post.

MAGALANG AND BANDOENG

In 1923, Magelang was small, surrounded by high mountains on the island of Java. Often, there were earthquakes in this area. Most of the time, though, they were small, and the people who lived there were used to them. But I remember one time when one of the surrounding mountains started to shake and spew an "ash rain". The results were unpleasant to say the least. For days the whole town was covered with grey ash. My mother became desperate that time because everything was covered with the sticky grey ash which was quite difficult to remove. Altogether, life was somewhat primitive in Magelang.

Our bathroom was some distance away from our house. When we wanted to go there in the evening, we had to carry a small petrol-lamp. A long open corridor led to it, and just before we reached the door, we had to clap our hands before opening it. Often we saw large rats running in different directions and disappearing into small holes in the corners of the bathroom. Our toilet was a wooden board, stretched about four feet above a small stream running underneath. A small bucket, filled with water, was used to wash ourselves. Quite primitive indeed, but we were used to it.

I was only eight years old, but I loved to hike and I was able to walk sometimes five to six hours in a stretch. Father often took me with him when he inspected neighborhood villages. He would walk through jungle spots across small mud paths which divided the rice fields called "sawahs". All kinds of animals could be seen everywhere. Monkeys in the trees, frogs, snakes, turtles, wild pigs and numerous insects. We walked often for hours. There never was a dull moment. When we passed through Indonesian villages called "kampongs", we saw many small children who were totally naked, like cherubs in a Christmas painting. They seemed to be happy with their simple lives. Sometimes I envied them their freedom, not being bothered by clothing.

On one of those walks something happened which had a lasting effect on me, and showed me one side of military life. We approached a village where we saw a group of soldiers, sitting in a circle on a patch of dirt. They were playing a gambling game. When they saw Father, they were startled. They all got up, and some even started to run. My Father ran after one of them, and caught up with him at the moment when the man fell backwards into a sawah. Father took out his revolver, pointed it at the man, and told him to get up and walk in front of him. The other man came back, stood in a row, and waited for my Father to talk to them. He scolded them, told them to go back to their garrison. They all were soldiers of the Indonesian army and they were caught gambling, which was forbidden. We left after the soldiers marched back in the direction of the army post. This episode scared me, especially since I had never seen my Father being a military man before.

There were a few Dutch children in Magelang which was wonderful for me. On my eight birthday, my mother arranged a birthday party which was the best I ever had. She organized games, offered prizes and prepared a very special treat of ice cream. To make ice cream was a chore at that time. Because it had to be prepared by hand, it took hours before it even looked like ice cream. Soon after my birthday, I had a chance to meet my cousins, who were the three daughters of my mother's sister. The older one was my age, the youngest one was my baby sister's age, and the middle one was five. I loved having my cousins there to keep me company, but soon they had to leave. My Father was glad when they went because he used to say that five women around him was just "a little much of a good thing".

KOTA RADJA 1925

Our stay in Magelang was too long. We had to leave again, this time to Kota Radja, in northern Sumatra. The trip took us by boat to Sabang, an island near Sumatra and from there by small boats to the mainland. Like Magelang, Kota Radja was a small town, with a lot of history because the Atjeh people who lived there were the last people who kept on fighting the Dutch. This made Kota Radja one of the more dangerous spots for the military forces.

Something awful happened when we lived there. One evening when my Father came home, he was terribly upset, close to tears. His face was very white. Obviously, he forgot that I was standing next to him and could hear every word he spoke. He told my mother that he had bad news about another officer who was a close friend. His name was Captain Paris. Father had been sick with another malaria attack. His superior officer had asked him to go to a place south on Sumatra to check on a disturbance there. But Father could not go because of his illness, so Captain Paris was sent instead. I don't remember exactly what happened, but Captain Paris was killed by angry Atjeh people. His body was chopped into pieces which were then sold at a marketplace. If my Father had not been sick, we would have lost my Father.

We stayed in Kota Radja for about a year, and because there was a basic but adequate school available there, my parents decided to send me. It was the first time I attended a real school.

Most of the students were native children, only a few were Dutch. The principal of the school was extremely strict. I heard stories of how he punished students by using a whip. I did hear the screams of kids who were being punished. Then one day I witnessed a real fight between the school principal and the father of one of the students. Students ran away in all directions, but some of them stayed back to watch the fight. When I came home, I told my Father about the fight and he became very angry. The next day, he went to the school and told the principal that he would see to it that he would be discharged from his job if he ever dared to touch another student or have a disgraceful fight with a student's parent again. Some time later we heard that the school drastically re-organized. My parents, however, had taken me away from the school, and my mother was teaching me herself again.

Kota Radja was a pretty town with several beautiful parks, and a graveyard that was beautifully kept and landscaped. Many Dutch military men were buried there. The natives honored the dead, and even many years later, after the Dutch lost their colonies, the graves were still well taken care of.

Water Buffalo in Rice Fields

Parasol Sale

Indonesian Soldier with Saber

Street in Boeloe Blanc Ara

BOELOE BLANC ARA 1926

The next outpost was Boeloe Blanc Ara, a small jungle dwelling with only two officers homes and a small garrison. Boeloe Blanc Ara, means parrot white feather (like McCaw parrot feather). My Father and one other officer were the only white people around. Father was away on patrol with his native soldiers for two weeks at a time, and then he would be home for the next two weeks. When he was away on patrol, the other officer took care of the garrison and our family. I remember seeing Father taking off for his patrol duty, paying visits to several villages where he kept the peace and made sure the villagers were behaving themselves. Sometimes he had to act as judge and jury when problems arose.

He also visited the leper colony close to Boeloe Blanc Ara on Sumatra to make sure the patients stayed in their compound. I remember my father telling me that the lepers had disfigured faces. Father said that sometimes the lepers were allowed to get married, which helped them to feel less ostracized from normal life. If they had a baby they had to give the baby to someone who lived out-side the compound. This helped to keep the horrible disease from spreading. I often saw the damage done to those pitiful patients in advanced stages, as their faces deteriorated, and their hands and feet became totally deformed. But on the whole their lives were the best that could be expected under the circumstances. They were taken care of by twenty coolies or sometimes other soldiers when

Father was on patrol. The soldiers had to carry quite a lot of gear with them to be able to survive the jungle, often having to hack their way through dense jungles to open new trails as they went.

The Indonesian jungles were abundantly filled with roaming animals. The largest ones were elephants, which crushed everything in their path. Elephants caused much destruction in the villages and on the plantations. Unfortunately, there wasn't much that could be done to avoid this trampling, and it was considered part of living there. My Father loved trekking through the jungle, sometimes up to ten hours a day. He walked so fast that his pace was hard to keep up with when he took us along with him. Sometimes he brought home wild boar that he had shot to supply the troops with food. Then they burned the hair off the carcass and skewered the beast on a wooden pole above a large fire. The meat would be rotated and basted for hours until it was tender, producing the best tasting pig feast you could ever imagine.

One time when Father came back, he brought me two wild baby piglets. Their mother had been shot by accident, so Father brought the little ones home, hoping we could keep them alive. When they were small they were very tame, like dogs, and very intelligent, so we kept them until they were large enough for their natural instincts to make them too dangerous to keep. We ended up donating them to a nearby zoo.

One of the more unpleasant things about jungle walks were the bloodsucking leeches, just waiting to attach themselves to a human body. Father wore a so -called "puttis", long strips of dark green cloth which were wrapped around both legs. This supposedly prevented the bloodsuckers from reaching human skin. But when Father came home from a patrol and unwound his puttis, he often found that he had bloody legs anyway because the leeches had managed to penetrate the cloth and bury their feet in his skin. I hated to see those leeches falling to the floor, all of them bloated into brown-black balls. A burning cigarette eliminated them fast enough after they engorged themselves.

One of the many stories Father told us concerned a time when he was climbing a steep mountain and one of his coolies fell into a ravine. Father was sure they would find the coolie dead but after hours of descending the mountain they found the coolie and all that was wrong with him was a broken toe. A more serious accident occurred when the whole troop was crossing a wild river. While crossing, the soldiers grasped each others hands to create a human chain, but the water was too swift and their gripping hands were torn away from each other, sweeping the men downriver to their deaths. After several days of searching, parts of their dead bodies were found along the riverbanks. The rest had been a meal for crocodiles.

Sumatra jungles were wild and dangerous, and even the more advanced techniques could not prevent mishaps. On another patrol trip, Father found a nice resting place near a forest, where all his men could bivouac together. One man was placed on watch duty that night, but he was so tired that he fell asleep. When morning came, everyone was accounted for, except one man. Nobody knew what had happened to the missing man until one of the soldiers found some tracks near the place where the missing man had slept. There were footprints of a tiger, leading towards a nearby river. It took the group two days of tracking before they finally found what was left of the soldier who was taken away. The tiger had picked the easiest prey and silently dragged him away while the watchman slept. This reflected badly on my father because he was responsible for his troops. The watchman was severely punished, but that didn't bring back the dead man.

Life was in many ways quite rough for all the military men, especially for those who were just beginning their careers and had to prove themselves worthy by performance. Even then there were enough men who loved the army to fill the ranks. Enticements to enlist were the pension they would get in their future, free room and board, free medical treatments, and protection wherever it was possible. They also gained the respect and camaraderie of their fellow soldiers, and the bonding of the surrounding community.

In those days the tropical splendor of the jungle was still mostly intact and my father loved it. The Indonesian people lived in villages, sometimes quite far apart, making them dependent on their own resources. One of the many problems they had were visits by wild tigers and elephant herds. The wounded tigers who couldn't fend for themselves very well, presented a real danger. Once tigers killed and had made a meal of human flesh, they would continue to prey on people. In one instance, the villagers asked the army if they would please help them find and kill a man eating tiger. Father ordered some of his men to build a platform in a tree near a spot where the tiger had been seen.

For two nights Father and another soldier waited patiently on the platform for the tiger to return, hoping to get a chance to eliminate the predator. Before they stationed themselves in the tree, they tied a goat to a nearby tree hoping the goats cries would draw the tigers interest. On the third night the tiger showed itself, the beasts body silhouetted against the rising moon. My Father told me later that it was such a beautiful sight to behold, he almost forgot why he was there. In that moment, the tiger smelled his would be killers, and disappeared in a flash, back into the safety of the jungle. At first Father was embarrassed about his failure to catch the beast, but a few days later, he managed to kill it by tracking it to its lair.

My parents befriended a German couple, who were living on a coffee plantation high up in the mountains not too far from where we were living in Boeloe Blanc Ara. These people were living a lonely life, and were happy to receive company once in a while. My parents decided to visit for a few days, but our only transportation was a large truck normally used for transporting sacks of coffee. On the way to the plantation, our family was the only cargo of the empty truck. Sitting in the back on top of a pile of empty coffee sacks, we were anything but comfortable, not to mention clean, but even so I enjoyed the new adventure.

My mother was quite afraid of the trip, especially when we

passed over a very large river by way of a very small bridge built solely of bamboo tied together with ropes. Somehow we made it, as it creaked and wavered as we moved over its hurdles. We arrived safely, and our hosts were more than happy to see us. They lived in a house built high up on bamboo poles, making it necessary to climb a primitive bamboo ladder, to enter their living quarters, which terrified mother even more.

On the first evening we were told what it was like to live in these primitive conditions. It was not an old plantation, so there was a lot of work to be done. Several servants met all of our needs and when they were done for the day, their own homes were close, but not built on stilts, so they had dogs for protection, although this did not always keep them safe from wild creatures. Our hosts told us that once in a while they would see a tiger under their house and the dogs would bark like mad, making such a racket that the tiger would decide to leave in favor of easier prey.

Then, our hostess, Mrs. Kuent, told mom to check the support poles which held up the mosquito netting around her bed. Earlier a large snake had been found curled around one of those poles on her bed. By this time, my mother was feeling quite anxious about hearing these stories. Being as young as I was, I loved the excitement of it all. The second day we spent with the Kuent's and their small son we walked for miles through the plantation. An elephant herd had passed near their home a short time before, and they wanted to show us the terrific damage these huge animals could cause. Huge trees were trampled to the ground and many precious coffee shrubs had been destroyed. When the rain came, it filled the many holes made by the huge elephant tracks, leaving alternate rows of miniature ponds in their wake.

Mr. Kuent told my Father to take his gun with him because he wanted to show us the sleeping place of a tiger he had discovered some time earlier. We walked for miles through dense jungle, crossing wild rivers called Kali's, hiking over small primitive jungle paths. We had two German shepherds with us, supposedly, to protect us.

This turned out to be quite ridiculous.

As we approached the end of the trail, on the left side there was such dense forest that you could not penetrate it without the help of a machete, called a "klewang". The right side of the path fell steeply to a ravine, and at the bottom there was a raging river. We noticed that all around us there was complete silence, a sign, Mr. Kuent informed us that the tiger was near. The dogs behaved in a peculiar manner. They clung to us, pushing themselves against our legs, sensing danger was close. Their hair stood up on their backs, and they bared their teeth, growling. My Father drew his gun as we turned the corner, where we saw a huge rock overhanging the trail. Underneath was a small platform covered with tiger fur. At the same time we saw the rock, we heard a big crash in the nearby woods and we saw a flash of orange quickly disappearing into the jungle followed by total silence.

We were all quite upset, belatedly realizing that we had been in great danger of being pounced upon and torn apart by this hungry tiger. Mother was angry at Mr. Kuent because there were three children along, my sister, his son, and myself. But Mr. Kuent told us that he was sure the tiger had eaten enough earlier at the plantation, and that he was satisfied, hence there was nothing to fear. Also the dogs were a deterrent for the tiger, reported an assured Mr. Kuent. I had to admit that those dogs even scared me, they were so large for their breed.

Life on the plantation was primitive, but with the help of five servants it wasn't too bad. There was no running water, and we used outhouses, often located over a small river or stream. The mail was brought in by ship three times per year and what we finally received was outdated. There were no newspapers. The servant had their own lives in the local area. I remember that they always seemed to very happy, singing and dancing while they worked. They were very industrious, and they earned a good wage working for the "Blandas" (white people). The houseboy served the food and kept the house clean. The Kuents also had a gardener who tended the flowers, and who trimmed the grass with a scythe or a machete. Baboe chouchi did the laundry and the ironing. I remember seeing her by the riverside soaping up the clothes and slapping them against the rocks. The cook prepared all the meals. Breakfast was served at 5:00 to 5:30 AM and consisted of bread and cheese and jam. At around 1:00 PM, the cook made the main meal, usually an Indonesian Rice Table. Supper was very light and consisted of bread, cheese and jam. Normally we went to bed in the early evening at around 8:00 to 9:00 PM when it got dark. The next morning everyone rose at 4:00 to 4:30 AM.

We stayed a few more days with the Kuent family and they were glad to have the company. Mr. Kuent had a job to do and was gone most of everyday, so his wife had to deal with loneliness. Sometime later we heard that some of their dogs had been killed by a roaming tiger, right underneath their house. Father was transferred soon after our visit and we never saw the Kuents again.

My mother had a Luger pistol which she kept under her pillow at night. She had taken shooting lessons and could shoot quite accurately. One evening I saw her with the pistol in her hand. My Father was away on patrol, so mother had to deal with the daily affairs. Our neighbor, another officer, was home though, so we felt quite safe.

On this particular evening though mother was fearful. There was a married couple, natives, who were our servants. They were arguing angrily, and soon the woman ran towards our house, screaming and asking for help. Mother ran to her bedroom, got her gun, and went outside to meet the woman. By that time the husband had caught up with his wife, and as Mom approached them, hiding the gun in her skirts, she saw the husband holding up his wife by her long hair and he had positioned a long knife against her throat, while yelling that he was going to kill her. The wife yelled over and over again that she was a "Christian". Obviously, she hoped that my mother would help her. I knew that my mother was a strong woman who coped with whatever faced her, but this time I was especially proud of her because she aimed the loaded Luger at the mans head, and said in Indonesian, "drop the knife, or I will kill you", and she meant it. The husband took one look at my mother and dropped the weapon. Mother ordered the wife to come inside, and yelled at the man to pick up his belongings and leave the premises at once. The next morning she sent the wife back to her own village, and we never saw either one of them again. When my Father returned he felt badly that mother had to deal with the situation, but he was very proud of her bravery and the action she had taken.

All Dutch nationals were trained and warned of situations that could arise in these colonies and how they could handle them. Sometime later we had trouble with our cook. Much too often, she would burn the meal she was preparing for us, so mother was thinking of getting rid of her. Then one evening, mother had a question for the cook, so she went to her room and knocked on the door. When there was no answer she pushed the door open herself and saw the crouching woman, oblivious to her surroundings, as she smoked her long opium pipe. She hardly noticed mother at all, and the next day mom let her go and found another cook. Many Indonesians used opium in those times, it was a common practice to smoke it. It was illegal for the Dutch officers and military personnel to use opium, and some officers who were caught using opium were dismissed on the spot. But the Dutch did not prohibit or regulate opium use among the Indonesians.

In Boeloe Blanc Ara there were many dangerous creatures. There were so many snakes, for instance, that Father decided to curb the reptiles, or at least make them more visible to us. To do this, he ordered several of his soldiers to clear a large field behind our house of snakes. Many snakes were harvested. One large burlap sack was filled to the brim with dead ones of all shapes and sizes, some of them very poisonous.

One soldier was bitten by a poisonous snake on his thumb, and without hesitation, he picked up a stone from the field, placed his thumb on it. and quickly hacked off his thumb with a machete. His fast action saved his life, so missing his thumb had definitely been the lesser of two evils.

In the year of 1926 I experienced something which was very exciting to me. Father called me one morning to do something for him. I had to take a bucket and fill it with water. When I asked him why I had to do this, he told me that on that morning the sun would vanish for a while, causing everything around us to be covered in darkness. So it would seem as if the daylight had vanished. I should not be afraid, Father continued, because it was something which was caused by nature and would not be dangerous in any way except for one. Father told me that I should not under any circumstances look directly at the sun while it was getting dark, or during the darkness. Instead, Father told me to place the filled bucket on the ground, and position it so that I could see the reflection of the sun on the surface of the water. When I asked Father why I could not look at the sun directly, he answered that the light from the sun would blind a person who looked directly into the sun during this event. I believed Father and I waited next to my bucket hoping to see the daylight vanish. Quite soon, but slowly, this did happen.

Slowly, it became darker, which was really upsetting if you did not know or understand what was really happening. When the daylight really started to disappear it did cause some reactions among the Indonesian servants. The animals around me also reacted strangely. Our houseboy and his wife were both very frightened. They came running to my mother, asking her if the world was going to collapse. Mother was very calm and told them that it was something of nature that was happening and that it would be dark only for a short while, and that the daylight would definitely reappear some time later.

Of course we could not tell the animals all around us the same story. The animals were really frightened by the unexpected darkness. Our cats all came running to the house where they hid under the building. The chickens all stopped what they were doing and headed for the chicken coop perching on their night-time roosts as it got darker. They obviously thought that somehow night had appeared even though it came at the wrong time.

I watched the sun slowly disappear on the surface of the water in the bucket. Father warned me several times to only look at the surface of the water, and not to look up directly at the sun. He was very stern with me as he said this, and I knew that he meant it. I was terrified of looking directly at the sun, for fear of being blinded. In amazement, I watched the sun slowly disappear, leaving us eventually in total darkness. It was really scary, and it amazed me to be quite frightened, even though I knew that it was something which was explainable and not really frightening. Pretty soon I saw the reflection in my bucket lighten up and slowly the reflection of the sun reappeared. Daylight returned all around me. It was quite an experience, one which I will never forget.

It took some time before our servants believed Mother's explanation of why the world seemed to be vanishing, but then came back again. Of course, it was very wise of Father to insist that I watch the reflection of the sun on the surface of the water instead of risking blindness by looking at the sun directly.

Our neighbors had a rather funny problem which had everybody who knew of it, screaming with laughter. There was a pet monkey that belonged to the neighborhood, and he was tied with a long chain to a pole. On the top of the pole was a seat where the monkey could sit, relax, and enjoy his surroundings. Quite a few chickens roamed around the pole every day. They were looking for scraps that the monkey would drop on the ground. Somehow the monkey learned how to catch a chicken. He would hold them and, one by one, pull out their feathers. Of course, the chickens were screeching with pain, but they always seemed to survive their ordeal. Somehow the chickens weren't smart enough to stay away from the pole, resulting in quite a few naked chickens roaming around, already plucked and ready for the cooking pot. It was an amusing sight to behold and had the benefit of the plucking being taken care of by the monkey.

The disposition of pets collected by officers staying at this outpost created a problem when families were sent to another place. One problem was that many of them had children who loved to have pets, especially cats, and that they didn't want to give them up. The larger problem, however, was that they didn't take the cats with them when they left. As a result there was a huge cat population in the area. At night the cats would howl and fight. Father loved animals but he couldn't stand missing his rest at night, so he decided to do something about it.

He ordered several of his soldiers to round up all the stray cats and kill them instantly so they wouldn't suffer. Of course, this was upsetting to everyone, but we knew it had to be done. The nights were silent after that, and all the new families were told they had to take their pets with them when they left.

Another unusual circumstance in the army life was dealing with sentenced criminals. To work out their sentences, these men were used by the army as laborers. They were called "bears" and they did all kinds of work such as construction, gardening, carrying heavy equipment, or whatever the army needed them to do. I befriended a bear that took care of our garden. Mother being the fantastic gardener that she was, always created landscaped gardens, wherever we lived. The bear who helped us was a big fellow who seemed so gentle. One morning he found a baby bird that had fallen out of its nest, so he picked it up carefully, climbed the tree and returned the fledgling back to its nest. I didn't understand how he could be a criminal, but later I found out that he had killed his wife, who had cheated on him by having an affair with a white man.

Sometimes bears were punished when they misbehaved. The punishment consisted of a certain number of whiplashes, according to the severity of the infraction. I remember several cases where bears were punished. Father decided the number of whiplashes that had to be given, and he hated this, so when he had to order ten or twenty lashes, he would have them stop about halfway through the punishment. In later years he was reprimanded for being too weak, but I admired him for it. It was upsetting to hear the whipping sounds followed by the screams we heard from the garrison, and I would put my hands over my ears to keep from hearing the torture below. It reminded me of the middle ages and I was glad to hear later that they had abandoned that practice. In contrast, the local population was often more retributive. Killing was quite often their way among themselves.

One time we witnessed an exciting event when we were having dinner at home. We were looking out the window as we ate and the chickens in the yard were running all around, enjoying themselves when suddenly we heard a big thud caused by a large green snake that had fallen from a nearby tree. The snake was beautiful to look at, but also one of the deadliest in the area. As soon as it reached the ground, it reared up right in front of a large chicken. We watched the two creatures because it was fascinating to see how they interacted. It was amazing to see how the chicken was totally hypnotized by the snake. The chicken followed the swaying motion of the snake's body with its head. About this time Father foresaw that the snake intended to eat the bird, so he called our houseboy, who quickly ran outside with a machete and killed the snake.

One morning, we found all of our chickens dead, blood everywhere, and chicken parts strewn about the yard. We found tracks that had been left by a musang, a type of weasel, that had feasted on an elaborate dinner of chicken. This was a big loss because the chickens were one of our main food sources. We had to buy a whole new flock of birds and tried to build a safer chicken coop. This was difficult because weasels can penetrate the smallest holes, but luckily, there was not another raid during the time Father served at that outpost.

One thing I did not enjoy was the local betting sport of cockfighting. I was walking around our neighborhood when I happened

Elephants on the Rampage

*Myself, My Sister,
and Baboe in Boeloe
Blanc Ara*

Mischievous Monkey

Our House in Boeloe Blanc Ara

onto a match. I hated to see these birds trying to kill each other, ending up all bloody at the end, if not dead. Worst of all, the owners of the birds didn't seem to mind if the cocks were maimed or killed, and the natives loved to gamble. The Dutch people were not allowed to stop the cockfights altogether, but there were areas where it was not allowed.

I had my tenth birthday in Boeloe Blanc Ara. It was one of the loneliest I've ever had because there weren't any children to play with me, and I didn't get the birthday present I had wished for. I was hoping for a baby goat, a kid, which had been promised to me by a villager. I was so disappointed, especially since I didn't have many material things of my own. I guess it was for the best, even though I was disappointed. I was sorry when we left Boeloe Blanc Ara since it had the distinction of being one of the most charming primitive outposts. We led a peaceful life there with interesting wild. My mother schooled me at home 2 to 3 hours per day. I remember these days as being very restful. We had a small vegetable garden, with egg-laying chickens running through our yard. My mother read a lot and I started drawing with pencil on a sketchpad. This was a peaceful and happy time during my childhood.

The next place the army sent us to was totally different, a place called Lhoknga.

LHOGNA

Living in Lhogna in 1927 was a real treat for a little girl. Not far from our house was the most beautiful beach in the world. Nearly every afternoon in the dry season, my mother, sister, and sometimes my Father and I spent several hours at the beach. It took fifteen minutes to walk the long avenue of Australian pines, called Tjemara's, which ended by crossing a bridge over a river where I would stop to watch the native fishermen throwing out their circular nets in a never ending procession. Most of the time they would catch quite large fish, but the small colorful coral fish were mixed in with the big ones. They came in the most brilliant colors and shapes, and sometimes I would be given a few of these to take home, so I always took a bucket along. Sometimes the fishermen were harvesting sea water to make salt. It was interesting to watch them pouring sea water into large flat containers, then exposing it to the hot sun. Several days later only the salt was left. It looked a little brown, but it was very acceptable for use in cooking.

After we crossed the bridge, we would walk through a field of so-called "touch-me-not's". When you stepped on them, the leaves would fold up right then, and if you looked back where you had walked, their would be a flat path in your wake. The beach was wide with pure white sand, bordered with Tjemara trees and tall spider lily plants underneath. Those lilies bloomed most of the time, forming a carpet that looked like old white lace. Not far from the shoreline were small islands, occupied by a wealth of animal and plant life. You could see monkeys swinging from the trees in the distance. At low tide there were beautiful shells everywhere and it was difficult to decide which ones to collect.

One sunny afternoon I was walking along the beach when I suddenly saw two huge animals running out of the jungle. They looked like two lizards as large as alligators, and, of course, I was curious, so I ran after them. The monsters saw me and they ran towards the ocean and swam away. Not knowing if they were aggressive or not, my Mother was frantically calling for me to come back. Later we found out that they were called Komodo Dragons. These prehistoric looking animals were about ten feet long and weighed about two hundred fifty pounds, and we heard they were very capable of killing a full grown horse. With no hearing capability, these beasts detect sounds and odor with their tongues.

I was told I was very lucky that I was not attacked. But I will never forget the first moment I saw them against the pristine beauty of the tropical beach; these huge, graceful reptiles running and slithering back into the ocean were a magnificent sight.

Another incident at the beach which left me unsettled, happened one day when we were swimming and a fisherman told us to get out of the water fast. He pointed at two black triangular shapes in the distance which were moving towards us. Luckily we got out in time, before the sharks reached us, but our parents were always afraid after that, for fear we would be too busy playing to see them coming. My Father had been swimming there with his soldiers, and kept a sharp eye on the water since he was responsible for the welfare of his men.

Some time later we found a perfect place at another beach where we could swim without the fear of sharks. A large coral reef had shaped a pool where the sharks dared not come in. One afternoon at the beach, we were surprised by a sudden thunderstorm. The rain was coming down in buckets. Just as we tried to make a run for the shelter of the trees, another fisherman called us to come to his primitive hut on the beach to get out of the downpour. This hut was made of overlapping palm fronds on a wooden frame, built so low that our only choice was to sit on the sandy floor. Our host was very kind, telling us about his family, in a nearby village and how hard it was for them to make a living. From then on we bought our salt from him and when we left mother gave him some money.

Sometime later this man gave me a crab which he had trained. This crab was living in a hole in the sand. When he called it, the crab would appear from it's hole and come to eat some meat out of his hand. For quite awhile I kept the crab in our yard where he made himself a new hole, gently accepting food from me with the very best table manners.

Those were wonderful and exciting years in Lhoknga. We had the nicest neighbors, who had four children. One of them was a girl my age, eleven, and her three brothers were six, eight, and sixteen years old. Very often we would play American Indian games using our imagination from books we had read. It was a treat for me because I had not had any playmates for quite a while.

In our neighbor's yard there was a huge fruit tree. When the fruits ripened, we would climb in the tree and eat so much fruit, it gave us stomach aches. There was a large stone wall next to the tree and when we climbed high enough we could see the back of the garrison next door. Quite often there would be soldiers there begging us to throw them some fruit. It was fun to see how happy they were when we picked our crop, and challenged ourselves throwing the fruit down to them at the right angle.

My eleventh birthday was not a happy one. The month before my Father had come home one afternoon, looking very upset. He had news for my mother. Her mother had died, of a heart attack, she had always had high blood pressure. She died in her sleep, it was 1927. Upon hearing the news, Mother screamed, threw a hairbrush at father, and then fainted. I had never seen her so upset. It was weeks before she acted normal again. The funeral occurred in

Holland, and no one of the immediate family could go, not any of the four children could attend, all of them were somewhere else in the world.

The stress at home was terrible, and this was the first time that I became aware that there might be something wrong with my mother and father's marriage. Father was not able to console my mother, she did not want anything to do with him. After a while, Father stopped trying to console her and just went about his way.

It was time for my birthday, and I did appreciate her efforts to be cheerful. The neighborhood kids came over and we even had ice cream, which was a rare treat in those days, and we played our games of hide and seek and blind man's bluff.

One afternoon, not long after my birthday, the family was sitting on the porch, looking out over the yard, when they commented on how quiet it was. We all listened and indeed there was silence, until suddenly the teacups on the table started to rattle. Father told me to stop kicking the table, and then it dawned on me that it was another earthquake. I jumped up, yelling "earthquake", and ran down the stairs into the yard, followed closely by the others. As we stood there, the ground all around us was moving and it was hard to stand up. The Tjemaras in the distance were swaying back and forth so far that the tops of the trees almost reached the ground. The chickens in the coop were flying wildly about, and the cats were hiding under the house. The servants were holding onto anything they could find as big cracks appeared in the ground around us, and everything around us seemed to be disintegrating.

For a few minutes it looked as if the end of our world was coming. Then suddenly, everything stopped. We didn't dare go back to the house for fear of an aftershock. We had been lucky this time too, and after awhile we climbed the stairs to see how much damage the quake had caused. A few things were broken or askew, but on the whole, we were relatively untouched. We didn't see the cats for several days, and the servants slept outside for a week, but eventually our routine became normal again. We found out later that this was not really an earthquake, but a so-called seaquake, only without the tidal wave, which we were thankful for, but on the shoreline there were a lot of fallen trees and flotsam from the aftermath.

We had quite a few animals in Lhoknga. Twenty chickens, two ducks, four cats, one hundred pigeons and a large tame owl. A native woman at the garrison had a white cockatoo which she was willing to sell, so after a lot of pleading, mom bought it for me for the paltry sum of five guilders. I was thrilled and named the bird Jacob.

Jacob could mimic Indonesian words such as "Slamat Djalan", which loosely translated means "God bless you" or "blessed your walking". When our cook went to the local market, Jacob would say "Cockie pigi die pasar", meaning "cook goes to the market" Teaching Jacob new Dutch words was tiring, but after a while I succeeded. Eventually, Jacob spoke Malayan to the houseboys and Dutch to me and my family. He would say "Goeje Moregen" (Good Morning), and "Ik ben Jakob" (I am Jacob).

He did cause one problem though. Jacob was able to mimic the sound of chickens when they were about to lay an egg, which caused an uproar, especially when the chickens weren't ready to lay their eggs. He also learned to imitate my mothers voice when she called our houseboy, Oesin. Several times Oesin came running only to find out that it was just the bird calling him. For some reason Jacob decided to target Oesin, so he would torment the poor man by letting out a startling scream just as Oesin passed by, usually carrying something. Sometimes he would even chase after Oesin, trying to bite his heels.

I needed to discourage this behavior, so sometimes he was free to roam around and other times we would put a chain around his ankle. It was amazing that he never left us, though his wings had been clipped, so he really couldn't fly that well anyway. Jacob trusted me, so I was never bitten, but once he bit and made a hole in Father's earlobe. Father was furious, but allowed me to keep

Jacob because he meant so much to me. I promised Father that he would never be bothered by my feathered friend again.

I enjoyed all the animals immensely. Our owl would sit in his cage by day and sleep, but at night the bird would fly away, and then the next morning, there he would be, back in his cage. There was no shortage of mice to keep him well fed during the night, so he would return to his cage during the day.

We'd had chicks before, but I'd always liked the baby ducks even more, which gave me an idea. Our ducks were ready to breed, so I took three duck eggs and put them under our breeding hen instead of her own eggs. The whole family was giggling about my trick, as we wondered what would happen when the eggs hatched.

After several weeks the ducklings broke out of their shells, getting their first look at their mother and the world around them. Amazingly, they accepted their hen-mother from the beginning as their rightful mama. Within a few days, the hen had accepted her strange babies. We were wondering whether her chicken brain had registered that her babies looked foreign, especially compared to all the other chicks in the coop. We had a small pond in our yard, and as soon as the ducklings discovered this, they plunged right in as nature intended. But the mama hen started to scream and run around the pond in circles, frantically trying to call them out, with no success, of course. Nature had taken over and finally she gave up and was starting to walk away, when the ducklings came out of the water and followed her after all. Since that first swimming episode, the ducklings came back every day while their mother watched from dry land, never trying to follow them into the water.

Another time, our houseboy, Oesin, was pouring boiling water he had used for washing dishes, into a small gutter in the yard. Before he noticed, one of the older ducks had waddled into the gutter and ended up with scalded feet, which made all of us feel quite badly about the accident. We quickly scooped up the duck and took it to mother. She knew quite a lot about first aid and natural cures, so she put some lotion on the ducks feet and bandaged it. Needless to say, the duck waddled around, looking like Charlie Chaplin with bandaged toes. Luckily, it survived, but I did notice it avoided walking near that gutter again.

Even though I was young, I was always gardening. My specialty was raising carnations in discarded petrol cans. But in my garden there were some nasty bugs that frightened me. I still shudder thinking of these creatures. There were centipedes six inches long with thick bodies. When you stepped on one of them, they gave off a florescent light. The tropical moisturized fauna attracted them. They were dangerous, so I always called the houseboy to kill them before I worked with my plants.

Scorpions were also plentiful. Sometimes you would see a mother carrying her young on her back with their tails entwined. Scorpions were interesting so I hated to see them killed, but their sting could also be deadly, so there was no choice.

Along the coastline were many beaches. They were deserted, and had a bountiful supply of beautiful shells stacked everywhere. Sea turtles were swimming nearby and monkeys watched us while swinging from one Tjemara tree to another. I will never forget the beauty of it all, and I feel very grateful to have seen the tropical seashore in all its magnificence, so long ago, still in its primitive form.

I felt that I was a part of eternity when I was there, with the sounds of the sea, the calls of the monkeys in the Tjemara trees, and the wind blowing through my hair. It felt timeless, like it had all always been there and always would be there, and that I was part of that place, and always would be. In later years, when life was difficult and frightening, I learned to find peace by thinking again of that beach, placing myself once again in that period of my life, when I was young, happy, and felt the protective shield of being one of God's children.

My father was an excellent photographer. He always wanted to take pictures of Indonesia "au Natural", and of the family too, so one day all of us were at one of the secluded beaches in Sumatra, when Father suddenly told my sister and I to take off our bathing suits and stand out on one of the reef rocks, so he could take a picture of us. At first, I refused him, but he was not a man to be disobeyed. I was ten years old at the time, and modest about being seen in the nude. The native children were used to running about with nothing on, but not us, so we very reluctantly took off our bathing suits and stood where Father could take the picture of us looking out at the sea. Then we quickly put our suits back on.

Soon after that I forgot about the incident, until Father got a letter from the Netherlands telling him that he had won a medal in a photo contest of the pictures he had taken of my sister Meta and me. Many years later, several pictures were sent to the Colonial Institute of Amsterdam, where they remain to this day. They changed the name of the museum when Indonesia was liberated, and today they are valuable as historical data of that period, and of course, to our family.

There was one thing that frightened me every time I had to deal with it. My father had a motorcycle, which he loved to ride. Often he would insist that I go with him, sitting on the duo seat. I just hated traveling with so much speed, my arms encircling Father's waist. The roads in Lhoknga were mostly dirt with potholes everywhere. Being shaken up and down constantly made it hard to keep one's balance, so I was always afraid we would be thrown off and be hurt. But the worst part came as we approached our home, and Father stopped the cycle suddenly, creating a loud bang. This would make me burst into tears, and Father would get mad and call me a "sissy". In later years I found out that he had really wanted a son when I was born, and was very disappointed. Remembering this, I hated motorcycles for the rest of my life.

Very often Father had to go on patrol with his soldiers to survey large areas around Lhoknga. He had to check villages in the jungle, and correct any problems that occurred. The Atjeh population in North Sumatra had been hostile for many years and fought many battles with the Dutch army. When we lived there from 1926 through 1929, the Atjeh people were more subdued towards the

Dutch, but they would war between themselves. So these trips Father made were not without risk and we were never sure whether he would come back alive or not. Mom worked hard at staying flexible through all this, but she did arm herself with a Luger, which she kept under the pillow in her bedroom. The army taught her how to use it, and she was a crack shot, winning several shooting competitions. I discovered the gun for the first time when I was ten, and she warned me never to touch it. I learned at a very young age that firearms were never to be played with, and could go off unintentionally, creating much damage.

The priorities of the natives and what we were taught as Europeans were quite often worlds apart. One morning I was crossing a small road next to our home when an old man approached, pushing a go-cart. The old man didn't even try to stop and ran right over a dog, cutting him nearly in half. It was just horrible because the dog was still alive and howling with pain, while trying to get up. The old man looked at me and said "It's only a dog", and at the same time he picked up the limp body and threw it into the gutter next to the road. By that time I was crying and asked the man if he would kill the dog to put it out of its misery. He said "why bother, it's dying anyway." So I ran home to ask the gardener if he would help me, but by the time we returned, the dog had died.

When we had chicken dinner, the gardener would kill the bird. I always tried to stay away when the servant slaughtered the animal, as I had seen a rooster running around without it's head, after one axing. When you live in a primitive country life and death are not hidden from your eyes, and you have to learn to deal with it. The best game meat we had was when Father came home from a hunting party with wild boar. They were large wild pigs with fierce looking tusks and very stiff hairs on their muscular bodies. The carcass was placed on a rod which could be rotated above a huge fire. It took hours before it was roasted to perfection on all sides. The taste was very different from domestic pig, and just as good, if not better.

My taste buds come alive as I recall the lobsters we bought from the natives. We strung the lobsters on a beam under the roof, where Jacob had his perch. The poor bird was afraid of them. He probably saw them as a predator trying to catch him with their large claws. At the time it was fun to watch him screeching at them and flapping his wings.

SECOND TRIP TO HOLLAND: 1927

We would have liked to stay in Lhoknga longer, but too soon the day came when Father told us that he had been transferred to yet another outpost. This time we would not come with him because it was Tangsi Lokop, primitive, and high up in the jungles of North Sumatra. Since there were no schools, children were not allowed to come. As a result, it was decided that my mother, sister, and I would go back to Holland and stay with my maternal grandfather. I was eleven years old then and it was time for me to prepare to enter high school. Mother had been teaching me up till now, but she wouldn't be teaching me at the high school level. So when the time came that Father had to leave, we said our good-bye's to him and for several weeks we stayed in a bungalow in Kota Radja, waiting for a ship to take us back to Holland.

I remember our stay in Kota Radja because I had a terrible infection in one of my front teeth. There were no dentists in Kota Radja, only a man who had assisted a dentist for a few months, so when he treated the cavity in my tooth, I came away with an infection. I developed a very high temperature and my face became terribly swollen, but I did survive. In those days, this was the risk you took living in those circumstances. Finally we were told that our ship, the John de Wit, was ready to sail, so we boarded a small boat and took a rough ride to the island of Sabang.

At Sabang we stayed overnight in a hotel which overlooked the bay, and we could see our ship anchored in the distance. The view was just beautiful as we watched the coolies walking back and forth carrying sacks of coal for the ship. In those days the ships were fueled by coal and everything was covered with coal dust. Even the hotel was dirty. The sheets on our beds were gray looking, and we even felt sooty ourselves as our hands and faces started showing blackish spots. We looked like clowns and laughed about it, but mother, being the neat and clean person she was, hated being there, and was very glad we had not been stationed at this spot.

Our trip to Holland took five weeks. We had a very nice cabin, and the dining room was clean and simple. We had to watch ourselves on the decks though, because they were narrow and slippery. It was a treat when we reached a harbor, as hundreds of vendors would crowd around our ship in their small boats, showing their wares. Some would come aboard with chicks in their hands, which they would make disappear and reappear in different peoples pockets. When we asked them what they did with the chicks when they grew up, they said that most of them never grew up. They died after a few days, but who cared because there were plenty of chicks available. This thought horrified me.

A lot of the time the voyage was not easy for us. Mother was seasick most of the time and couldn't leave the cabin, and there was nobody to supervise the children. Everybody had to take care of their own children, which wasn't easy, with little ones that liked to run around. So when mother was seasick, I took charge of my little sister, Meta, who was three years old, at the time. I had a great sense of responsibility and was afraid of losing Meta. What worried me most were the slippery decks outside where a child could easily slip and fall into the ocean. If a child fell overboard, there was no way to save them.

A story went around, which was true, about two children traveling with their parents on one of those big ships. The mother scolded her little girl and threatened to push her out of one of the portholes if she didn't behave herself. Her brother, who was just a little older thought his mother really meant what she said. One day the mother wanted to leave the cabin for awhile, and she asked the boy to take care of his sister, while she was away.

When the girl became naughty, so the boy took her, and pushed her out through the porthole, thinking this was the right thing to do. When the mother came back, she asked him where the girl was, so he told her what he had done. This story circulated throughout the ship and it gave me nightmares. There were quite a few other children around and often they would ask me to join them for games, but I never would join them. Even at eleven years old, I felt very responsible for my sister. This was a great relief to my Mother, and she praised me for my efforts.

The journey through the Suez Canal was fascinating. On both sides of the canal were little villages surrounded by date palm trees. Most of the buildings were painted white reflecting the bright sunshine. Caravans of camels driven by men in white robes with turbans on their heads, looked as if they had just stepped out of a Bible story. The canal itself was quite narrow, and in the sea water you could see the brilliant colors and shapes of many species of fish and jelly fish.

A young man came aboard from his small boat, offering to show us how well he could dive if we gave him some money. Some passengers obliged him, so he climbed to the highest deck of the ship, positioned himself and dove gracefully from a height of approximately one hundred feet into the sea below. How he dared to dive from such a height was astonishing and very dangerous, but it the young are willing to take such risks without any fear.

The harbor of Port Said was also enchanting, like a fairy tale come true. I was allowed to join a group of passengers visiting the city. Countless beggars swarmed around us the moment our feet touched the wharf. They were pitiful, but we had been warned not to give them anything till we left, or they would have robbed us.

Vendors crowded around us, showing us their merchandise. What I liked best were the beautiful necklaces made of hand blown glass in brilliant colors and shapes. I still regret that I didn't buy more of them because I've never seen them for sale anywhere else.

We paid a visit to a mosque, leaving our shoes outside. Not a bad idea when you want to keep your floors clean! The serene atmosphere and intricate designs on the walls of the mosque were beautiful, going back many centuries, and all the tiles were hand set, taking a considerable part of somebody's life.

It struck me as funny that all the merchants were standing in front of their shops saying the same thing over and over again in several different languages. It was probably the only thing they could say outside their own language, but it was very effective. They were chanting "look-look without buying". I even heard it in Dutch, much to my surprise. A lot of our group did look and were buying quite a few goods to take back to the ship.

Cock Fighting

Meeting Komodo Dragons

Duck Tending

Natural Pose for Father's Photography

LIFE IN HOLLAND: 1927

A few days later we docked in Marseilles, France. My mother decided she'd had enough of rocking ships, so we boarded a train and we were in Holland within twenty four hours. We took a sleeper train so I really enjoyed the trip, with it's constantly changing scenery from the countryside to the cities of France and Belgium. When the conductor came to punch our tickets, I was proud to be able to speak to him in French.

Grandfather Kooreman, my mother's father, was very happy when he met us at the station in Amsterdam. He was lonely after the death of his wife, and now that I was with him I felt the loss of her even more than before. I remember how nice she had been during the short time we had spent with her when I was six. But that's the price you pay when you leave your own country to live somewhere else. It was sad that when my grandmother died, none of her children or grandchildren could attend her funeral. Two sons and two daughters with their families were living in Indonesia, and her youngest son, who wasn't married, lived in America.

It took some time for me to get used to the Dutch culture and cooler climate. Now, my mother only had one girl to help her with the household, and she was only there five days a week. In those days we didn't have the modern conveniences in our households, like washing machines, refrigerators, and dishwashers. Sheets and blankets were sent out to a laundry man. Quite often the things you sent out were not what you got back. It was not unusual for you to get something that belonged to someone else. I still remember how mom used to make a list of all the items she sent out, so there would be no errors.

There was a small cellar in the house where we would keep some fresh food for a few days, but perishable foods had to be bought almost every day, therefore you had a baker, a milkman, and a grocery and produce man coming to your door. In a way, it was nice to have so many different people to talk to everyday. We would also have our neighbors over in the afternoon, especially around tea time.

There was only one small bath and toilet available in my grandfathers house though, and most of the time we only took a bath once a week, on Saturdays. This took a little getting used to after all the water that had been available to us in the islands.

In September of 1927, I went to a regular school for the first time which was quite an experience for me. I loved it because now I had more playmates than I had ever had before. In May of 1928, I had to pass an exam required to be accepted into high school. Over the previous years I had learned five basic subjects. They were arithmetic, history, geography and the French and Dutch languages. According to the correspondence course which I had followed with the help of mother, I had done well. My grades were above average, so I had high hopes of passing the exam.

When it was time for the exam, however, I found, to my horror, that I didn't know enough and wasn't able to answer many of the questions, especially in arithmetic. When the teacher took me aside with another girl for a oral exam, he asked us the following question. When 180 birds are sitting on a rooftop, and a hunter tries to shoot 72 of them, how many are left sitting on the roof?

We had to answer him in a split second, so I tried frantically to figure out the right answer. But the girl sitting next to me had a answer right away. She told the teacher, while laughing "None of the birds are left, because they all flew away." I was dumfounded

because it never dawned on me that this was one of those aptitude tests of your intelligence. Those were trick questions that one
learned in regular school, which I missed. The teacher laughed
when the student gave the right answer. He gave her a good mark
and gave me a bad one.

The day after the exam I had to go to the high school where I
had taken the exam to find out the results. When I was told that I
didn't pass and that I would have to do a whole year over again, I
burst out crying and just couldn't stop. I was desperate because I
had studied so hard and had done my very best, wanting so much
to succeed. The same teacher that had given the oral exam tried to
console me, telling me that it was not so bad, and certainly not the
end of the world. But I told him that my Father would be so disappointed and that I was so ashamed of myself.

The teacher asked me where my Father was and where I had
gone to school. When I told him that Father was in Indonesia, and
that I had never gone to school before we came to Holland, I could
see that he was surprised, to say the least. He asked me if I had ever
heard of the so-called joke about the birds on the roof, and when I
said "no", he felt guilty for embarrassing me. He even apologized,
which made me feel a little better, but it did not change the fact
that I would have to repeat the sixth grade in school. I felt so stupid that year and was dreading that fact that I would have to take
the exam over again at the end of the year. Three weeks before the
time to retake the exam, my paternal grandfather, who had been a
principal of a school, came over to help me prepare for the oncom-
ing exam. We worked on arithmetic the most, and he taught me
some of the tricky problems one had to learn. My correspondence
course had never handled problems like these, so I was grateful for
his assistance.

Two problems I still remember: When you sit in a train that is
100 meters long going from A to B, which is a distance of 15 kilometers, with an average speed of 90 kilometers per hour, and a fly
is flying in the train in the same direction, starting at the back of

the train at the same time as the train starts, at a speed of 10 meters per minute, how far does the fly get in the train when the latter passes station B? (Answer: The fly reaches the front of the train when it passes station B.) The second was: A leaking faucet drips in a bathtub that can contain 90 liters of water. The faucet drips 10 drops per second, and each drop is 1/20th of a milliliter. How long will it take for the leaking faucet to fill the tub to the point of over flowing? (Answer: Two days and two hours.) Working with grandfather was a treat. He was such a good teacher and I got to know him a lot better.

One of the happiest moments of my life was when my grandfather Leeksma told my mother that there was no question about the fact that I was smart, but that there had been a lack of education in my correspondence course, which was neither Mom's or my fault. I passed the second exam with flying colors and felt elated when I started high school. It helped me to realize that I was not stupid after all.

Winter in Holland was something new for me, especially when it had been snowing, covering everything with the "white stuff". I couldn't believe my eyes when the canal in front of the house froze over and people could walk on water. An old pair of skates were hanging in the tool shed and they fit me quite well, so I tried to skating "on water". I tried my hardest to learn to skate well, and after falling many times, I did manage to stay upright, albeit slightly bent over, skating some distance with outstretched hands and arms, but I was never very good at it, especially when it came to stopping. This little "handicap", often sent me headfirst into piles of snow or ice, which was a painful experience. But when we were young we overlooked the bruises of pursuing new challenges.

My skates were tied with strings to flat heeled shoes and were held tightly to give me the support I needed, but I had to wind the strings over and over again which was really frustrating.

Most of the kids around me could skate already, so they teased me but it didn't bother me because I always had the good excuse of having lived in the tropics. Winters in Holland are quite miserable, with a lot of fog, rain, and somber skies, especially when the snow was falling and the waterways were frozen up, making most of the young people very happy.

The winters of 1927 and 1928 were exceptionally cold, even to the point that the sea was frozen over near the shoreline, shaping some waves into giant sculptures. Some people even crossed the Zuidersee (southern sea), a near inland sea on horse and buggy. I used every opportunity to go skating in front of our house on the canal, the Leidse Vaard. I was warned to be careful though because ice could be thin and crack in some places. One afternoon I found out how dangerous thin ice could be. I happened to be sitting on the edge of the canal, tying my skates, when three soldiers came skating by very fast. Just when they started to pass under a small bridge close by, we heard an enormous resounding "bang". The surface of the ice had started to crack and a large hole appeared right in front of one of the soldiers. In a split second, he disappeared under water. Luckily, he surfaced and tried frantically to hold onto the edge of the breaking ice, yelling for help. The two other soldiers had managed to scramble out of the canal. On the bridge was a long rope, which was placed there on purpose, in case of an emergency such as this.

Several people were standing on the bridge, watching the skaters. They grabbed the rope and quickly lowered it to the struggling soldier, who grasped the rope with frozen hands and was hauled out. The rope saved his life and everyone was cheering, even my mother, who came running out of the house, anxious because she thought something might have happened to me. She was so glad to see me sitting there on the embankment, safe and sound, that she gave me a big hug. Of course, nobody skated any more that afternoon anywhere near the spot of the accident.

The spring of 1928 came and it gave me the opportunity to go outdoors more often. I used to go to some nearby meadows, where there were several ditches. There were so many interesting plants and animals to find. Salamanders, green frogs, small fish, were all present, and I would try to collect them for an aquarium.

Whenever I came home from a fishing trip with a bucket loaded with aquatic creatures and water plants, Rika, our part time maid, would start yelling at me as soon as I entered the kitchen. Most of the time she had just finished cleaning the kitchen floor and didn't want me to step on it with my muddy shoes. I knew she was a little bit afraid of frogs. Often I had a small frog in my bucket, and I'm ashamed to say that I chased after Rika with a squirming frog in my hand. She would run and scream, but at the same time, she would laugh because she liked being chased. When I stopped chasing her, she always wanted to see what I had caught, and help me do whatever with it, I have never forgotten Rika, and keep her close to me in my "memory" treasure chest.

We used to sit in front of the house on summer days, watching the constant flow of boats on the canal. The old fashioned tramway sped through at regular intervals in the near distance, running between Amsterdam and the sea resort of Zandvoort.

On one of those days we saw a bad accident. An old man was pushing his ice cream cart when a motorcyclist approached him from behind. The cyclist was wavering as if he were drunk. He hit the old man, and before you knew it, the force of the impact, which sounded like a cannon shot, propelled man and cart into the air. When the cart came down it was shattered in many pieces. In no time the police were there and a crowd had gathered. Later we heard of the sudden tragic death of the ice cream vendor.

We had very nice neighbors, the Bouwers who lived to the left of our house, and who went on hikes in the dunes if the weather was good. They knew how much I liked nature and hiking, so they asked me to go with them. I would go by tramway halfway to the beach resort of Zandvoort, and would get off at a certain stop near the dunes. We had a special ticket which allowed us to cross the affordably. The Dutch dunes are beautiful, covered with white sand, wildflowers of all kinds, and graceful grasses. In springtime "brem" (genista) bushes bloom with their golden yellow clusters of flowers everywhere. Colorful lizards were jumping in and out of the vegetation. I wanted to catch some for the terrarium that grandfather had built for me at home, but it wasn't that easy. Sometimes I would just watch them, digging their holes and sunning themselves, but eventually I caught a few and took them to school with me to show the biology class, which always earned me some extra credit.

School work and my hobbies kept me pretty busy. I had started to take piano lessons because my mother played at Grandfather's house, and she thought it would be good for me to know how also, so I practiced faithfully, but I knew in my heart, that it wasn't right for me. I just didn't have the desire or talent for it, though I did sing all the familiar Dutch songs with my mother when she played.

After a year of piano lessons the teacher happened to notice some of the drawings I'd done for school. She couldn't believe that I had done them, and asked me "do you like to draw or paint?" When I told her that I had been drawing since I was four years old, she told me that she wanted to talk to my mother.

Mother told me later that the teacher had advised her to stop my piano lessons, and find, instead, somebody who could teach me art. She said "Hanny is not very musical, so it would be a waste of time and money for her to go on playing the piano." This suited me just fine because I could spend more time on my real love, art.

Soon afterwards I found out that my high school art teacher was giving private lessons to some of his talented students. He had seen my drawings and happily accepted me into his private class. His art lessons were just wonderful. I remember one of the subjects I had to draw, which was a portrait of the Egyptian King Tutankhamen, along with still lifes and landscapes.

Grandfather gave me money on my birthday and on St. Nicholas day too, which was the fifth of December. I was thrilled to possess some money, especially because I was allowed to spend it on whatever I wanted. After thinking about it, the choices came down to some drawing supplies or walking two hours to and from the pet store in Haarlem. I felt like a millionaire at the pet store. Deciding what to buy wasn't easy. Would it be a mouse for a quarter, a lizard for seventy-five cents or possibly a fish? Once I bought a pair of mice. I kept them in a large jar with woodchips on the bottom. Milk, bread and nuts were easy to get to feed them. They were so graceful in their movements that I tried too draw them, which was not that easy because they move very quickly. Not too long after I got them, they had babies that were born looking like little rubber erasers with no hair on them.

Mother and grandfather weren't too happy having mice around the house, so I was careful to keep them in the jar with some netting on top. At that time I didn't know much about mice, and due to my lack of knowledge, I made a fatal mistake. One sunny summer day I put the jar out in the yard, thinking the mice needed some fresh air! Two hours passed, and I went to get them, but the mice were gone. I'm sure the neighbors cat had managed to open the jar and have a fantastic meal. Of course I felt terrible and decided not to buy any more mice.

Two old ladies who had been our neighbors for quite a while, moved away, and a new family named Alexis moved in. It was a lucky break for me since they had two children. The youngest was a boy, sixteen years old, two years older than I. His name was Arnold and I soon found out that he and his Father competed between themselves painting and drawing. This delighted me, and pretty soon we organized competitions in art between the three of us. We would choose the subject, like a bird, portrait, still life or maybe a landscape and we would all create in the same subject. It didn't have to be the same picture, as long as the category was the same. When we were finished with our work, we would compare them and decide which one was the best. Sometimes we would ask an outsider to decide for us. Only once did I win, mostly because they were more advanced in art than I, but it was a good challenge for me.

Once in a while I played soccer on the street with a group of boys. I loved the exercise, but Mom wasn't thrilled about it, and would say "You should behave more like a girl." Whenever she found an excuse to keep me away from the street, she would use it.

The time I spent in Holland was not without sickness. Several times I had bronchitis. When I was thirteen I came down with double pneumonia, which was very painful. It took quite a while to get over it and I nearly died. In the 1920's the medical world was not as advanced as it is now, but after six weeks, I finally recovered. In addition, I had the usual childhood diseases – measles and chickenpox, but these only slowed me down for a short while. During the rest of my teens I was quite healthy, thank goodness. I never liked the Dutch climate, somber and cold for so many months of the year, and I longed for the warm sunny climate of Indonesia.

After I had the chicken pox Mom decided to send me to the Saadmans, friends who lived in the sea resort of Zandvoort for two weeks. I wasn't too happy about this, but Mother insisted. Luckily, she allowed me to ride there on my bike, which took about an hour. I knew my way as I had been there before. Their house was beautiful and surrounded by dunes, which overlooked the sea in the distance.

I didn't have to worry about missing school because it was August and I was on vacation. The Saadman's were nice people who had three children, all older than I. We went on long hikes over the dunes and on the beaches, and I helped them with their beautiful garden. They had quite a large fish pond with hundreds of fish in many colors. Unfortunately, I didn't have much in common with their children who were 20,16, and 15 years old. But the sixteen year old showed a special interest in me, trying to hug me, and I panicked.

The Saadman children had an advantage over me that I could not overcome. They could speak languages that I could not. Many times when they were talking to each other and I approached, they would switch languages so I couldn't understand them. I knew a little French already, but English and German were new to me, and I felt this was very rude of them, but I didn't complain. Instead, I decided to go home after a week there, telling them that I was homesick. At first they tried to convince me to stay, but then they realized that I wasn't very happy. I thanked the lady of the house and left on my bike. In those days it wasn't dangerous to travel alone on the roads in broad daylight. Of course, Mother was surprised to see me back so soon, but understood when I told her how shabbily the children had treated me. Interestingly enough, the oldest daughter of the Saadmans, came over to see me a few months later, and told me they were sorry for having teased me, and that she had realized how cruel it had been of them. Ever since that experience, I've made sure not to speak a language that the people around me cannot understand.

A few times we were invited to stay for a couple of weeks in Bussum. A very good friend of Mother's lived there. I called her Aunt Vinny, although she wasn't really my aunt. Bussum is a lovely town south of Amsterdam. The scenery is very nice, with vast fields of purple colored heather and dark pine forests. There were bicycle paths everywhere too. We enjoyed taking picnics to the nearby villages and settling ourselves in the heather fields for a marvelous repast.

Those were the only vacation times we had, and at last, word came from my Father. He was coming back to Holland on furlough.

FATHER COMES HOME: 1930

Everybody was excited. We had not seen him for quite a while. My sister could hardly remember him. I will never forget when we went to the railroad station to greet Father. The train pulled into the station at Haarlem and, as the passengers started to disembark we spotted him right away. He was a very tall, handsome man, with a deep brown tan from the tropics, which really stood out against his snowy white uniform. Everybody looked at him, and I was so proud and happy to see him again, but Meta took one look at him and hid behind mothers skirts, asking "Who's that man?". Mother explained that it was her father, but it took Meta a while before she came forward to give him a hug. When it was my turn to hug Father, I suddenly stopped in my tracks because the first thing he said to me was, "Do you have too wear those ugly glasses?" I had been wearing them for awhile now, since the school had insisted that I have an eye exam. I had been having trouble seeing the chalkboard, and after the exam, it turned out that I was nearsighted and needed glasses. I hated them, especially when a boy in class told me he liked me better without them. I already thought I was ugly with them on, so I felt deeply hurt that the first comment out of my father 's mouth was an additional invalidation of my looks. Tact was never one of my Father's strong points His tactless, nonchalant comment stayed with me for years afterwards. He had no idea that his comment hurt me so.

Our lives changed drastically when Father came home. He was a real sportsman and we went on hikes, bike trips and swam when the weather permitted. I even got my swimming diploma on one very cold September day. I had to swim with all my clothes on, shoes too, which was not easy because they dragged me down with their weight. Mother had never learned to swim, so she took lessons with me, and we graduated on the same day. I was proud of her because she had been afraid of the water all her life. She always told me to do something about anything that was an obstacle in my life, even if it took a lot of willpower to overcome the problem.

Father was a lot more generous than Mother when it came to presents. I guess Mother had learned to be thrifty from her childhood. My sister and I only got presents on special occasions, like birthdays or feast days like St. Nicholas. The origin of the St. Nicholas feast dates back 1700 years. St. Nicholas was born in 270 in a town called Myra, in Turkey. When he grew up he became a bishop, who did a lot of good for his people, especially sea faring skippers. After his death, his body was moved by Christians to Bari, which later became a part of Spain. On Christmas we didn't get presents because it was considered a holy day. We did have a Christmas tree though, decorated with real candles and ornaments. We could never leave the tree when the candles were lit though because of the fire hazard. On Christmas day we would have a special dinner of wild rabbit, called "hare". Just before the holiday a man would come to the door with a pole over his shoulder. Several hares were hanging from the pole and mother would choose the best looking one. It took quite a while to skin and prepare the hare, but it was delicious to eat. Sometimes we would have chicken, but never a turkey in those days.

St. Nicolas feast, the fifth of December, was the most important children's festivity of the year. Everybody bought or made presents with a funny poem attached to each. There was a lot of laughing at the practical jokes played on one another. I remember one occasion when I got a present that looked like candy, but when

I took a bite, it turned out to be made of soap. I didn't like this joke very much because it tasted terrible, and I really didn't think it was funny.

Many stories were told of St. Nicolas, and how he rode to the rooftops of the houses, dropping presents through the chimneys. On the first day of December, four days before the feast, the children would put a wooden shoe in front of the fireplace, along with straw and a piece of bread or carrot for St. Nick's horse. Early the next day they couldn't wait to see if he had left them a small gift in place of the straw and goodies they had left in their shoes, only if they were good, of course.

St. Nicolas often visited small children's' groups. His assistant, Zwarte Piet (Black Peter), would have the big book with him with names of all the children and a report next to these names indicating if they had been good or bad. After each child's name was called, St. Nicolas would praise or scold that child. For those children who had been behaving badly St. Nicolas would call over Zwarte Piet who would scold the child and threatened to carry the child away in his big gunny sack if the behavior did not improve. This made a very strong impression on the younger children who were terrified of the "big book". Each child with good behavior would also receive a gift also mentioned on the list. Of course the children's parents all carried knowing smiles when the judgments from St. Nicolas about the children's behavior were uttered. I believed the whole St. Nicolas story for many years and I was disappointed when later I learned that it was just a children's fable.

Father and I went shopping in Haarlem. I forgot what Father needed, but it took quite awhile before he found what he was looking for, so while we were passing several stores I stopped to admire some necklaces in a shop window. Father stopped too, and seeing how interested I was in the jewelry display, he asked me if I would like to have the necklace. I couldn't believe it. Father took me by the hand and pulled me into the store. He asked the salesgirl to show us some of the necklaces. They were made of colored glass in bright hues, and all of them were just beautiful, in my eyes. I liked two necklaces especially. One was blue and the other green, my favorite colors. I couldn't make up my mind which one I liked the best. Father got impatient, so he asked the salesgirl to wrap up both of them. "Here is something special for you" Father told me, as he handed me the package and said: "I'm glad you like them so much". I couldn't believe my luck. This was the first time in all of my life that I got a present for no special occasion at all! I was beside myself with joy and told Father that I would never forget this moment, and I never did. I wore those necklaces for years and whenever I look at them I feel elated.

Father's furlough went by quite fast and soon it was time for us to go return to the Dutch East Indies. About the same time, Mother's sister and her three daughters came back from the Indies to stay with my grandfather, Opa Kooreman. We said good-bye to my grandmother, Father's mother, and a few friends. My Father's father, Opa Leeksma, had died a short time before Father came back to Holland. He'd had a long life, and reached the age of seventy-six, but we really missed him when he died. He had been an excellent school teacher, who had been a great help for me to study for the exam I had to pass for my high school certificate. My father never talked about the death of his father, Opa Tine de Boer-Leeksma. Father was much closer to his mother, Oma Tine de Boer-Leeksma. She lived to be 96, and passed away in 1946. My husband, Bram met her during World War II, just before she died. They got along very well, even though they knew each other only a short time.

VACATION IN SWITZERLAND: 1932

My parents decided to leave Holland early because they wanted to have a vacation before we went back to Indonesia. We went to Switzerland and stayed in a small hotel in Montreux, on the Swiss end of Lake Geneva. I don't know why they decided to go back to Switzerland, maybe because mother had a happy vacation there once when she was a teenager. Father had done a favor for a friend, whose daughter was the same age as my mother at the time. To return the favor mother was invited to spend a vacation in Switzerland with his daughter. Mother talked about that vacation for years after that.

The view from our hotel was spectacular, overlooking snow capped mountains in the distance. Actually there was a lot of snow everywhere because it was February. We went hiking or shopping everyday. There were a lot of ski slopes nearby, crowded with ski-ers. I saw many kids taking ski lessons, practicing coming down the slopes or just having fun in the snow. I had always been good in sports, and I wanted to learn to ski so badly that I begged my parents to let me take lessons. But they said "no" because it was very expensive and it didn't make much sense for me to learn how when we were going to go live in a tropical climate, where there was no snow.

A guest in our hotel showed me a doll that she had made of cloth, which really impressed me. I wanted to make one for myself, and I was very handy with my hands and knew I would be able to copy it. So I begged for the material to make the doll for quite a while, and finally mother bought me what I needed to make it. I spent a lot of time in the hotel room working on this project, and I remember my parents complaining about me wanting to work on the doll for hours instead of being out with them. But I was getting tired of plugging through piles of frozen snow and ice in freezing weather. It was such a relief for me when I could stay inside for a while.

It was a small doll made of wool, and standing on skis. The hotel manager complemented me on having made such a finely detailed doll. I kept it for years until it fell apart from wear.

When we did go out, we would walk for hours. My sister was still very young then, so mother had to carry her because Father would walk ahead much faster than we could keep up. Mother used to complain about this and Father would get mad. I hated those quarrels and couldn't understand why Father was so selfish.

We stayed in Switzerland for six weeks, which was entirely too long for my sister and me. We were very happy to board the train for Marseilles, where we would embark on our journey back to Indonesia. Our boat was waiting in the harbor when we arrived, and what a wonderful feeling it was to get aboard the ship that would take us back to our beloved Indonesia. We sailed for three weeks before reaching Batavia.(this area is now called Jakarta). The trip was a very pleasant one. There was another girl, Lily, who was two years older than I, who befriended me. She was proud of the fact that she could speak English, because her Father was a teacher. It was an incentive for me to learn English in high school as soon as possible, because it was frustrating not being able to understand several nice young men from Spain who spoke with my girlfriend, Lily.

Of course, they couldn't speak Dutch, although they tried to communicate with me, which made us all laugh. I felt stupid when Lily tried to interpret what they were saying. It was too much of a bother though, so from then on, when the Spanish fellows approached us, I left and went somewhere else. At any rate, some good came out of it, because I really wanted to study English when I entered high school in Indonesia.

BACK TO THE INDIES: 1932 BANDOENG

Something happened on the boat trip over that I never will forget. A group of Catholic clergymen were also traveling to Indonesia. One of them was a Cardinal. They were very nice and talked to all the other passengers. I admired the red cap and wide attire of the impressive looking Cardinal and told him so, which pleased him, coming from a teenager. One afternoon my parents and several other passengers, including the clergymen, were sitting together on one of the ships decks. There was a lively conversation going on between them while they were enjoying the sunny weather and the smooth sea. I had gone to the ships library to find an interesting book. The librarian gave me a book she thought I would like. Happily I found a chair on one of the decks and started to read. After a while I came across a word that made no sense to me, so I got up and went to my parents, and asked them in a rather loud voice what the word "brothel" meant? As soon as I asked, everyone stopped talking and stared at me. A terrible sense of doom came over me, but I didn't understand why my question was wrong.

My Father stood up quickly and taking my arm, pulled me aside. He asked where I got the book I was reading? and who gave it to me? I told him the librarian gave it to me and that I didn't understand what was wrong. Father didn't say another word to me, but both of us went to the library and Father told the lady that he thought she had given me a book that was too mature for a young girl. When she told him that she thought the book was right for me, he scolded her. She was quite embarrassed and apologized. For the rest of our time aboard the ship Father chose the books I was allowed to read, but mostly they were children's books. Neither he nor mother ever told me what the word "brothel" meant, and I didn't dare ask again. Only years later when I found out what the word meant, did I smile when I remembered how embarrassing my question had been. In those days people didn't talk openly about things like that.

Finally we reached Tandjong Priok, a harbor of Batavia and everybody was more than happy to disembark, and be on their way.

Father got a message from the army that he was to be stationed at an outpost again, instead of a more civilized place. My mother was very upset about this because she had spent several years on these tropical outposts where she felt cut off from communication with people and the world at large. I had reached high school age and mother couldn't teach me anymore, so I needed to be near a school. Also mother's health wasn't good, so Father asked the army to reconsider his placement. Because his military record had been so good, the request was granted, and we were sent to Bandoeng, a beautiful city, high up on a plateau between two mountains. Bandoeng, in those days was considered one of the largest and best cities on Java, with a wonderful cool climate and beautiful scenery everywhere.

For about six months we stayed in a rented house because there wasn't military housing available. I remember my first days there, a beautiful new bungalow with nice rooms for us and a nice yard with orange trees. There was also a separate building in the back where the servants would stay. I was glad to be back in the tropics, with all its splendor around me. It was such a luxury to have servants again, who kept the house and garden in perfect shape.

Soon thereafter, the Christian high school where I was enrolled, started a new year, which was great timing, as I wouldn't lose any precious time. The high school was quite a distance from our house, and on top of a steep hill. Every morning I would bike to my school, which was good exercise, but very tiring. But when school was out, it was a thrill to race all the way down to our house. I loved the school because it was new, and had large rooms which overlooked the perfectly landscaped grounds. When class started, I was happy because I could keep up with the other students now and I liked the nice teachers, especially in my favorite subjects, art and biology.

My French teacher was very strict though, and I had some difficulty in keeping up in his class. In Holland the schools had different French study books than they had in Bandoeng. I knew a lot of French words from Holland, but I didn't know the one's being taught in Bandoeng, so at first it was hard to catch up so that I could understand what was happening. But I studied hard and the teacher was understanding when she found out how many times I had changed schools. With German I had more luck, as those books were the same as I had used before.

I started to learn English too, which I was anxious to absorb because I had observed how much this language was being used everywhere I went. But in a way, I was out of luck with my English teacher. She was young and quite good as a teacher, but she had trouble keeping order in her class. We called her Miss Prit. When we had a test, nearly all the kids cheated, except me and a few others. Not because we were such "good" children, but more because we were serious about learning how to speak and write English. We knew that when you cheat in class, you are really cheating yourself in the long run. One morning the kids in the class were noisy and difficult to manage. Suddenly Miss Prit burst into tears and left the classroom. Everybody was shocked and became very quiet, just as the principal slammed open the door and gave us all a lecture about how stupid we were and how inconsiderate and cruel the class had been to Miss Prit. He pointed out that we were really the losers and how in later life we would regret our actions. He punished us by giving all of us extra homework, which he would personally correct, and demanded that we apologize to our teacher. At the next lesson we all apologized, and she took it so graciously, that it put us all to shame.

Our class behaved much better after that, and we enjoyed our lessons more. I found out some time later that our teacher was a very sweet person, who had to take care of a sick mother and was having a difficult time, financially. After a few months, she took a leave of absence and our new teacher just happened to be my aunt Ko, my mother's cousin and sister-in-law. I was delighted and very proud of my aunt, who kept such order in class that you really learned a lot from her. She was a tiny person with dark, piercing eyes. Her method of teaching was to praise you if you did well in her class, and if a you dared to be difficult, she would ridicule you. Such a student she would praise for being so daring and interesting and stupid, that she was sure that the student would become a famous pillar of Dutch society in the future. I was amazed at how cleverly she made the class laugh, leaving the culprit "standing in his undershirt" as they would say in Holland, meaning ashamed. When our aunt was pleased with our class, she would have us stop our lesson, and she would tell us interesting stories in English, about the time she stayed in England. She was an excellent storyteller. Everybody loved to listen to her, and she was one of the best teachers I ever had.

A group of boys and girls I knew at the time started a small club. Every Saturday evening we would get together at one of the girls homes. Her parents' home was spacious, especially the living room with its marble floors. We would roll up the carpet, sprinkle powder on the floor, start up the record player, and dance until ten. It was such a treat! We had the nicest group of young people, five boys and five girls. Once a week we would also play tennis together, and one time we all went on a picnic. We drove high into the mountains in two cars, with my girlfriends parents as chaperones. Of course, there was some competition between the girls about who would dance with the most handsome and best dancer of the fellows in the club, but the competitiveness was all in fun because we all got along very well. I knew that most of the girls were prettier than I was, because I needed to wear glasses, and that wasn't considered to be a mark of beauty. However, I was a good dancer and a pretty good tennis player, which made up for the loss of "looks". I remember reading a book that helped me a great deal at the time. The title was "In the background", and it described the life of a girl who was always in the background because she wasn't popular or pretty, but in the long run she found happiness in life with what really counted. I wish I had kept that book, but it would be considered very old fashioned now.

Our club lasted for a year. It dissolved when the school year ended because most of the boys graduated and went back to Holland to further their education. I often wondered in later years what happened to those wonderful teenagers. This was the sad part of belonging to a military family because we were always on the move, which meant that lasting friendships were hard to come by.

A military house became available to my Father, so we moved to a different section of Bandoeng, far away from where we lived before. This time our house was near a swimming pool. It was a private club though, so you could swim there only if you were a member. Because the membership was quite expensive, I was only allowed the opportunity to join during summer vacation. In those days I loved to swim and would spend hours almost every day in the pool. Soon I found a new group of friends, several boys and girls who would get together to swim and chat at the pool by the hour. There was always music from the record player which created a great ambiance for all of us. I renewed a friendship with a girl named Dini Groen, who was one year older than I. We had known their family in Sumatra, so all of us resumed our friendships, catching up on our lives since we had last seen each other.

A young man named Will joined our "swim group" after a while. He was very handsome and the girls liked him a lot, but the boys resented him. To my surprise, he seemed to like me because he asked me if I would like to go out with him. I knew my parents wouldn't like it because he was twenty years old, four years older than I, but I was so impressed that this young man was interested in me that I did go bicycling with him one afternoon. We took a rest after a while near one of the rice fields on the outskirts of Bandoeng. We talked about a lot of things and admired the beautiful scenery around us. Tall mountains in the distance, and bright green rice fields with a few native huts nearby, all a delight for the eyes. I liked it when he asked me to go out with him again, and said I would. My mother asked me where I had been, and for the first time in my life, I lied. I told her I had gone to a girlfriends house.

A few days later I went out with Will again. This time he kissed me. This was the first time for me, and I felt so grown up. Will asked me about Father and what rank he held in the military, and also questioned me about a girlfriend and her father. I didn't understand why he asked me all those questions, but when I asked him why he was so interested in my Father, he told me he was in the military himself. He asked me several times, "What would happen if we were all alone together somewhere?" I said "well, I guess we would talk a lot more and you would probably kiss me again". He laughed and said "I've never met a girl as naive as you before". The word naive was new to me, so I looked that one up when I came home. When we parted, Will asked me if I would write to him because he had to leave town for a while. He gave me his address, and I did write him a note, telling him how much I liked him and was looking forward to seeing him again. Just for fun, I also wrote him that he probably wouldn't dare to pay my Father a visit, because he seemed so interested in him. Two weeks later a young man in a military uniform came to our house, asking for my Father, because he was a messenger delivering some papers. I was shocked when I recognized him from a distance. He was talking to my Father, and it was Will. So he did accept my challenge, after all!

The next day we met again and we laughed about it. Will told me that he loved challenges in life. He thanked me for my note and we talked for a while, then it started to rain, so we headed home. Will lent me his cape he had with him for me to keep dry. He also told me that he hadn't been completely open with me about the fact that he was in the Army division of the service, and I believed him. But when he took his cape back as we reached the house, I had a sudden negative feeling of something being wrong. I watched him when he left, with his black cape flying around his shoulders, with the rain pelting down on him. I remember clearly that his vanishing silhouette looked to me like the devil in person.

At this point in time, I must have had a premonition of unpleasant things to come. I never saw Will again and my anxious premonition did come true. As the years went by, I had premonitions like this more and more often, which scared me, but sometimes it helped me to overcome or deal with whatever I had to face in my life.

When I got home, I was soaking wet and feeling anxious. Mother was home, but Father came home later, just before dark. I had taken a shower and started to tidy up my room. Suddenly my door swung open and Father came in, ordering me in a very angry voice, to come to the dining room. I followed him and saw that mother was already there sitting in a chair, with a very tentative expression on her face. Father pulled out a chair for himself next to mother's chair and told me to sit right across from them. The way he looked at me was frightening. It was obvious that he was very upset. "Where have you been?" he yelled at me, and when I started to say that I was at a friend's home, he interrupted me, and said "Enough of your lies. I happen to know that you went out with a soldier, who is a scoundrel that recently served a prison sentence". I felt as if lightning had struck me.

I knew that I had to tell the truth, so I confessed that I had been lying because I liked Will so much and was afraid that I wouldn't be allowed to go out with him because he was so much older than I. Father asked "Did he touch you?" I answered that all we did was talk, and that he had kissed me only twice. Once again Father asked "Are you sure that's all he did?" I was petrified and said once more "yes, that's the truth, I swear. I'm so sorry and I promise that I would never do that again, but I was so glad to have a boyfriend, like the other girls. Mother, who knew me well, said "I believe her and I can see that she is telling the truth". Father glared and yelled at me "do you want to get pregnant by a scoundrel of a common soldier?". I was so innocent and naive, and certainly I didn't know anything about sex, so I said "Is it possible to get pregnant from a man kissing you?". My parents didn't answer me and had never informed me about sex. I felt so awful and frightened that I burst into tears.

Father ordered me to go to my room, and when I got up, he said "you are not leaving that room for a long time, and certainly, not until I give you permission to do so. You can only leave your room to shower or eat, and then back you go." So that's what I did for several weeks. It was vacation time, so I didn't have to go to school. But then school started again, and I was allowed to go to school, but then I had to come directly back home and go to my room. I kept myself busy with homework, reading books and, of course, drawing. The girls in school started asking me where I had been because they hadn't seen me for a while. I was so ashamed that I told them that I hadn't been feeling very well, which was true, in a way.

We had the use of a car for a short while and sometimes my parents allowed me to go with them for a drive around Bandoeng to admire the beautiful scenery. Mother was the only person at home who talked to me. Father totally ignored me. Mother told me that Will had been transferred to an outpost far away. Father's superior reprimanded him for permitting his daughter to befriend a soldier, which was just not allowed. The military ranks were very strict in those days. Mother also told me how Father had found out about my stupid "affair". It turned out that Will had a friend, another soldier, who had seen me from a distance, and Will had shown him my letter. His friend had made fun of how ridiculously naive I was and how easy it would be to manipulate me. Will hated the army, especially his superior officers, whom he blamed for his recent prison term. He didn't know my Father, but wanted to take revenge on any officer. Starting an affair with an officer's daughter and trying to make her pregnant, would be the perfect revenge. So when he met me and noticed how vulnerable I was, he chose me for his dirty plans. Will's friend saw how innocent I was, and decided to warn my father about the danger I was in. It was not until some time later that I realized how grateful I should have been for the protection I got. I felt terrible for having lied and I didn't blame Father for being mad at me. I tried to talk to him, but he didn't want to talk to me. For the longest time he ignored me completely, which was the worst punishment that he could have given me. I did find out that Will had dated another Officer's daughter, so I told my mother, and she told Father, and Father warned the other officer of the situation. So, at any rate, some good came out of my experience.

About this time, I developed severe stomach aches, caused by nervous tension, not to mention the severe case of acne on my back, not uncommon to teenagers. Mother sent me to the Army doctor, who turned out to be a very kind man. He said he thought my physical problems were caused by tension and mental stress. I told him it was true that I was very stressed, but I didn't want to tell him why. I felt like a criminal and tried not to think about it.

Vacation time came at last, and my parents decided to send me to stay with friends, Frits and Elly van Lent for two weeks. They lived and worked on a tea plantation, and I was so grateful to have met the van Lents, as they were a most gracious couple. Frits van Lent was a planter, who helped supervise the planting of young tea shrubs, and the harvesting of tea leaves. Each morning he got up at dawn and walked for hours, all over dirt roads and mountains slopes. The best growth took place in a cooler climate. The scenery was breathtaking with its beautiful vistas between the mountains.

Far away, in the distance you could see the ocean. Nearly every morning I walked with my host, and once in a while his wife would join us. The plantation was surrounded by jungles where a lot of wild animals lived. We saw wild pigs crossing the dirt roads, and as long as you didn't bother them, they would leave you alone. Monkeys were everywhere, swinging in the trees, and one even tried to throw a coconut in our direction.

We always had three dogs with us. They were trained to attack in case of danger. I remember that one of them was called "Pecco" after one of the teas produced in Indonesia. We would stop occasionally when we saw a group of women plucking tea leaves from the shrubs. They were very pretty and most of them were young. My host pointed at one of the girls and told me that she had given birth to a beautiful baby the evening before, and here she was, back working the next morning. It was amazing how strong these young women were, even though the young mother was only thirteen. I wondered how she could take care of a newborn when she was working. It turned out that she had made a deal with another mother where she would feed both babies in the evening, and the other woman would feed the infants in the daytime. This way they both had free time to do other things. This made quite an impression on me because I was already three years older than the new mother. I just couldn't visualize myself as a mother at that age. In those days parents arranged marriages for their daughters even before they were six years old. Amazingly, most of these prearranged marriages turned out to be happy ones, perhaps because the parents were careful in choosing a suitable match in the young men they chose for their daughters.

Indonesian kids were quite happy. I loved to watch them playing in the river, or gaming with their homemade clay marbles. They loved to dance and sing. At a young age they were taught to become part of the working unit, creating a close bond with their families and the villagers, and they loved it. The tea factory was fascinating. It takes quite a long time to cure tea leaves, and there are many different types and grades. I never knew how much work was involved before the tea is ready for the marketplace. When you walked through the factory, the smell was heavenly, and you could see that workers were very happy. The pay was good, and the so-called "picking girls" were paid by the pound for the leaves, which gave them an incentive to work fast. Most of the time they worked in groups, and you would hear them talking and laughing together.

A WILD PARTY

One evening I had a very unpleasant experience. The administrator of the tea plantation invited us and the van Lents to a dinner party. I had never been to such an event and was looking forward to it. It turned out to be quite a big party, with a few couples and a lot of single men, whose wives were in Europe most of the time. The party started with cocktails and then dinner afterwards. It was a very elaborate meal called an "Indonesian rice table", which consisted of large amounts of rice served individually, accompanying that were separate little dishes of meats, fish, eggs, vegetables, and many condiments such as coconut, nuts, spicy chutneys, and generous amounts of hot peppers, which could all be mixed to make a taste delight.

Everybody seemed to be having a good time. The servants kept filling the glasses as soon as they were emptied. As the evening wore on, quite a few of the guests were getting drunk. I was also served liquor, but I didn't like it after taking a few sips, so I left my glass filled, which was a mistake, because several of the guests were urging me too imbibe and "be happy", which irked me.

There were men on both sides of me. One was Chinese and quite polite and nice, but on the other side was an older man, who started to bother me, calling me "Blautje" (Little Blue One), due to the blue dress I was wearing. He kept teasing me and urging me to take a drink, so I decided when he wasn't looking, to empty the glass in a potted plant just behind me. But as soon as I emptied the glass, the servant would fill it again. The Chinese man saw what I was doing, and thought it was very amusing, as I emptied glass after glass. Later that evening I looked at the poor potted palm tree and thought that it had started to sag over its unwelcome drinks. I often wondered if that plant survived that evening. When, at last, dessert was served, things got out of hand. One planter jumped on top of the table and started to dance right between the dishes, breaking some of them, while he sang a dirty song. Everybody started clapping and laughing, except me. I hated to see a grown man behaving so crudely.

Luckily, everybody got up from the table when he started to dance, which gave me a chance to try and find Frits and Elly.

But I didn't get a chance because several men wanted to dance with me at the same time and started to argue about it. The young Chinese man tried to rescue me, but was shoved away. Just when I was really getting upset, my hosts found me, and took me with them. I pleaded with them to take me home. They decided that the party was getting out of hand too, especially for me, so we started to leave. Several guests tried to hold us back, but we managed to reach the front door. As we stepped outside we heard a lot of the group singing, and the lyrics were "good riddance to them".

Indonesian Transportation

Tea Plantation

Village Bathed in Moonlight

Our House Servants

FRIENDS IN BANDOENG 1931-1933

It is amazing how some people can behave without any real feeling for their friends. For years my parents had very close friends, whom they saw quite often in different places because they were also a military family. Like my parents, they were transferred to different places in Indonesia. Several times friends happened to be stationed in the same place at the same time as my parents. This happened when we were living in Bandoeng. My parents were delighted to see their friends, whom I shall call Mr. and Mrs. Verbeek. They had a daughter that was one year older than I, and she was a sweet girl, whom I liked very much. Her parents were very concerned about her because she had diabetes and had to take insulin shots every day. Then there came the time for the Verbeeks to go back to Holland for their six month furlough.

Most people would travel back to Holland to see their relatives, and the Verbeek's were excited and looking forward to the trip. Winter was approaching, though, and they realized it would be cold in Holland. They didn't have warm clothing, so they bought some at a special store. Mrs. Verbeek came over one afternoon and asked my mother if she could borrow her fur coat, saying she would take very good care of the coat, and they would be back in only six months, and after all, mother didn't need it in Bandoeng.

Mother was reluctant to give her the coat, as this was her most prized possession. Her parents had given her the seal skin coat, and she always had it stored in a special bag with mothballs. She checked quite often to make sure the coat was still in good condition. But after some thought, Mother didn't want to be selfish, so she gave Mrs. Verbeek her fur coat, asking her to take good care of it, and to return it as soon as she returned to the Indies.

Mr. Verbeek had a 1928 Chevrolet, which he offered to sell to my Father for a reasonable sum. My parents had never owned a car before, so they thought it would be fun to have one for a while, so they bought the car. The Verbeek's and their daughter left, and we were sorry to see them go.

Soon after that we found out that the car was a wreck. Father had trusted his friend because Mr. Verbeek had assured him that the car was in top condition. Of course, Father should have checked out the car, but he didn't. So many things were wrong with the car, that it was nearly impossible to get it in working condition. The repairman worked on it for months, and the bill for repairs was almost as high as what we paid for the car originally. Father wrote Mr. Verbeek a letter telling him of all the troubles he'd had with the car, but he never got an answer. After six months, when the Verbeeks were due to come back to the Indies, we tried to locate them. Through the military files Father found out where they were and wrote them, but never got a response. Mother was very upset about her fur coat. She couldn't understand why Mrs. Verbeek didn't return it.

Ten months went by, and Father got word in 1933 that he was transferred again, this time to Malang, a town on the west coast of Java. My school year wasn't over yet, so my parents decided that Father would go on ahead, and Mother, Meta, and I would stay for two months with my Uncle John, my Mother's brother. He happened to be alone at that time because his wife had to go to Holland for some reason. I was not very happy because I loved Bandoeng. I had made a lot of friends that I didn't want to leave. Starting all over again in another town in another part of Java did not appeal to me very much. But, so far, our lives had been like that, relocation was a part of the lifestyle we led, and you just had to make the best of it.

One afternoon my Mother and I were sitting in the front room of my uncle's home when somebody came up the steps to the front hall and approached us. To our utter amazement, to turned out to be Mrs. Verbeek. Mother looked at her with an expression of shock on her face that I'd never seen before. When she got up and approached Mrs. Verbeek I could see how upset she was, as she stopped short before reaching the woman and asked "Where have you been all this time? I have tried to reach you and you never bothered to contact me!". Mrs. Verbeek peered at her with a startled look on her face, saying "I'm so sorry, I just couldn't bear to write you because we had a lot of problems." "Where is my fur coat?", asked Mother. Mrs. Verbeek started to cry and said, "I sold it. We needed the money badly and I thought you didn't need it in the East Indies, so I decided to sell it." Mother's face turned to stone. "My God, you sold it?", she cried. "How utterly unethical. At the very least, you owe me the money you got for it". Sobbing, Mrs. Verbeek said, "I cannot pay you because we are so much in debt". Mother looked at her then with so much anger on her face that it scared me. "Get out of my sight" she yelled in a high pitched voice. "I never want to see you again. Your husband also cheated us out of a lot of money, because the car he sold us was a wreck. You are both crooks." Then she turned around and went inside without another look at Mrs. Verbeek, who had started to run away, still crying. That was the last I ever saw of her or her family.

Many years later, when I was grown up, we heard what happened to the Verbeek's through a mutual acquaintance. They went back to Holland after his retirement, and one summer their daughter went to Russia on vacation. There she met a Russian soldier, and as far as anyone knew, she married him. They never saw her again. She just vanished behind "the iron curtain". For years they tried to find her without any success. In the end, Mrs. Verbeek spent her last years in a mental institution, outliving Mr. Verbeek, who had died earlier.

When my Mother heard this, she said. "God presents a bill to everybody, and whatever you do in your lifetime, somehow you will be responsible for your actions." But then she added, "It doesn't give me pleasure to hear what happened to the Verbeeks. I do feel very sorry for them." I felt sorry for my parents because it is terrible when you have been cheated by people you love and consider to be your best friends.

Just before we left Bandoeng, Uncle John promised to take us to see a famous crater, the Rangoeban Prahoe, high up in the mountains. This place could be reached by car, but it would be rough going. On the day we were supposed to go, Uncle John overslept, and then told us that he decided not to go because it was too much trouble. Mother was furious, so she managed to rent a taxi to go the next day. We did make the trip and were lucky because it was a beautiful day, unlike the day before. The view from the mountain crater was fabulous. The bottom of the crater seemed about a mile deep, and you could see people walking on the bottom who looked the size of ants from that distance. The crater wasn't active, or else we wouldn't have been there investigating the precipice and getting dizzy as we peered into the gaping hole. I was grateful to have seen this beautiful spot, but this was also when I discovered that I had a phobia of heights. Forty nine years later I went back to that same spot, taking a guided tour, and nothing had changed in all those years, giving me an understanding of what "eternity" meant.

I was mad at Uncle John, who could be very selfish, so I confess that one afternoon I gave him quite a scare. He was reading the newspaper in the living room and when I came in, I saw a chance to tease him. I had caught a large chameleon in the garden because I had wanted to show it to my sister. I placed the creature right on top of the newspaper he was reading. The chameleon was agitated, and it lunged at my uncle, who in turn, jumped up screaming and swearing. Then he chased me, as the chameleon disappeared under the chair. I was faster than Uncle John, so he couldn't catch me. Later I told him why I had startled him, and much to my surprise, he started to laugh.

Uncle John's favorite hobby was hunting. Twice a year he would gather up his guns and go "big game hunting" with some friends. Most of the time he would come home with wild Buffalo, and sometimes game from the "cat" family. In those days, between 1920 and 1930, wild life was still rampant on Java. A huge tiger skin covered the marble floor of one room in the house. One day the maid came in that room with a basket in her arms that was full of laundry. I heard her coming, and crawled under the tiger skin. As she came close, I stood up with the tigers head on mine and roared. The maid screamed, and, dropping all the laundry, ran from the room. Mother was mad at me, of course, but when you are young, sometimes you do crazy things just for a giggle.

When Uncle John was in the right mood, he could tell fascinating stories about his hunting adventures. One time he was on a small jungle trail, when a huge wild boar came out of the bushes and attacked one of the natives. The animal was aggressive and used one of his dangerous tusks to rip open his victim's stomach. The man's intestines fell out of his middle as he fell to the ground in pain. Everybody was horrified. Some men tried to help the wounded man, while the others killed the boar. One of the hunters took a piece of bamboo and started to rip off small strips the size of thread. Another got water in a helmet from a nearby brook, and when he came back, he washed the wound, pushing the intestines back into the natives abdomen. Then they took the bamboo and used it as thread to close the wound. Some cow manure mixed with dirt was later placed on top of the wound and strips of cloth were used to bandage the whole area. A stretcher was made and several men took the man a long way to the nearest village. My uncle and his friends were very upset, but they were grateful that the native carriers seemed to know what they were doing. None of them thought the man had much of a chance of survival though.

A year later, Uncle John went hunting again. He and his hunting party started to recruit several men from the village where they had been the year before. When some men came forward to offer their services, the hunters couldn't believe their eyes when they saw the same man that had been so mortally wounded the year before, volunteering himself again. He greeted them with a big smile and then took off his shirt, showing them a huge ugly scar on his stomach. It was a miracle that he had survived the ordeal. Not until much later did the scientists discover that some chemicals in cow manure help to heal wounds. I didn't like the fact that my uncle was a hunter, but on the other hand, he did come in very handy when there was a man-eating tiger loose, plaguing the villages.

My school year ended at last and my mother, sister and I left Bandoeng. We traveled by train for a whole day to reach our destination. The train was hot and dirty, and had wooden benches which were quite uncomfortable. We were very glad to leave the train, especially when we saw Father waiting for us on the platform.

Malang was also a beautiful place high up in the mountains with a cool climate, and like Bandoeng, Father had rented a house near the high school. The school area was encompassed in a large circle of trees on the outside and a small park in the middle, with the school positioned on one of the borders. When I visited many years later, the Banyon trees had grown, creating such an enormous canopy over everything that I could hardly find the school.

MALANG

The year was 1934 and I was happy to start school so I could make some new friends. Soon I felt at home in Malang and settled down to a new routine. I befriended a young man in my class and later dated him for two years. He was my first boyfriend and I was happy to have someone to date. We would often go cycling in Malang after school. The traffic was not dense and it was a treat to enjoy the scenery, although the roads were quite steep here and there, challenging our physical strength. I also had several girlfriends, and for about a year, I was happier than I had ever been before. I was doing well in school, the teachers were nice, and my parents were friends with the principal and the biology teacher. One thing I did regret though, was that the English teacher was the same one I'd had in Bandoeng. She had been transferred to Malang, and when she saw me there, she was embarrassed thinking that I might tell the other kids what had happened in Bandoeng. I tried to put her mind at ease by telling her how nice it was to see her again. I felt so sorry for her that I enlisted the help of my friends to make her feel more comfortable, and it did help. Some time later I found out that she loved our class and considered it the best she had ever taught. We also had the highest marks in English, so my classmates were paid for their cooperation and kindness.

Our neighbors were the military family of Dr. Strong. He and his wife were very pleasant neighbors. Each week, the doctor went for a day to the native villages, called campongs, to take care of the sick. We had a cook who had an enormous goiter on her throat. We asked the doctor if he could help her but he said he couldn't in this case, so our cook asked Mother if she could take a leave of absence because she wanted to go to see the medicine man of her village. When Mother asked her if she thought the medicine man could help her, she said she was sure of it. Mother believed her and let her go. Mother cooked for us that week, and after a week had gone by, the cook came back, and we couldn't believe our eyes. The goiter was gone, and the only thing left of it was a loose flap of skin hanging beneath her chin. Of course, Mother was curious to know what the medicine man had given her. The cook told her that all she had to do was eat a particular type of soup every day. The soup consisted of all kinds of herbs and spices taken from the jungle. The goiter shrank more and more each day until soon it was gone. Some time later, Mother told our neighbor about the cure and the doctor got all excited and wanted to find out where this medicine man lived, so he could ask him what kind of ingredients he had put into the soup. But our cook left us because she was homesick, and she wanted to return to her village, and Mother was sorry she hadn't told the doctor sooner because nobody seemed to know which village she was from. The natives of Indonesia had many ways of fighting disease, and it wasn't until many years later that scientists became aware of, and started to study natural ways of curing illnesses.

We had quite a few animals in Malang. We always had chickens so we could have fresh eggs. It was my job to gather the eggs and I loved it. The chickens were very clever about hiding their eggs in odd places. Even in the coop you could have trouble finding their hiding places. One of our hens had started to breed and in a few weeks she had six chicks. We all enjoyed watching them, but one was Meta's pet. She played with it and carried it wherever she went in her free time. Late one afternoon, she came home and noticed that her chicken was very nervous. It was running around in circles, and seemed to be looking for something. So she tried to quiet the chicken by putting it on her lap, and lo and behold, the chicken, still agitated, laid an egg in her lap. And that was the start of a ritual of the chicken laying an egg in Meta's lap. As soon as Meta would come home from school, the chicken would come running, settle itself in her lap and lay her egg. It was the talk of the neighborhood, and my sister was so happy to have such a smart chicken. But then a day came when the family went on a trip with friends, to the seashore in south Java. We all had a wonderful time and didn't come home until late in the afternoon. When we came into the yard we saw something quickly moving towards us in the twilight. It was my sister's hen, all puffed up, running back and forth excitedly. So Meta sat down and the hen immediately hopped on her lap and proceeded to lay her egg. Imagine her holding that egg inside all that time, poor bird. Soon after that, the hen stopped the ritual when she matured and started to breed. Chickens are not very intelligent, but this one must have been special.

Jacob, our cockatoo, could be a real nuisance sometimes. On a very special day my Father had to attend a parade. His beautiful white uniform had rows of shining brass buttons, and Mother had hung it on the back porch before Father put it on. Jacob happened to be around because we let him loose most of the time. It was just bad luck that Jacob noticed the shiny buttons of the jacket and started to peck at them. Our houseboy, Kario, discovered Jacob's misdeed when he saw all the buttons lying damaged on the floor. He came running inside, babbling about the catastrophe. Luckily, Mother had a whole extra set in her sewing kit and sewed them on very quickly. Father made the parade just in time, and we all breathed a deep sigh of relief. Kario felt quite guilty because he was in charge of keeping the uniform in perfect shape.

One day we took a trip to a resort in the mountains to have a look at real Dutch cows. We admired the clean fat beasts but fell in love with a flock of baby geese. Little yellow fuzz-balls, blue eyes and bright orange flat feet. We convinced my mother that we couldn't live another day without two baby geese. We named them Hans and Greta. They soon became the sole property of my sister Meta. I never seemed to have time to play with them or cuddle them, what with all the school homework. Hans and Greta adored Meta and followed her everywhere. Always waiting for her the gate when she came home from school. Within a few months they stood almost three feet tall. The most preposterous sight was when she put them on their backs, side by side, in her doll pram, pushing it all over the yard. They loved it, their slender necks bobbing up and down and their orange flat feet flapping in the air. They were the best watchdogs one could wish for. When strangers approached the gate, they flew into a rage and chased them off. They tolerated the servants and my parents, they adored Meta, but they hated me. We never understood why. It must have been quite a funny spectacle for anybody who was fortunate enough to see me running to the bathroom, all the way chased by two hissing and cackling geese. My legs were always covered with black and blue bruises where they had bitten me. One day we heard a bloodcurdling scream and saw our laundress going after Hans and Greta, wildly swinging a broom. There was no love lost between them but it never had come to blows until that day. We had a beautiful lawn, and as usual, the laundress had spread the freshly washed sheets spread out on the grass so the sun would dry and bleach them. This was an open invitation for Hans and Greta to leave their call of nature in the center of each sheet. From that day on they were locked up in the chicken coop on laundry day. The chicken coop was a large shack in the backyard, its walls were chicken wire and it had a solid roof. We lived in peace and harmony for a few weeks, everything seemed to be under control. Then the old woman came to the gate, she carried a small basket in which three small white rabbits huddled together.

As luck would have it Meta was home, there was no way she could live without the little rabbits. They were 50 cents each. After much begging and promises my mother gave in, although she was filled with dark forebodings. She must have heard all the stories about little white rabbits? Room was made in the chicken coop, cozy and snug nests were created for the newcomers. All this turned out to e a gigantic disaster. With in a few days we had 14 rabbits. One had given birth to six babies and to other to five. The third rabbit must have been a male. May was in awe and beside herself with excitement. So was my mother but not for the same reasons. She threatened to drown them all. So all these stories she had heard about little white rabbits were true.!! But not to worry, May would look after them, feed them, clean up after them, no problem...

After a few weeks when all the commotion has died down, and our lives had resumed the normal routine of everyday life, the world exploded. We were awakened that day by a strange muffled scream. We saw our mother staring out of the window, her hand over her mouth, pointing to the backyard. We looked. What used to be lush flower beds had been turned into a desolate kind of no-man's land. A few rabbits were still there mopping up the last remnants. Neither my sister nor I remember what happened next. We must have suffered from some type of amnesia. Even now, after all these years, we can not remember the aftershocks. Later that day we discovered the tunnel the rabbits had dug under the chicken wire and so discovered the flower beds. A few weeks later the rabbit problem was solved in a tragic way. A Loewak (civet cat) had managed to get inside the chicken coop and had killed them all. A few remnants of rabbits were still scattered over the lawn. We never talked again about rabbits.

Another time Father asked Kario to white wash his tennis shoes. Kario forgot about it and when Father asked him if they were done, he had to tell him that they weren't ready. Father was very mad and told Kario that he had thirty minutes to get his shoes polished. When the time was up, Kario was nowhere to be found, and when we called him, we heard a voice, but when we looked up in the direction of his voice, we saw Kario sitting on top of the roof of our house. There he sat, in the hot sun, with a shoe in each outstretched hand. When we asked him what he was doing, he said that he thought the shoes would dry faster if he were sitting closer to the sun.

We were very fond of Kario and his wife, Sarina, who was our housemaid. After a while we noticed that she wasn't very happy, and asked her why. She told us she missed her family in Bandoeng, and that she wanted to leave us to go back home. So Sarina and Kario said "good-bye" to us. They had been with us for several years, so they were both crying and we all felt bad about their departure.

Mother wrote them a glowing letter of recommendation to show prospective employers in Bandoeng. Mother tried to place them by asking friends and neighbors if they had positions available for two people. A few days after Kario and Sarina left, we got up one morning and were surprised to find a long line of natives waiting patiently in the yard. There were at least twelve young men wanting Kario's job. Mother had the difficult task of deciding which one to choose because they all had excellent recommendation letters from their previous patrons. They were all very eager to get the job because Mother was well known as a nice and gentle "Nonja" (Mrs.). We also got a new maid, but we never forgot Kario and his wife.

Our gardener was special too, but in a different way. One day I noticed that his feet were very wide and so I started to count toes and it turned out that he had six toes on each foot. I hadn't known that was possible.

Our servants had their own living quarters which consisted of two bedrooms and a kitchen. Their bathroom was a small enclosure with a well in the middle and the same convenience of a toilet that we had. Our kitchen was also quite primitive with two holes in a cement ridge, covered with a grill and charcoal or wood beneath and when the fuel was burning, the cook would fan it constantly to keep the fire going. We didn't have any electricity, but I didn't mind because I loved the smell of burning wood. Every evening we had to pump up our kerosene lamps, which gave us sufficient light. Our beds were enclosed by mosquito netting to keep the insects at bay. Sometimes I would catch fireflies and let a few of them go inside my netting. It was fun to watch the moving lights, and you could even read if you caught enough fireflies close together.

School hours were different in Malang with classes between 7:30 and 1:00, with two recesses. The family got up at 5:30 am, and then we took a nap in the afternoon from 2:00 to 4:00. Dinner was served in the afternoon about 1:00 and a bread meal was served at 8:00 PM. Everybody went to sleep quite early. I loved to get up early in the morning when it was still dark and the air was still cool. Almost every afternoon we would drink tea on the front porch of the house. Neighbors and friends would stop by to visit and exchange news, which was an enjoyable pastime. Once in a while we had guests, mostly military folks, stay for dinner, and our houseboy would serve us our meal wearing white gloves. Mother had the dinner table set beautifully, with a damask tablecloth and napkins, silverware and crystal, and a bouquet of flowers in the center of the table to add the finishing touch. Most of the people around us didn't bother to entertain in such grand style, but Mother loved it that way.

Every so often a seamstress would come over to help with sewing new clothes. Mother would cut the patterns and materials, then the seamstress would sew according to Mother's instructions. She also did a lot of embroidery and smocking. My sister and I were always well dressed. In those days, all the European style clothes were homemade. The sheets on our beds were changed every day and washed by our special laundry maid, who also ironed our clothes daily. Our wardrobes were mostly cotton, with silk being used for special occasions. Life was very special in those days for a housewife, even in the more primitive areas compared to what life became in later years.

My parents befriended the Van der Valks, who lived nearby. They had two daughters about the same age, as my sister and I. Our parents wanted so much for us to get along, but I couldn't stand the girl who was my age. I had my own girlfriend from school whom I liked, but the Van der Valks were always very critical of her, degrading her because she came from a simple family. I resented that and tried to avoid these people, but it was hard because they were my parent's friends and were at our house a lot. What I learned from this is that you can never force people to like your friends. I called the Van der Valks my parent's friends, but not necessarily mine.

Mr. Van der Valk worked on a pineapple farm on the east coast of Java, not far from the Island of Bali. He asked me several times to come and stay with him and his daughter on the farm for a week or so. My parents wanted me to go, but I was quite unhappy. I didn't like his daughter Josje very much, and I knew it would be very hot there because the farm was in the lowlands, far from the mountains where we lived. My parents kept insisting that I should go because their friends wanted a companion for their daughter. So I gave in and accepted the invitation. It took several hours of driving to reach the farm. The farm was interesting, with its endless rows of pineapple plants. The landscape was as flat as a pancake and seemed quite dull to me, but at one end of the farm was a large river with huge boulders and some woods around it. A small pond bordered the woods, and Jane and I spent several hours there one day. We climbed all over the boulders that were larger than we were, and tried to catch some of the colorful fish, small shrimp, turtles, and frogs that were in the pond. But Josje was always complaining about something, which spoiled any fun I might have had.

We had been exploring for a while when a native farm hand came over, and warned us that not long ago a tiger had been seen sitting on top of one of the boulders in the river. I was fascinated by his story, but Josje ran back to the farmhouse immediately. The farmhouse was quite primitive and hot. Mr. Van der Valk tried to entertain us in the evenings with stories mainly about himself, in which he played the hero every time. His jokes were dull and vulgar, which I disliked. The place itself lacked variety and there was nothing to do but walk between the rows of pineapples. Mrs. Van der Valk, was very pretty but empty headed and vain. All she could talk about was clothes, makeup, and hairstyles.

The first night we spent on the farm was very upsetting and embarrassing for me. Josje and I were sleeping in a large bed surrounded by netting called Klamboo. In the middle of the night I had to go to the bathroom, but I didn't know where to go. In those days, you would go to a so called "pot de chambre" in your bedroom because it was dark outside and not that safe to go to the outhouse. I frantically tried to wake up Josje to ask her where the pot was, but she pretended to be sound asleep and I really didn't want to wake her up. I crawled out of bed and went to another room that had a door leading to the yard. I opened the door, after quite an effort, and stepped on a small rug which was laying in front of the door. Our host had several large watch dogs that slept in that room. The dogs had gone to the bathroom on that rug, so when I stepped down, my bare feet oozed through the middle of their filth. Then I was knocked forward by the dogs, who wanted to go outside and ran me down in their exuberance. By now, I was desperate, so stepped outside and hid in some bushes to relieve myself. But then I didn't know what to do with my messy feet. It took me quite a while to clean myself on a small patch of grass and with the help of some leaves, I managed to get rid of most of it, but when I went back to bed, I dangled my feet over the edge of the bed so I wouldn't spoil the sheets.

The next morning I was up early and went straight to the bathroom to take a bath. Our host asked me at breakfast how his dogs had managed to run off in the middle of the night. When I told him my story, he and Josje screamed with laughter. They thought it was so amusing that they teased me all week about my misfortune. I was thrilled to leave and when I told my parents what had happened, they were furious, not only because my hosts had not provided a convenience for me, but because there were many very poisonous snakes around the Indonesian plantations. Mr. Van der

Valk apologized to me later, but I never did like him. I had another bad experience with this family later, to boot.

St. Nicolas and Christmas were coming, and my parents invited the Van der Valks to get together on the evening of December fifth, St. Nicolas eve. In Holland, the custom was to give small presents with a funny poem to each person. My parents gave me a small allowance each month, and I had saved enough money to be able to use it for presents. I always made presents by hand with materials I bought with my allowance money. For two months I had been making all sorts of things in my spare time. There were bookmarks, handkerchiefs, necklaces of glass beads, and more. I had worked very hard and I managed to finish each present for my parents, sister, and the Van der Valk family. I was very proud and looking forward to seeing if everyone liked their gifts. When the evening came, we were all having a good time at our bread meal, but when everyone started to unwrap their presents and read their poems out loud, I got quite a shock. The Van der Valks made remarks about how silly and time consuming all my work had been. My Mother was furious, but she was too much of a lady to call them on their rudeness, so instead, she said that she thought it was very sweet of me to work so hard and that she liked my creations.

The rest of the evening was strained, and we only saw this family once more when we left Malang. Years later I had another encounter with them, which was also unpleasant. It was then that I discovered that they were jealous of me because I was more active and more creative than their daughter. I had taken a course in sewing in the later part of our stay in Malang. I loved it because I could make my own clothes and choose the colors and patterns I liked, not to mention, I got a diploma for my efforts. I remember making a gown for a social evening at the high school, and was really looking forward to wearing it. But when the night of the dance arrived, I came down with an attack of dysentery, so my beautiful evening dress didn't get used, at least not that evening.

Not too long afterwards we returned to the Netherlands. It was a traumatic experience for us all and I don't think we ever got over it. No more mountains, exotic flowers, lush jungle, pristine beaches covered with wonderful shells, no more anecdotes, smells, sounds, and worst of all, no more pets, just memories. The homesickness has never left us. The memories of our former lives helped us in times of need, when life was dark and uncertain.

COURT MARTIAL

During our stay in Malang, I'd noticed that my Father wasn't himself at all. Sometimes he was very quiet and other times he was very difficult to get along with. He had always been strict with me and my sister, but during this period we were more afraid of him than ever. We tried to avoid him as much as possible. It wasn't until much later that we found out what was happening to him, and that he had good reason for being disturbed. We tried to understand him, but we were never close to him, partly because he never confided in us about himself until shortly before his death almost 30 years later, which was very tragic. Mother and he had decided not to confide in us the problems they were having with the Army, because they didn't want us upset about the darker side of life's realities at such a young age.

My Father's job in Bandoeng had been to train 100 young men, who had come straight from Holland, not having the slightest idea of how different the lifestyle would be, in this strange place where nobody spoke Dutch. Having come from a protected environment, most of them were out of their element, not just with learning a new language, but with a climate that was totally the opposite of what they were used to. Especially in the jungles, where it could be brutally hot and humid, they had to be disciplined, learn how to protect themselves, and obey their commanders, even though they were young.

Many of them became homesick in a short time, and some of them who just couldn't face the regimen, started to resist, and of course, had to be punished. Often Father would talk to them and sometimes he didn't punish them, instead giving them another chance. He managed to shape his large company into a well balanced, and drilled group in just eight months, which was much to his credit. I remember him coming home one day, and as he sat down with a big sigh, he told us that a superior officer, a Major, was going to take over his troops, and it was all out of his hands now. And at the time, the superior officer had commended my Father about his company.

When we left Bandoeng, a Major took over the troops that my Father had trained, and took them to Surabaya, where they began disintegrating as a group, due to the lack of leadership from the Major. My Father was unaware of the rumors that were whispered about the cruel treatment of this Major towards his men, which would eventually result in the mutiny of my Father's troops.

But what had happened to my Father after that was just dreadful. He was falsely accused of something he didn't do. The new Major blamed my Father for the unrest among the men of my father's former troops, The major claimed that had my father done a better job training the troops, they would not have mutinied under the Major. As a result of this accusation, my Father now faced a court martial. After the court martial he was found innocent and was exonerated, but the accusations created a situation which ruined his military career and beyond. I will translate official documents, so whoever reads this material, will understand how difficult military life in the colonial days could be if you lived in the Indies. The end result was that Father was given a chance to stay in the Army without any chance of promotion, or retire with an honorable discharge. I cannot blame him for choosing the latter. He had suffered from enough unfair treatment and corruption, and his health was failing him. He had thrombosis in both knees, which bothered him when he had to walk long distances. He also had severe headaches, probably caused by tension, and on top of all that, he had recurring attacks of malaria. He was forty five years old when we left Malang, and he was bitter, knowing that he had been used as the "scapegoat" by an officer unable to continue Father's good work.

A general translation of some of the documents of Captain KWK Leeksma's Career and Court Martial appear below.

The judgment of Captain Leeksma's career was good throughout the years 1913 to 1934. It was not until the year 1935 that his career came under the scrutiny of a court martial. In 1926, the judgments of him were as follows: Upbringing, Good.

Order and discipline, Good

Administrative abilities, Excellent

In 1927, the judgment read; Job done by Captain Leeksma throughout the three years he served in the army in Atjeh has been considered to be good in all respects.

All the rest of the reports gave him the same positive criteria, until 1935, when an unbelievably unfair assessment distressed our whole family, and was devastating for our Father.

Complaints were made by a Major who had taken over my Father's troops. This man was an incompetent leader, but he did have connections with the highest officers. He managed to get their support, making my Father the scapegoat for the lack of performance on the part of the Major during his tour of duty with the troops that had just been under my Father.

When the Court Martial took place, Captain Leeksma did not get the support he should have had. He was being accused of delivering his troops to the Major in a disorderly, untrained condition. In fact, the report at the time of his release of command said that Father had the respect of his men, and the unit was running smoothly and efficiently.

The only thing that the court could find any fault with was that when one of Father's men got out of line and had to be punished, he would sometimes cut the punishment short, when he felt the soldier had learned his lesson.

One time, one of his colleagues had been punished with a half year prison sentence because he had left the place where a whip lashing punishment was taking place, resulting in the death of the prisoner from the severe flogging. Since the commanding officer was responsible for all that happened, and the fact that his counterpart should have been present during the punishment, this also came back to haunt Father.

Finally the court martial took a turn, and the truth came out about the Major's deficiencies, so he quickly took an honorable discharge from the Army and left, without having to answer for any of the trouble he had caused.

Father was finally exonerated, but he was told that he would never get another promotion, and he was advised to leave the Army with an honorable discharge, and a Captain's pension, which he did, but he was very distressed at the injustice he had been handed.

In some ways, the court marshal was a blessing, because of events that occurred in Indonesia during the Second World War. Most likely, had Father stayed in the Dutch Army, he would have been sent to Timor, where many Dutch officers died at the hands of the native Timorians. If Father had stayed even longer, he would have been placed in a Japanese concentration camp when the Japanese overran Indonesia, early in the Second Word War.

PART 2: HOLLAND AND WORLD WAR II

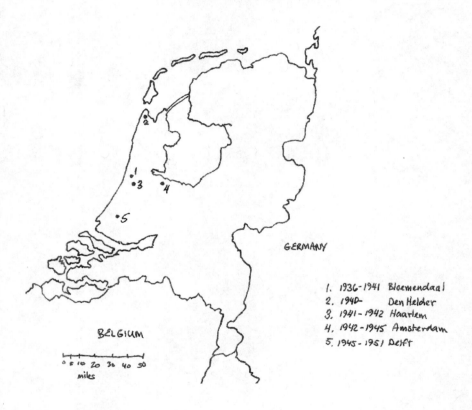

GERMANY

BELGIUM

0 5 10 20 30 40 50
miles

1. 1936-1941 Bloemendaal
2. 1940-   Den Helder
3. 1941-1942 Haarlem
4. 1942-1945 Amsterdam
5. 1945-1951 Delft

BACK TO HOLLAND 1936

I hated to leave Indonesia because I considered it to be "my country". I had loved everything about it – the lifestyle and the beautiful tropical splendor, the fascinating animals and plant life, the climate, and the innocent warmth of the people. Following Father's military career, however, we had no choice but to return to Holland. The trip back to Holland was quite discouraging. We traveled first class and everything on the ship was luxurious, but I could not enjoy it as I should have. My parents were at odds with each other, now worse than ever before. I suffered from my recurring stomach aches, so Mother gave me some 'Milk of Magnesia', and that helped. She had been a pharmacist's assistant before she married, so she knew quite a lot about medicines. Those stomach aches were with me for the rest of my life, but I was grateful that I could take something to ease the ailment.

On the ship, my parents befriended a very nice man named Mr. van Daal, whom we all liked very much. He was so enamored with Mother that at the end of the trip he asked her to divorce my Father and marry him. But she told him that she thought it would be cruel to leave her husband at such a low time in his life.

This was not the first time such a thing had happened. She had been asked to marry someone else several times when she was young, but she kept trying to make the best of her marriage. She always told my sister and I that my Father had a lot of good qualities which we should appreciate. What bothered me was that Father was much too interested in other women, openly flirting with them, which was embarrassing, especially for my Mother. Father was handsome, tall, and very good at sports. He loved dancing and parties. My Mother was beautiful, but a real housewife, in that she didn't care so much about the parties. Father was also musical and used to play the violin and the banjo. Sometimes he would whistle whole symphonies. Mother played the piano a little, and her voice left something to be desired, so music wasn't her forte.

Even though both my parents were good people, their marriage had been a fiasco. When I was five years old, my Mother wanted a divorce, but Father refused to allow it unless she found someone who would be a good Father for me. Mother even asked her youngest brother, who lived in America, if we could stay with him for a while, but he was a bachelor and didn't want the responsibility. I loved my parents, even though my Father was so strict, but my sister and I suffered a lot because our parents were so unhappy. In those days couples didn't get divorces easily, but I often wondered if it would have been better for all of us if they had been separated.

When we arrived in Holland, my mother and my sister went to stay with my mother's father again. Opa Kooreman was living in a large home with his other daughter and three grand daughters. The house was large enough to accommodate all of us for awhile. Opa Kooreman was dying, and he knew it. His doctor was amazed that he was still alive, but he wanted to see my Mother and her family once more before he died. I remember being in his sickroom, where he was lying in the same bed where his wife had died eight years before. As my sister and I stood at the foot of his bed, he looked so frail, but managed to lift himself up somewhat, so he could see us. Looking at us intensely, he whispered softly, "You have grown a lot, and I'm so glad to see you ", and then he laid down again. I stood over him, and kissed him, saying "Opa, go to sleep and rest." "Yes, I will, for good.", he said. He closed his eyes and looked very peaceful. He was such a good person, and we all admired and loved him for the special individual he had been. He died the next morning and was laid to rest next to his wife.

For a short time my Father and I stayed with my aunt Lies, Father's sister. Her family lived in Hilversum, a nice town south of Amsterdam. Their house was large, but even so, it was quite crowded. Besides my aunt and her husband, there were two sons, a daughter, another girl who stayed with them, and my paternal grandmother, Tina. So, with us too, it was very crowded, and there was a pall in the family, as my Aunt Lies and her husband, Bert, had lost their second son Koentje (Koenrad, their only son from their own marriage) quite recently. He had been born grossly deformed, but was very smart. When he was ten years old, he fell off a swing and died several days later from internal bleeding. Although the death was a blessing because of his deformity, they all missed him very much because he had shown so much courage in his short life. A short time later, Father and I moved to a boarding house for a while. We had no sooner moved there, when we got news that Mother had been rushed to the hospital, to undergo a hysterectomy in the middle of the night. The operation was complicated by the development of a pulmonary thrombosis. She barely survived, but thank God, she made it. She was in the hospital for quite awhile, and Father and I went to visit her nearly every day which was a long commute for a round trip. Both my parents had blood clotting problems. Mother had difficulty with a physiological problem that developed, which the doctors called "open wounds" on both legs, which she would have to deal with for the rest of her life. In those days, the medical world didn't know much about treating thrombosis.

Being split into two households was not good for our family and we'd all had a bad time of it since we came back to Holland. My sister came over to stay with Father and me. We had a difficult landlady who complained about everything. The food she served was barely passable and we weren't allowed to have visitors often. I had to keep an eye on Meta, who was thirteen. I really didn't know what to do with myself at that time, but I tried to keep busy sewing and knitting. We had to wait for Mother to get well before we could even think of finding a house for the family.

When the time came for Mother to leave the hospital, she was still so weak that she moved into the boarding house with us for another three months. Once in awhile, I would stay for the weekend with our old friends, the Kamps, in Amsterdam. They had two sons, one a year older than I. The parents were hoping that we would fall in love, but he wasn't that interesting to me. I had my eye on going to art school in Amsterdam. Besides, it was the middle of the school term. It wasn't the right time for me to decide what kind of study I would pursue. About six weeks later, when Mother was feeling a little stronger, we moved to another boarding house, which was worse than the first, but we made the best of it. By this time my parents had decided they wanted to live near Haarlem, and they started looking around for a house to rent. I helped them, but it was a difficult time for all of us. The summer was coming and I was told that I could start playing tennis again, so I took some lessons, and much to my delight, I discovered that I was good at this sport. My tennis instructor promised to look for a tennis club I could join.

When he told me that there was a club that would accept me on a trial basis, I was very grateful. I went twice to the club and tried my best to play well, knowing that I was at least as good as several of the members I had watched. On the third visit though, I felt something was wrong. Everybody looked at me with funny expressions. The head of the club approached me and asked what I was doing there? So I asked what he meant, because of course, I was there to play tennis. Whereupon he said "Didn't you get the note telling you that the club had not accepted you as a member?". I shook my head no, and he retorted, "Well, I'm very sorry about that", and then he turned on his heel and walked away, leaving me standing there, embarrassed, while everybody was staring at me and shaking their heads as if I had done something wrong. So

I left the court feeling humiliated and mad that people could be so tactless and cruel. When I asked my tennis instructor later, why this had happened to me, he said that there were already too many girls in the club and they felt that I would be too much competition for them. For some time I tried to find another club, but they were all booked solid, so I reluctantly put my tennis racket back in the closet.

I was very unhappy for awhile, and my parents started to worry about me. Then I saw an advertisement in the paper, offering a two week camping trip to England for a reasonable price. I got in touch with the group and when they told me about their plans and they asked me if I would like to come. I readily accepted because I needed to do something to get me out of my depression. I joined a group of young people in Amsterdam that August, and we traveled by train to the province of Zeeland, and from there took a ferry to Harwich, England. The campsite wasn't far from there by bus. We slept in tents, and there was a large building nearby that housed the bathrooms and dining room. The weather was perfect and each day we had something new to do. There were bus trips to London and neighboring villages, as well as picnics at various beaches. We were joined by campers from other countries too, such as Austrians and Germans, and it was fun to exchange information in other languages.

I befriended a handsome English boy and his older sister. They invited me to visit their home at Christmas time. I wasn't sure that I could go then, but I was tempted to try to visit later on. Our Dutch group was very nice, but when we came back to Holland, we parted, and never saw each other again. I remember two very nice Jewish boys in the group and often wondered, in later years, how they fared during the war, and if they survived the German occupation. We never had an inkling of the terrible years we would have to face in the near future.

I did see the English boy and his sister some time later when I accepted their invitation. Unfortunately, the boy, who's name was

Bill, wanted to get serious with me, but I decided that he wasn't "the one" for me. When the war was over, I saw him just once more when he came to Holland to ask me if I would marry him. But by that time I was already engaged to Bram.

BLOEMENDAAL

My parents found a home for rent in Bloemendaal near Haarlem. They had to furnish the whole house which was fun, but it took quite awhile. Luckily, we could stay at my grandfather's house for two months. When grandfather died, my Aunt Ploon decided to use her inheritance to go back to Indonesia, where her husband was living with another woman. Their marriage had been "on the rocks", but my aunt hoped that she could salvage their relationship. By the time she got there, however, it was too late for them because he was unwilling to leave his new common law wife. My Aunt Ploon and her daughters Fransje, Medi and Hetti, lived in Bandoeng for two years. Just before the war broke out in 1936, she came back to Holland with only two daughters. The oldest, Hetti, had met and married an Army officer in the Indies. Aunt Ploon and her two daughters Medi and Fransje were penniless, and so father agreed to let them stay with us in Bloemendaal. They stayed for two years, until in 1938 Aunt Ploon succeeded in obtaining some of her husband's pension. She and the girls then moved away into an apartment in Den Haag and lived separately.

In the meantime my parents had finished furnishing our new home and we moved into it after my grandfather's house was sold. Our home was a show place because my mother had excellent taste. The furniture store owner, who had sold them most of the new pieces they bought, asked my Mother for her permission to show our new home to some of his customers. Of course, Mother was very proud of her success, and we were happy for her, because her life hadn't been very easy.

The end of the summer came and I needed to establish what I would do next in planning my future. I needed to have a goal or something worthwhile to do. Most of the young people in those days, went to college after high school, but I had always wanted to study art, so I asked my parents if I could try to enter the Art Academy of Amsterdam. They told me that I could apply, and I did. I took my portfolio to the academy where I had to show my artwork, and the director told me they would consider my application, and that he would let me know if he thought I had enough talent to be accepted. I was so excited because I was pretty sure that they would give me permission to study there, and that would make me so happy, especially after the difficult times I had been through lately.

Two weeks later the letter came informing me that the Academy would be delighted to have me and that they had found my work far above average. Needless to say, I was elated. At last I would be able to study what I had wanted for so long. But then I got one of the worst disappointments of my young life. Mother told me that she couldn't afford to send me to the academy and pay for the train fare from Haarlem to Amsterdam. My parents were helping my Mother's sister financially, because she had no income since her husband had left. I loved my aunt, so I resigned myself to the fact that I wouldn't be able to study art at that time. I tried to console myself with the thought that I would be able to do it in the future. My Mother suggested that maybe it would be nice for my education to go to a home economics school for two years. At least I would know how to run a household then.

In Indonesia we had several servants who did all the household chores. Of course, this was wonderful at the time, but on the other hand, I never learned how to take care of myself without help, so I agreed to enter the school. We learned how to cook, do the ironing, polish shoes, wash clothes, etc. It was an all girls school, and most of the students were engaged to be married, so they had a good incentive to do the best they could. It made me feel very lonely because I didn't know anybody in Haarlem. I missed my friends in the Indies. Most of the girls lived in Haarlem and they all knew each other. I was an outsider who had no roots. I tried my best, but I didn't like the school. Ironing was especially a nightmare. It took an hour to iron some clothes and some sheets and they had to be folded so perfectly it was irritating. When you polished shoes, they had to shine like a mirror, and when a room had to be cleaned, you were in big trouble if the teacher found even one speck of dust on anything. The dirty laundry was brought in from outside the school, and sometimes it was disgustingly dirty. But I did like our cooking instructor, who was an older woman with a great sense of humor, so I did survive the basics of cooking. In later years, I discovered that I didn't do any of these chores as well as I had been taught, nor did I care. I especially hated ironing and disliked the woman that taught the class. I seemed to distrust her for some reason which I couldn't explain. But after the war was over, I learned that she had turned out to be a traitor to her country. She was responsible for the deaths of a lot of people, so I guess my intuition was working well after all.

After spending a year in that school, the principal, who was a strict old spinster, told my parents that I was a very bad student, which was true. This intervention turned out to be a blessing in disguise for me, because it gave me a chance to quit. I had found out that in the very same building in which I was painfully taking classes, there was another section, which was associated with the Amsterdam art school. After pleading with my Mother to let me leave the "household" school, I was allowed to register at the art school. Mother realized how unhappy I had been and how much I really wanted to study art. In those days most parents were much more strict with their children. You just obeyed your parents. When I entered art school I was really happy for the first time in more than a year. The art school was just for girls because they taught not only painting and drawing, but also needlework, knitting, weaving, macramé, lace making, a full scope of the arts. I loved it from the start. Some of the prerequisite courses were of great interest to me also, like psychology and philosophy, for which I had a very good teacher, who taught us about teachers of philosophy and teachers of history. We were also taught how to handle classes of children. After four years I received a teacher's degree, which certified me to teach in any school.

Most of the time I traveled by bike to the school. This took about half an hour, but when the weather was bad, I went by bus. At lunch time I could walk to a nearby restaurant for a cup of coffee, which cost a quarter at the time. But I had to take my own sandwich with me for the sake of economy. Quite often I even saved the coffee money, just to have some money of my very own in my pocket.

I did very well in this school, getting good marks and I got along with the teachers very well. I also liked the other girls in my classes and because I already had my sewing certificate, I didn't need to take those lessons again. This gave me some extra time, so I signed up for some dancing lessons in Amsterdam. I loved to dance and was good at it, but there was one setback. Most of the girls in the class were very pretty and they were always asked to dance by the boys. I had to wear glasses, and it made me feel ugly, not to mention that this wasn't a very popular look with the boys, so I ended up being a wallflower, or was asked by the boys who were left-overs, and they didn't interest me much either. Once in a while there weren't enough boys and I would end up dancing with the teacher. That I did like, because the teacher was a heavenly dancer. At any rate, I did learn how to dance, but I never went back after that.

I suffered a lot because I wore glasses. Sometimes boys would tell me outright that I wasn't very pretty with glasses. But when I didn't wear them, I couldn't see very clearly in the distance. So I decided that it was more important for me to be able to see all the beautiful things the earth had to offer than to be vain about my appearance. This was a hard decision because it is so important when you are young to look well to others. Some of the boys were interested in me, but I wasn't fond of them, especially one boy that was in my class who had a harelip that made his face disfigured, and I am ashamed to say that I hated to dance with him.

During this time in my life in 1936 I dated two young men who were the sons of my parents' friends. They were both nice fellows, but as I got to know them better, I realized that neither of them was the kind of man that I wanted to spend my life with. I felt badly because I wanted to get married and have children, but I wanted to make sure that the man I married was the ideal man for me. I had experienced, through my parents, what it was like to be involved in an unhappy marriage, and how badly an unhealthy union can affect the children. What amazed me was the fact that both sets of grandparents were happily married, but practically all their children were unhappy in their marriages.

When I had just started with art school, I met a young man, the son of a family lawyer friend. His name was Dick Keuskamp, and I had known him in Indonesia, as a small child, years ago. It was so good to see an old friend. He introduced me to some friends of his in Amsterdam, because I was new and did not know anyone. Through him I met Kieks Bakker, who became my best friend. Kieks and I remained friends, writing and visiting for decades, until she finally died in 2004 in Hollland. Kieks Bakker had a very nice family, and to my surprise, I found out that the minister we'd had in Malang, Dominee Bakker, was Kieks Bakker's uncle. Kiek's mother came from South Africa, and her brother had become our minister in Malang. Kieks Bakker and her sister Toos and I became good friends.

Dominee Bakker stayed in Indonesia during the war and returned to Holland after the war. His son fought in the underground, was picked up by the Germans, and taken to a concentration camp. The Dominee learned later that that son had been hanged in a German concentration camp. After all his wartime experiences, Dominee Bakker lost his faith and became depressed and despondent in his later years.

In the summer of 1939 I was asked to join Kieks and Toos for a vacation they were taking to Belgium. It wasn't very expensive because we were planning to use bicycles and stay overnight in youth hostels. To my surprise, my parents told me they thought it would be good for me to have a vacation because I had studied so hard. Belgium is a beautiful country with its low rolling hills, farms, and forests. Wherever you turned you could enjoy the art in museums, and the beautiful architecture of the old buildings. Kieks and Toos and I had a wonderful time. I wrote down everything in a small journal and illustrated it with pictures, dried flowers, and included all of my thoughts at the time. At the end of our two week trip, I experienced an ironic event. We had already had our last dinner the day before we had to go back home, when the waiter of the restaurant, asked us if we had heard the bad news. We hadn't listened to any newscasts while we were on vacation because we just wanted to relax and enjoy ourselves. So we were very surprised and shocked when the waiter told us that we should leave quickly for home because England and Germany were just about to declare war.

We had no idea that these political events would develop into such a serious situation. We left by train early the next morning. Of course, we were very upset, but we consoled ourselves with the thought that Holland wouldn't be involved in this war, as we had managed to stay neutral in World War I. Even so, we knew that a war would affect Holland in many ways, even if we were neutral.

THE INVASION BEGINS

Right after I returned from Belgium, World War II broke out. Everybody knew that it would change our lives drastically. We didn't know how badly Holland would be hit, and we couldn't even imagine at the time how utterly horrible the next five years would be for millions of people. We followed the news intently. Our anxiety grew with each passing day, as we heard of countries being swallowed up by the Germans. We felt as if a giant monster was gradually approaching us, eating everything in its path. The radio newscasts kept us informed that the Dutch government was still hopeful that the Netherlands would stay neutral, but when Germany invaded Czechoslovakia and, later, Norway and Denmark, we weren't so sure any more.

On the 30th of April, 1940, all furloughs were canceled and our military forces were put on alert. I spoke with a young man, the nephew of our neighbors, who was stationed in Rotterdam. He had planned to come over for a visit, but he'd gotten strict orders that he wasn't to leave the garrison. We knew that the German forces were getting closer and closer to Holland. Later we heard that part of Holland had been flooded, on purpose, to slow down the invasion of the German forces.

My Mother had just left Bloemendaal a few days before to visit a friend of hers who lived in Den Helder. Our Navy was stationed there and Mother's friend's husband was the head of the Navy dock yard. Mother wasn't gone very often, but we were glad that she stayed with her friend for a few days. Those days turned out to be the worst of our lives. I will never forget the date, May 10th, 1940. It was a beautiful spring day with bright sunshine and warm weather. Father, my sister, and I had an early breakfast that morning, and were just getting up from the table, when we heard shots outside. They sounded so far away, that we couldn't figure out what was happening, so we went outside to investigate. Several of the neighbors were already outside on the street, looking at the sky. Some planes were circling around and seemed to be shooting at each other. Father said "Well, they are probably having exercises", and just as he made this comment, all around us we heard funny tinkling noises of something falling from the sky. I picked up a small metal piece with very sharp irregular edges. When I showed it to Father, he started to yell for everyone to go into their homes quickly, because the metal piece I had found was a piece of shrapnel from a gun shell. "It looks serious" Father yelled. "There is real fighting going on up there." Then everybody started to run. It was a miracle that nobody was hit because pieces of shrapnel were falling to earth all around us. When we went inside, we immediately turned on the radio and heard the bad news for the first time. The German forces had invaded our country and so we, too, were at war. It was such a shock to us because we really believed we would be able to stay neutral, but it wasn't meant to be. As it turned out, the Dutch government had known for some time that our country would be involved.

We were worried about Mother. I had an older friend at the time, who had a car. I took my bike and told my Father that I was going to ask him if he could drive me to Den Helder to pick up Mother, and he agreed that it was a good idea. Luckily, my friend was home and agreed to take me right then. On the way, we didn't see much out of the ordinary, so it was hard to understand why the government had given us such distressing news of war. When we arrived in Den Helder, Mother's friend told us that the war had, indeed, started, so she had sent Mother home by taxi, and that we had only missed her by a half hour. As she told us, I watched her in amazement as she ripped her white sheets into ribbons. When I asked her what she was doing. she said, "I just found out last night that we are really at war with Germany. Our Naval fleet managed to leave the harbor in the middle of the night, just in time, thank God". Then she explained that she was making bandages out of old sheets because she expected that there would be a lot of wounded people needing them. Now, we were truly convinced that we were at war, and it gave us such an eerie feeling, never imagining that this would happen in our homeland. We said good-bye and good luck to Mother's friend and quickly raced for home.

Soon after we left, we were stopped by a group of military men. They were wearing the Dutch uniform, which gave us a feeling of safety. They asked us who we were, what we were doing, and where we were going. We told them, but I could tell that they didn't really believe us. Then they asked us to say the following words quickly. "Scheveningsche schipper", which translated means "Fishing Boat Skippers from Scheveningen", (one of our shore towns). It seemed strange that they would order us to say these words, but they looked so mad that we obliged them, blurting out what they had requested. It was amazing how their demeanor towards us changed after we pronounced it correctly. They started to smile and told us to go home fast. Later we found out that this was the method that they used to find out whether we were Dutch or German. Only real Dutch men and women can pronounce these words correctly. The Germans were landing in our country by parachutes, right behind the areas that had been purposely flooded to keep them out. Then they would dress in Dutch clothes, and mingle with the Dutch population. This way they managed to infiltrate the country behind the fighting zone. Because Germans had difficulty pronouncing "Scheveningsche schipper", the Dutch could pick out the infiltrators quickly and detain them. We were stopped three times on the way back home and were asked the same question each time.

The third time we were stopped, the officers asked us if we could take a wounded man with us to a hospital in Amsterdam. We were glad to help the man, who had a bleeding head wound, bandaged with an old piece of cloth. Unfortunately, it wasn't a good enough bandage, because the blood had seeped through and was running down his face. He was in a lot of pain. He moaned as we drove, but didn't tell us what had happened. It turned out that he was a farmer who had been on his way to market to deliver his produce with his horse and wagon, when, suddenly, a German fighter plane dove right down at him, strafing the area he was passing. Luckily, he managed to jump off his wagon, and crawl underneath, but his horse was killed and he was wounded. When the plane disappeared in the distance, some people stopped to help him.

After three hours of driving, we were stopped once more by the Dutch military. When we told them that we had a wounded man with us, they knew we were okay, and one of them took the man to the hospital for us. We were glad we could help him, if only a little, as it was a terribly helpless feeling to hear the man moaning, and not be able to do more. We didn't see any fighting during our trip, but we did see more wounded people along the way. Coming home was such a relief, finding Mother had arrived safely an hour before. At any rate, we were all together again to face an uncertain future.

The second day of the war, the news worsened. The radio stations were still in Dutch hands and there were horrible tales of fighting, especially in Rotterdam and the east side of the country, near Arnheim. We knew we didn't have a chance of winning. Our Army was small and not very well equipped, even though our young men would fight like lions. There were stories of our soldiers, in hand-to hand combat, physically biting the throats of the enemy. For five days we stayed home and all normal activity stopped. At night, most of us slept downstairs, as the house shook once in a while from bombings along the north sea coastline. This was way too close for comfort. A large crack appeared on the front wall of the house, which remained there unrepaired, as long as I can remember.

On the third day I couldn't stand being cooped up in the house anymore, so against the protests of my family, I went outside. It was a beautiful day and everything seemed quiet in our small town. Others left their homes to walk about, some to a nearby park which overlooked a large expanse of dunes. On a clear day you could see to the north sea in the distance. An it was from there, for the first time, that I witnessed real fighting going on.

It was bright daylight, but the seacoast was lit by fires and bombs exploding everywhere. Planes were shooting at each other in the sky, and as they circled around each other, some would drop to the earth in flames. From some of the downed planes I could see parachutes opening. I prayed for those who had a chance to stay alive. The noise was so loud that I covered my ears. The explosions seemed unending. I thought to myself that if hell really existed, then this is what it must be like. There was quite a steep dune near to where I stood. A rabbit hole was visible on its slope, and just as I looked in that direction, a rabbit came out, looked around, and hopped up the hill. When he reached the top, he stood on his hind legs, perked up his ears, and stood motionless, watching the action. I was surprised to see how calmly the rabbit took in all the noise from the battle and the planes. He just turned around towards me, and started to preen himself. I guess he didn't see me, because first he pulled down one of his ears, fluffed it up, cleaning it with his teeth, and did the same with the second ear and on down his body, stopping once in awhile to observe the action near the shore. I watched that rabbit for at least a half hour admiring its composure. When, at last the rabbit decided to go back in it's hole, I felt a moment of peace as if time were standing still. I will never forget that rabbit because it taught me a valuable lesson. Take life as it comes. Make the best of it and don't worry too much about things. Accept with calm that over which we have no control.

After the war in Holland, I often walked to the same place that

I had seen the rabbit. The dunes in that area weren't damaged by the war, and the rabbit hole stayed there for a long time. Only once did I see the rabbit again going about its daily routine, as if nothing had happened.

The fighting days were especially hard on my Father because he had offered his services as a military officer, but he was told by the Dutch Army that he was too old to fight even though he could have helped in many ways.

Sea Coast Bombardment

For the first five days of the war, the radio was still in Dutch hands, but it didn't give us much information about the fighting because the Germans could use that information also. On about the fourth day, however, they reported that Rotterdam was being bombed, and there was a rumor that other cities like Amsterdam and Utrecht would be next unless the Dutch army capitulated. We found out how terrible the bombardment of Rotterdam had been. The whole inner city was flattened and on fire and we knew the Germans would carry out their threat to flatten other highly populated areas. The small Dutch air force had been mostly destroyed, and the remainder was in no position to be of any threat to the Germans, so on the fifth day the Dutch army capitulated. At the end of that day, the radio announcer told us that the fighting was over and that the Germans were taking over the country. Our Queen and the whole cabinet left the country and we had to accept our defeat. The announcers voice was all choked up and sad, as he said "God bless Holland, farewell, and good luck". The Dutch anthem sounded loud and clear and then the radio went dead.

It was not until some time later that we realized exactly what had happened, and how the war against my country had started. German Troops had started to attack our country. German planes had bombarded Dutch airfields. Paratroopers landed at several strategic places which caused a lot of confusion everywhere. The German ambassador to Holland had declared that German troops had entered the Netherlands in order to protect the Dutch neutrality against an impending Allied invasion. The Dutch Government rejected the German allegation and decided to defend it's country.

It would be five long miserable years before we heard a real Dutch broadcast again. Everybody was in tears. We didn't know what would happen to all of us. Maybe it was a blessing in disguise, because otherwise we might not have had the courage to go on, if we knew what was to come. On the fifteenth of May we could leave our homes. Everybody in the neighborhood went outside and all of us were very upset. The weather was beautiful, the birds were singing, and it looked as if nothing had happened, and knowing this wasn't true, made all of us feel very strange. Luckily, we had been spared direct bombardments. The Germans had left Amsterdam mostly intact, probably because it was considered to be an "open city'", which couldn't be defended. Some stores opened up for the public, which was wonderful, because we were all low on food supplies by this time. We were under the temporary illusion that we could go back to a normal life.

But early on the morning of May 16th, 1940 we heard heavy footsteps outside and when we looked out our front room windows we saw German soldiers marching by in a long, long line. Their heavy footsteps sounded like the thunder of an approaching storm, menacing and frightening. In a way, it was a sad sight because you knew that many of those young men would be killed in the future. What a waste! But at the time, we felt only anger at these strangers taking over our country, destroying our land, and murdering thousands of innocent people. We lost a lot of our Dutch soldiers, who had fought in the last five days. They didn't have a chance of winning the battle, nor did they have a chance of survival, because we were so small and defenseless, as it should be in a peaceful neutral country.

Our weapons were old and too few in number, but despite this handicap, our soldiers fought ferociously, making it harder for the German army, who thought there would be no significant resistance from our troops. The days following the occupation of the Netherlands, we heard all kinds of horror stories from people who had been in the middle of the fighting. My second cousin on my Father's side was missing. We feared the worst because he was a pilot, and we were sure that he had been shot down. His plane crashed after being attacked by a German fighter. This was only the second time he had fought. The day before, he had fought, crash landed and survived that ordeal. But the second day he wasn't so lucky. It wasn't until ten days later that we heard the whole story from the survivors of the crash.

My cousin and his crew got involved in a dog fight with the enemy, and they had the misfortune to be attacked by several planes at the same time. They didn't have a chance, so after the plane had been hit, my cousin ordered all of his crew to bail out as the plane started to fall. They all made it, but he was the last one to jump, and his parachute hung up on the tail rudder of the plane. While he was hanging there, helpless, the Germans riddled his body with bullets, so there was no doubt about his fate. For a while his body couldn't be found, but finally his father found his body lying in a ditch near the downed plane.

My uncle had lost his first wife during the birth of their fourth child, leaving him with four children to raise, two boys and two girls. Later he married my Fathers sister, even though they were cousins. They had one son, who was a deformed child Koenrad. Tragically, "Koentje" fell from a swing when he was ten years old, dying from his injuries a week after the accident. So now the loss of another son to the Germans was a terrible blow from my uncle Bert. In later years my uncle had to endure more tragedies in his life. It was unbelievable how this man was hit by catastrophes, and yet, he always managed to pick up the pieces of his life and go on living. He was a religious man, and this had a lot to do with his tremendous strength and courage.

My cousin's funeral was very impressive. He was buried with a military salute of gunfire with full military honors. The young men who had been with him who had survived were his pallbearers. Once in a while I still think of him and wonder what his life would have been like if he had lived. He was such a handsome young man with so many hopes and dreams. If there is such a thing as another life for all of us, maybe my cousin will have another chance. He had wanted to be a consul for Holland, and I'll bet he would have been a good one.

I had met and befriended a young man shortly before the war broke out. He was serving two years in the Army, the expected duty of every young man in Holland, if they were of sound mind and body. When the war broke out, he was stationed in Rotterdam, and he fought for days, right in the middle of the bombardments. I saw him again several days after the fighting stopped, and I was appalled to see how his appearance and demeanor had changed from a young man to a broken older person in those few days. For days he had been fighting just trying to survive the worst nightmare anyone could ever imagine. Most of the city of Rotterdam was destroyed, killing thousands of innocent people. He saw a woman standing against a brick wall, when a bomb fell nearby. All that was left of her was a large red spot on the crumbled wall. There was a hospital nearby where the dead and dying were brought. The dead were the lucky ones, because they didn't have to suffer any more. Their bodies were put in big piles outside the hospital. Occasionally, a moan could be heard among the corpses, and a hand would appear, faintly beckoning from the pile of human bodies. Frantically, other people would remove the bodies until they reached the person who was still alive. My friend had to pick up the human body parts, which were blocking the streets. He told me, that like a robot, he went about his work, blocking his mind from what he was doing, and he was surprised that he was still living when the fighting stopped. But he said he would never be the same again.

In later years I was told that he had saved a person from a fire, even though he was traumatized, and was considered a hero. When Rotterdam was rebuilt, many of the foundations and cellars were still intact, so the new buildings were constructed right on top of the old ones. Many bodies were left in those places because it made no sense to dig them out, so they stayed in their war graves. It was impossible to know exactly how many people were killed, but the estimate was at least 30,000 in Rotterdam alone. A lot of our young soldiers were killed, fighting the best they could against the formidable enemy. Right after the fighting was over, the German soldiers came in droves, marching in long columns, with perfect unity in their cadence, and creating a thunderous pounding with their duck walk marching. On and on they went, like an army of robots, menacing and frightening, and we knew the future looked bleak for us, as if we were living a nightmare without being able to wake up.

Gradually though, daily life started to function somewhat normally again. After all, we had to try to stay alive, and try to make the best of what was happening. There was a lot to do, especially in those places where the fighting had taken place. The fighting had caused just one crack on the front wall of our house, and we felt very fortunate that Amsterdam had been spared. My classes had been canceled for about a month, and then I got the word that they were going to begin again. For a while class met in an old building. I remember that we had an assignment to sketch, and later embroider a scene we had experienced of the Germans taking over our country. I chose to create a small scene of some wildflowers between grass, with a bee visiting the flowers. Underneath I embroidered "Spring 1940". It was a peaceful piece. My art teacher was surprised at my work and when she asked me about it, I said that I wanted to emphasize that no matter what happens to you or anybody else, you must always keep an inner peace, where no thing or no person can touch your soul. This inner peace can be found in the beauty of this world, whether it's in nature, a sunset or music, or perhaps the smile of a baby or an older person; there is love in all good people. I often found such peace in a field of wildflowers on a sunny summers' day. My teacher then understood how I thought and was pleased with my work.

Gradually our lives went back to the old routines. At first it wasn't too bad. There was still food available. and most of the townspeople went about the business of living. Soon my classes were held in the original building where we had studied before the war. Of course, we saw German soldiers here and there, mostly in the city, but at that time they didn't bother us. The news in the papers and on the radio was all how wonderful the Germans were, and how successfully they were conquering Belgium and France. We had a terrible feeling that a great monster was gobbling up most of Europe, including us.

The most dreadful fact was that we couldn't do anything to prevent it. The underground forces had started to develop and gain some strength. In the next few years, these forces made a big difference between life and death for many people, as they subversively countered the enemy's efforts. As time went by, the Germans issued more and more rules and regulations. Our food supplies dwindled because they confiscated whatever they could get for their own troops. During that time I was under a lot of pressure, as most of the Dutch people were, and as the bad news came to us of the war raging all over Europe, the pressure to stay alive until it was over rose.

And if the war raging throughout the country and Europe was not enough, what made it unbearable for me was the tension inside our home. My Father would express his frustrations and anger by making hateful remarks about everything and everybody. A lot of the time, he would take his frustration out on my sister, not speaking to her for months on end. When he had to say something to my sister, he would tell my Mother to relay the message to her. He would even do this if we were all sitting at the dinner table together, which was very humiliating. One day when it was his birthday, my sister wanted so badly to make peace with Father that she bought some cigars for him. When he entered the living room, she gave them to him, hoping her offering would end the dispute. But when she approached him, he took the present and flung it at her face, yelling at her, "I don't want anything from you". Then he stood up and stomped out of the room. Meta was crushed.

Years later, I came to realize that my Father was on the verge of a mental breakdown. He'd had such bad luck in recent years, feeling powerless about what life was handing him, and he didn't know how to cope with it. The rest of us were suffering from his actions too, which made my tension stomach aches come back. Mother had some powder that was like milk of magnesia, which had helped me before. She wondered why I took it so often, but when she asked me why, I said that it was because of the pressure of my studies and deadlines I had to meet. Both Meta and I started to sleepwalk at night, caused by tension. One night I dreamt that our house was on fire and that I had to escape or die trying, so I climbed out of my window. The problem was that I really was climbing out of my window. Luckily my parents heard the commotion I was making, and caught me just before I jumped from the second story window. Sometimes when I came home I would just sit on the front stoop for a while because I dreaded going inside.

Meta's sleepwalking was even worse than mine. One night we heard the front door bang shut, and when we went to investigate, we saw her walking down the street, walking quite fast, clutching her doll, still in her sleeping trance. From then on we made sure that she couldn't open her windows and that the doors to the outside of the house were locked securely.

We had a young girl who helped Mother with the house. She was a very nice and gentle person, and because she liked my Mother so much, she stayed with us for years, even with the upsets that occurred. She told me once that she felt very sorry that our family was so unhappy.

One evening I was so despondent that I wanted to die. In my room I had a gas outlet which could be used for cooking. That evening I put some clothes under the door, shut the windows tight, and turned on the gas. But when the room started to fill with gas fumes, I suddenly realized what I was doing. I thought of my Mother, who always called me "her ray of sunshine", because I always tried to console her when she was upset. I just couldn't leave her. It would have killed her, so I switched off the gas, opened up the room, and took a big breath of fresh air. The next day Mother was disturbed because she smelled gas in the house somewhere. But it was soon gone when I closed my door and kept the windows wide open. Nobody ever knew how close I had come to destroying myself. I made up my mind that I would never try this again, no matter what. I knew I was needed in this family, and it was up to me to be brave and make the best of it. Besides, I was convinced that as long as I lived, God had a plan for me. I also believed that as time passed, things would get better for us, and so I had to keep faith. I focused on working even harder getting my teacher's degree.

There was a shortage of teachers in my field of education. I had already been promised a job with a very acceptable salary at a fancy all-girls school in Indonesia. At that time we were sure that Holland would keep the colonies, and would be able to take over again, once the war was over in Europe. How could we foresee that Holland would lose Indonesia after the war?

During the first year of the German occupation was very bad because the Dutch people realized for the first time what it meant to be in the middle of a war. Every aspect of our lives changed into a nightmare. We couldn't believe what was happening around us. People we knew were disappearing and being killed. Most of them were totally innocent of any wrong doing. Our feelings of resentment grew to hatred which became stronger each day. It wasn't my nature to feel this way, so I had another battle with my faith. How could people be so mean to each other, although it was understandable why people became hateful themselves.

It happened to me too, and I'm not very proud of one instance especially. It is an example of why people behaved badly even though they were basically good. During my art study years, I befriended a fellow student who joined our art class. At first I got along well with this girl and enjoyed her company. But something happened that changed my feelings completely. One day I visited her home and met her Father. For some reason I had a negative feeling about this man even though there was no logic to back it up. I tried to put my feelings aside and ignore them because I liked my friend, who had lost her Mother, and had taken on the care of her Father and sister. A few months later I met a young man who was working for the underground forces, and he told me something about my girlfriend that I didn't want to hear. He said that I shouldn't see her anymore because the family were German sympathizers. In other words, they were traitors. Her Mother had been German and her Father was in the Navy, but pro German. By itself, this wasn't too bad, but when the Germans arrived in our country, she had gone to welcome them, cheering as they marched into town. She took them flowers and candy to make them feel welcome. This was the worst thing she could have done to the Dutch people. Needless to say, I was shocked, and I decided to cut my friendship short.

It was a hard decision for me to make, but I had to do it because it was dangerous to associate with anyone who was pro- German, and it was particularly dangerous for my Father because he was a former military man. I changed my attitude towards this girl, and of course, she felt it, and asked me if something was wrong. I told her that I had changed my mind about how I felt towards our friendship, and wasn't really interested any more in being with her. She took it very hard, and didn't understand what had happened, but soon after that, luckily, she found another friend, which made me feel a little better.

The time at the art teacher's school passed quite quickly, and soon we both graduated, going our separate ways. I never saw her again, but I did hope that she had a happy life for herself because she was really a victim of circumstances. Even though I knew I had to do what I did, for years after that, I felt guilty about my actions. I remember it all, and wish I could take it all back.

In the second year of the occupation, life became even more challenging. Food wasn't easy to get. In the evenings and early mornings we often heard the Allied planes flying over. German artillery tried to shoot them down. The noise was harrowing and we prayed for the safety of the Allied fliers. We were grateful for them trying to help fight our mutual enemy.

I had a girlfriend, a lovely girl that lived nearby, and her family was one of the nicest I had ever known. Quite often I would visit her home, and enjoyed the company of her family immensely. Her parents were very loving to each other and to the their children. They seemed to like me too, and I would help them around the house, sharing with them my knowledge of sewing. There were always young people around, and it gave me such a boost seeing how happy people could be around each other. It also gave me encouragement to clear the air in my own home, especially by helping to support my Mother more. But then something awful happened.

I noticed that Meta had been getting more and more difficult.

She was very moody and mad at the world. She even started to attack Mother. I noticed that more and more bruises appeared on Mother's arms, and I confronted her about it. At first, she said that she had hit her arm against the door jam, but when I questioned her further, she told me that my sister had gotten mad and hit her. She pleaded with me not to tell anybody. She said that my sister was so upset about the circumstances that we were living through. that she just couldn't help herself, so Mother became her outlet. Forgiving her right away was my Mother's way of coping with the situation, and her way of showing support for my sister's anger. She said she thought it was just a phase, and that it would pass eventually. Instead of trying to talk to my sister, I avoided her more and more, which was a stupid and a selfish way of handling the problem. I felt very guilty about that in later years.

And then the situation came to a climax one evening. My parents, my sister and I were having dinner together, when my sister asked Mother, "Mam, what would happen if a person swallowed too many aspirin tablets at once? Would it kill you?", and Mother asked her why she wanted to know. And my sister retorted, "Well, I was talking about it with a girlfriend, and we were wondering if aspirin tablets could be harmful". "Well", Mother said," you have to be careful not to take more than it tells you on the label". We finished our dinner, but I had a funny feeling about this conversation. I looked at my sister, and noticed how quiet and withdrawn she looked. I tried to ignore the feeling, but somehow it kept nagging at my subconscious mind. Then on an impulse, I went to our bathroom and looked in the medicine cabinet. I noticed immediately that the bottle of aspirin was missing. If I remembered correctly, the bottle had been quite full the last time I had seen it, and instantly I knew what was going on. I ran upstairs to Meta's room, which was on the third floor and tried to open the door. It was locked, so I knocked on the door, and trying to keep my voice calm, I asked her to open the door because I had something to show her.

Luckily, she opened the door for me, but when I stepped inside, she turned around and sat down on the edge of her bed. She looked very pale, very sleepy, and spoke to me in a monotone voice. I noticed the empty aspirin bottle lying on the floor, so I took the key out of the door and calmly told her I would be right back. Then I ran downstairs as fast as I could. Mother was just coming out of the living room as I reached the ground floor. I shoved her out of the front door, yelling at her to call an ambulance and the doctor, fast. I also told her that my sister had swallowed, God only knew how many aspirin tablets. We didn't have a telephone, but our neighbor was a dentist, and when we needed to call somebody, we could use his phone. In no time the ambulance arrived, taking my sister to a nearby hospital, where they pumped out her stomach. The doctor told us that if we had been five minutes later discovering what she had done, she wouldn't have survived. All of us were terribly upset about this, and when she came home, we all tried to be especially kind to her. She promised that she wouldn't ever try to kill herself again. This gave us new perspective, and cleared up some of the tension in the household, so something good came out of the trauma we all felt. At any rate, we all realized how unhappy my sister had been, and I could definitely relate, as I had been through a similar experience, myself.

Some weeks passed and I got another shock. One evening I went over to my girlfriends home and she met me at the door, but didn't invite me in. She told me that she was very sorry, but her Mother didn't want me to come to their house anymore. When I asked what the problem was, she told me that they felt that I was too much competition for her and her sisters, as far as young men were concerned. I couldn't believe my ears. It was quite a blow to my ego, and I felt so lost and lonely afterwards. Then some weeks later, I ran into this girl in front of a store, and she started to talk to me in a friendly way, and I knew she meant it when she told me that she was sorry for what had happened. It turned out that her Mother was a friend of the doctor's wife, who had told her of my sister's suicide attempt, so they came to the conclusion that I came from a unstable family. By this time everybody in town knew what had happened, thanks to the gossipy doctors wife. In the end, this doctor lost several of his patients because of his lack of confidentiality. What he and his wife had done was inexcusable.

A new girl entered our art classes, whom I befriended after a while, but I was learning to be careful with friendships. Later I introduced her to my cousin. They fell in love and later married, which made me feel wonderful. Just to see a happy ending was a boost I badly needed. The time approached for me to finish my studies and get ready for a difficult exam. I studied very hard because I wanted to be able to support myself and I was looking forward to a challenging job. The exam was to be given in The Hague, and it would last sixteen days with two weekends in between. Four of us girls were going for our degree, and we all had to find a place to stay nearby. I had wanted to stay with my Mother's sister who lived in The Hague, but my Father didn't like her, and insisted that I stay with another family. I didn't like them at all because they were the infamous Van der Valks that I had disliked so much in Malang. Besides the previous events, my Father was too fond of the lady of that family, and my Mother resented her because she responded to Father's flirting. This put me in a difficult position because I didn't want any friction with my Father, but I also felt loyalty towards my Mother, and in the end, I did accept the invitation to appease my Father.

FINAL EXAMS

When I boarded the train to The Hague, I had a large suitcase, which contained all my study materials, as I intended to study more in the evenings. The first day of my exam was nerve wracking, a normal expectation, with which I had to deal. We received a schedule for all the work we had to accomplish. In the beginning, we had to do creative art such as drawing, painting, sketching, and handiwork, such as embroidery, knitting, macramé and weaving. Later we had a written exam on art history, and after that, we had an oral examination. Each day when I came back to my guest house, I joined them for dinner. I gave them all my food coupons. By that time everybody in Holland had food coupons because the food was becoming so scarce. My hosts complained that I hadn't given them all of my coupons, which I resented, because it wasn't true. And then they wanted me to "go have fun" with their daughter after dinner each evening. I told them I needed to study for the next day's exams, but they said I was being ridiculous and dull. But I didn't give in, and excused myself from the dinner table and went up to the attic where it was quiet and I could study effectively until I was too exhausted to do anymore. But this made me feel uneasy and a little guilty since my hosts didn't appreciate my nerves, or the concentration I needed to accomplish my goal. I persevered though, because I had made up my mind to succeed as well as I possibly could.

In the afternoons, when I came back from another exhausting day of exams, the house was often empty. I knew where they had left the house key, but one day the key wasn't there, and nobody was home. So I sat on the doorstep in miserable weather, for more than an hour, and when they came home, they didn't even bother to apologize. The first weekend, I did go out with their daughter, but she kept complaining that I was no fun. Mrs. Van der Valk never asked me about my exams, in fact, they made fun of my work, intimating that art was a silly waste of time.

Then something happened that was worse than anything else. Every night we heard the Allied planes flying over The Hague, and we were even getting used to the drone of their machines, but then came the night I will never forget. I woke up in the middle of the night, hearing strange noises, and before we realized what they were, the house started to shake. High pitched penetrating whistling noises filled the air, ending in enormous explosions. We were being bombed, and it was very frightening. The bombs came closer and closer. The walls of my room were shaking so hard that the pictures fell from the walls, and my bed was jumping around the room. I held on for dear life, but then a bomb fell on the street next to ours, which knocked me out of bed. I crawled under the bed, expecting to be hit by the next bomb at any moment. The last bomb fell on another street near ours, and I thought for sure that was the end of all of us. But then it was suddenly very quiet again. The planes disappeared and I heard sounds of frightened people downstairs. Then I went to join them.

For a while we all stayed in the hallway, but then we decided to go back to our beds, although none of us got any sleep. The next day we heard that the damage from the bombardment was extensive. A lot of buildings had been destroyed and a lot of people were killed. We also found out later that the allied air forces had miscalculated the spot they were to bomb. It had been a terrible mistake, and, of course, the Germans gloated. In times of war, such errors happen, and human errors do occur.

When I went back to my exam the next day I was still shaking, but the examiners continued and I had to try as best I could to control myself. When I think back to that time, it's hard for me to imagine how I managed to struggle through those years. The test I was most worried about was chemistry. I had never done very well in that course in high school because it didn't interest me, nor did I understand it very well, so to be on the safe side, I memorized the book, and thank God, my memory at that time was very good. But when I took the chemistry test, I was in trouble, because the professor didn't ask questions that were in the book, so I didn't know the answers. Later, I asked why I had done so well in the beginning, but flunked so badly in the end. Then I told him my secret of memorizing, and he was dumfounded. "Let's see", he said, "if what you are saying is really true!". He found out that I could recite whole pages of the chemistry book. I could even tell him on what pages some of the material was explained. He was so impressed by my efforts to try to learn about chemistry, that he gave me a passing mark. In later years, I really didn't need much chemistry, so I didn't feel guilty about nearly flunking the course. When we finished testing, I was told to come back the next day to find out if I had passed, which I was pretty sure I had, but you never know with big exams like this one. The exam papers were handed out according to performance, and I was the second person to receive my results. This meant that I was ranked as #2 not only in the class, but in the whole country of Holland.

I couldn't believe it! For the first time in weeks I was happy, especially knowing that of the fifteen girls taking the exam, I was second in the class, and therefore second in the whole country! So all my studying and efforts had paid off. When I returned to my hosts, they seemed to be glad for me, but then said, "Now you can stay a bit longer and go out with our daughter". I wanted to go home as soon as possible, but I knew I owed it to them to stay a little longer. I sent a telegram to my parents, telling them that I had passed the exam and that I would come home in four days. I tried to be nice to the family, but I never did like them very much. When, at last, the day came that I was to go home, my host took me to the tramway in The Hague. My suitcase was so heavy, that I could hardly carry it. My host refused to help me with the heavy load, telling me that it was my own fault that I had brought so many books with me, so I was on my own. He disliked me because of the affinity between his wife and my Father, which wasn't my fault, but he took it out on me anyway. My Father knew the van der Valks from his service years in Indonesia. I never mentioned it to my Father because I didn't want to create more problems. Besides, he wouldn't have believed me anyway, having a blind side about this couple. The whole situation was ridiculous, and in later years, I realized that I should have said something. I got cards and flowers, and my name was in the paper, and everybody was congratulating me. I felt free again, as if I had escaped from a prison.

A few years later my Father was furious when he accidentally found out that there was such tension in this family where he had forced me to board for the 16 days of my final exams. I was a nervous wreck when I was taking my final exams also because of the fact that my Father flirted with the owner's wife, Josje van der Valk. Coming home was a great relief.

MY NEW FRIEND BRAM

No more studying nonstop, and I had achieved something worthwhile, so now I could take care of myself. I took long walks with my Mother, did some reading, went to the beach with my bike, and became a member of a rowing club. Rowing was the most challenging of these. It took a while before I learned how to row different types of boats. Later when I became a coach, I got into trouble because I didn't know how to handle the job very well. One afternoon I had two girls in my boat. At first everything went well, but when we approached the dock, I gave the girls the wrong command. This resulted in the boat's slamming into the dock as we hit it at the wrong angle. I felt very stupid, of course, and went to the president of the club telling him that I would pay for any damages. Surprisingly, he was very nice about it, and said that because I had come forward on my own volition, that I didn't have to pay for the damages. I was impressed with his generosity, and it renewed my feelings that it always pays to be honest.

My chemistry teacher told me some time ago that his wife knew me from the Indies. When he mentioned her name, Lilly, I was surprised, because I had known her quite well when we lived in Bandoeng, but I didn't know that she was married and had a little baby daughter. They invited me over several times, including when their daughter had her third birthday party. At Lilly's party I met a friend of my chemistry teacher. This friend talked about many things with me, and he was particularly excited about his high school chemistry class. He seemed to be a nice young man, and we had a lively conversation about sailing and rowing. He was a member of the rowing club, too. He told me that he had a small sailboat at the club and asked me if I would like to go sailing the next Sunday. I accepted the invitation because he was a lot of fun and I'd never had the opportunity to go sailing before. His name was Bram Bernard Simone Tjebbe Boonstra, named after his four grandparents.

When I came home, Mother asked me if I had a good time, and who had come to the party. I told her that a young man had invited me to go sailing with him. But I said to her," I like this young man, but I'm sure he's too young for me". I was twenty five at the time, and I didn't want to get involved with a teenager. My friend Lilly and I discussed Bram, and when I mentioned to her how I did not want to get involved with a high school student, Lilly started laughing. She said "Why don't you go out with Bram again, but then ask him about his high school chemistry?" So the next time when we went sailing, I asked him if he was still in high school and if he liked his chemistry classes, he gave me a puzzled look, and answered, "Oh, yes, I'm still in a high school in Haarlem". Then he thought a moment and also started laughing, and then he said "But you know, in my chemistry classes I am not sitting in the class, I am standing at the head of it!" At first, I didn't understand what he meant. But then it dawned on me that he was indeed in a high school chemistry class, but he was the teacher, not a student. I couldn't believe it because he looked so young. Then I asked him how old he was, and he told me that he was twenty nine and a high school teacher in Haarlem, but actually he had his PhD in Chemistry. For now, the only job that he could find was as a high school chemistry teacher.

This was a nice surprise for me, and immediately peaked my interest in this new friend. Bram was about 5' 10", a good height for someone my size, he had a slim muscular body, dark hair, light green eyes and beautiful skin. Although he wasn't very affectionate, he seemed to have a good sense of humor, and giggled at my teasing, exposing a beautiful set of teeth. He cared greatly for people, and right off I sensed a highly developed soul with deep faith, integrity, and loyalty, not easy traits to come by, especially with the hard times we'd been encountering.

In the weeks that followed, Bram and I rowed and sailed together more and more often, sometimes joining some other young members of the club. Once we rowed for several days, tent camping overnight. The girls were in one tent, and the fellows in the other, so it was all very proper. Another time we went sailing with two other couples in two sailboats for several days. We cooked our meals on a small wood stove, and stayed overnight in a large barn, sleeping on fresh hay. The boys slept upstairs in the loft, and the girls were downstairs. One night, when we were fast asleep, somebody touched my shoulder, waking me with a start. A policeman stood next to me, which scared the daylights out of me. He was holding a young girl by the arm. She looked frightened as she tried to free herself. The policeman asked me if it was all right if the girl slept next to me, and I said it was all right with me, and I was sure it would be okay with the others. I moved over a little and the girl settled in next to me. She looked angry and frightened at the same time, and of course, I was curious to know why she was there with us, so I asked her why the policeman had brought her. She told me that she and her boyfriend were sleeping in their boat near the lake shore, when the policeman woke them up, shoved them out of their boat, and told them that it was forbidden for them to sleep on the boat together when they weren't married.

In those days boys and girls had to be very proper, especially when they were young. It is shocking to compare what was expected of us then compared to the morals at the end of the twentieth century. Sleeping together, or worse, living together when you weren't married was considered very immoral. If you dared to live with a man outside of wedlock, you were considered an outcast by your family and the community, and it was totally scandalous if you had a baby under those circumstances.

The next morning I woke up and the new girl was gone, so I told the other girls about what had happened the night before, since none of them seemed to be aware of the situation. They were quite surprised that the policeman had brought the girl to us, so they supposed that he didn't know what to do with her. We never saw her again, and I never even knew her name.

We had a lot of stormy weather the next few days, and one day, Bram, my girlfriend, and I went sailing in Bram's boat, when a sudden gust of wind hit the sail of the boat at the wrong angle, overturning the boat ever so slowly. We were startled and all dove into the cold water with all our clothes on. After I went under, I tried to push myself up, but I couldn't because my legs were tangled in some rope. Luckily, I was a good swimmer and managed to disengage myself, surfacing just as I ran out of breath. After gasping for air I noticed that we weren't very far from shore, so I made a beeline for land, where we undressed, and put on some dry clothes our friends lent us.

Despite the capsize, we sat on the bank of the canal singing drunken sailor songs, relishing the adventure. Later, we all retrieved the overturned boat, bailed it out, and let it dry. When we went for food the next day, we all laughed because we had to pay for the food with soaking wet money. But we felt lucky that none of us were hurt or drowned. Everyone in Holland learns how to swim at an early age because there are so many lakes, canals and rivers everywhere.

Sailing and boating were about the only pleasures we had left during the war. There were so many terrible things happening all around us that we did some creative positive thinking to keep our morale, up, especially during the first years of the war. The Germans were so successful, winning more and more battles, that we had to work at our attitude. As far as the Dutch people could tell, it looked as if our freedom would be taken from us, possibly for good. More and more items we needed to subsist were taken from us. Food became scarce. Everybody received coupons for food, but these were quite often useless, because there was no food to be had with or without the coupons.

MY FIRST JOB

I had been looking for a job the fall after I graduated, but jobs were quite scarce to get at the time, so I applied for any job that looked promising. One that I applied for was designing children's clothing, but I was turned down because I was too late with my application. Another job possibility was to paint lamp shades, but it paid so little, it wasn't worth the effort to apply. But then, suddenly, I was told that a girls' school in Amsterdam needed an art teacher. Needless to say, I rushed to Amsterdam to meet with the principal. She told me that she was interested in me, but she wanted to test my talent because there was another applicant. When I asked who the other person was, I was surprised to find our that I knew the girl very well. She had studied art with me. In fact, she was the girl that had been collaborating with the Germans, and therefore, couldn't be trusted. My test consisted of standing in front of a class of thirty five girls and instructing them on a subject that had been given to me earlier. I knew I could do this, as I had been taught how to teach a class at art school. The test went well. I knew I had done a good job.

A few days later I received a note from the principal saying that she wanted to see me. I had high hopes of being accepted for the job, but when I talked to the principal, she said that she had not decided which candidate she would accept. Then she told me she had heard a rumor about the other applicant's association with the Germans, and she asked me if I knew anything about the girl. She wanted to know whether this other girl had an alliance with the Germans. This put me in an awkward position, because I didn't want to tell her what I knew of the girl. On the other hand, the school's good name was at stake, too. In those days anybody who was pro-German in Holland was considered a traitor, and feelings ran very strong about this. I decided to tell the truth about what I knew, and as a result, I got the art teaching job. My first real job! I was very happy. Even though my salary at the time was small, it was a beginning.

At first I only taught three days a week, and I was exhausted at the end of those days. I got up at 5:30 am. I had to leave the house at 6:30, riding my bike to the train station in Haarlem. The train took me to Amsterdam, and then I walked 20 minutes to the school so I could be at my job and ready to teach by 8:15. If the weather was bad, I took the bus to Haarlem, and then the train to the school in Amsterdam. I was always afraid of being late because the transportation in those days wasn't very reliable, because of disruptions from the war. I taught four classes each day, with thirty five girls in each class between ages 13 to 22. In the beginning, teaching wasn't very difficult, because all the materials I needed were available, but gradually it became quite difficult, as the supplies dwindled, and I had to use anything I could get my hands on. My students made handbags from strips of ribbons sewn together, or pieces of cloth, which were later embroidered with designs the girls had drawn beforehand. It was amazing how nice these left-over tidbits came together to create real works of art. My boss, the superintendent, was very pleased with my work. She said I was a magician to create such works out of practically nothing. I did get along very well with the other teachers, of which I was the young-est. The only thing I didn't care for too much was the fact that none of my daily interface was coed; only girls and women. Thank goodness, I had my friend. Bram, whom I saw on the weekends.

Life became more and more difficult though. Getting enough

food was a major problem. Coupons were useless pieces of paper since there was no food to back them up. Once in a while you could get food at "black market' prices. Bram wasn't feeling too well once, and I wanted to get him some nutritious food. I bought him an egg from a farmer at the ridiculous price of F5.-, a very high price for one egg. My salary was only F75.- per month! I had managed to save part of it, so Bram was very lucky to get half an egg.

We often woke up at night because of the Allied planes flying over us to Germany and back again. The Germans tried to shoot them down, which was very noisy. It was lucky that the trains were still running the first years of the war. Teaching my classes became more and more difficult though, especially in the winter, since there was no heat in the building where I taught. During those months I would wear layers of clothes, and I even wore my coat standing in front of the class if the weather was raw enough. Writing and drawing on the chalkboard was difficult when my fingers were so stiff from the cold. Once in awhile one of my students would faint from starvation, and I would try to revive them, so the student could be sent to the principal's office to be treated by the school nurse.

One little girl was always looking at her work too closely, and when I told her not to get so close to her work, she told me that she couldn't see the work from farther away. That told me that she had eyesight problems, and I told the principal, so she could help. A week later she told me that she had discovered that the girl lived with her family in the basement of a building where there were no windows. The only light for the girl to do her homework by was candlelight, and she could hardly see. The principal reported the situation to the authorities, and the family was relocated to better living quarters. Later I heard that the girl's eyes had improved in the new living conditions, just before any permanent damage occurred.

Once in a while I would have a problem with a student. There was one older girl of eighteen, who was always fooling around and upsetting the class. I had sent her to the principal's office several times because she was unmanageable. After thinking about it for awhile, I ventured to do something which could have easily backfired. When this girl became a problem again, I asked her to stay after school so I could talk to her. At first, I asked her all about herself. She liked that, telling me all about what she liked, and what her hobbies were, and about her family and boyfriend. I showed a real interest in everything she told me, and I could tell that I was getting closer to reaching her. When it was my turn, I told her that I wanted her cooperation in the class, instead of antics and loudness. I told her about myself, that I wasn't many years older than she, and that this was my first job, and that I loved it and wanted so much to become a good teacher. I could see that she was listening to me, and told me that she wanted to become a teacher too. She assured me that she wouldn't be giving me a bad time anymore, but would cooperate, and from that point on, we became friends. As it turned out, she was a nice girl, and I was fortunate to be able to reach her. It could have backfired, resulting in a lot of trouble for me.

There was something else to contend with when I was teaching. The emergency alarm went off when bombs landed near Amsterdam. My classes were on the third floor of the building and every time the alarm went off, my class of thirty five and I had to go all the way to the basement until the all-safe siren sounded. Then we had to climb all the way back up, which was not only tiring, but also time consuming. At lunch time I had to give coupons for a lunch consisting of, maybe, one small potato, a spoonful of vegetables, mostly cabbage, and very rarely a tiny piece of meat, if we were lucky. I was always hungry, as was everybody else. But one time I had a question for the principal, and went to her office unannounced. I knocked on her door and when I entered the room, she was sitting next to her desk with a small wood stove at her feet, and she had a plate of food on her lap. I could see she was embarrassed because she had told all the teachers that everybody was cold and hungry, herself included, and that we should not complain about it. I was shocked and then angry when I saw what she was doing. I thought how easy it must have been for her to tell us not to complain about the cold and hunger, but I couldn't blame her. She was much older than I, about fifty, I would say, and she had the opportunity, in her position, to obtain some extra supplies for herself. I didn't tell anyone what I had seen, because she was a nice person, and it would have been very destructive if I had told anyone.

Just when we were hoping that the war would end, there was a sudden change. The Germans decided in 1942 to evacuate all the towns near the seacoast. Without warning, everyone in town, including my parents, were told they had to leave their homes. Everyone who didn't have family or friends to go to, were placed with families in Haarlem. My parents were told to move in with a doctor's family in Haarlem. They could only take a few things with them, leaving practically all of their possessions in our house in Bloemendaal. It was devastating for my parents, especially my Mother, who loved her home. We had beautiful furniture and art objects in that house, and we didn't know if we would ever get them back because there was always the danger that the Germans would confiscate everything or it would be destroyed by bombardments. We were only allowed three days to pack our personal belongings and whatever else we could take with us. I knew a young man who belonged to our rowing club, who had a dry cleaning business in a large building in Haarlem. He offered some space in his building for my parents to keep some of their belongings. My Father made a cart with wheels to transport some of our belongings to this gener-ous man's building, and he offered to help us move, too. People were often so nice in wartime, trying to help out, without reward. Bram and I helped my parents move to Haarlem, and my sister found a room in Amsterdam.

I was lucky in finding lodgings for myself and took three small rented rooms which had been occupied by Bram's sister. She had just moved to Amersfoort with her new husband a short time before. The three days of moving were a complete nightmare for everyone who moved from Bloemendaal. People were running back and forth, crying and cursing at the enemy, while they tried to decide which of their possessions to take with them, and which they would leave behind. These were heartbreaking decisions to make. On the last day of moving, when my sister and my parents had already left, I entered our house, to inspect it for the last time. It was shocking for me to see additional unfamiliar furniture everywhere, like we had never lived there. Our landlord lived across the street from us, and he was still working in his house, so I ran up to him and asked him why there was someone else's furniture in our house. He told me that he had given permission to a friend of his to store their furniture in "his" rented house. I was furious, but there was nothing we could do about it. But I did find the people whose furniture was in our house and told them that we had not given permission or even known our house was being used by somebody else. They told me they were very sorry, but that they were told it was all right with us for them to use the house. Of course, I couldn't do anything about this, but it scared me, because I realized that we were being manipulated and that we couldn't defend our home anymore. Of course, it was a rented house, but nevertheless, some of the contents were ours. When our parents were able to move back in after the war, some of their furniture was damaged and some was missing, but most was salvageable.

ENEMY CONFRONTATION

Three days later, the town was sealed off. Only the German patrols were allowed to remain. At that time, the "blackout" rule was enforced. Nobody was allowed to show any light after dark, even candlelight.

I will never forget the first evening I spent in the rooms I had rented. They were on the second floor with a narrow staircase leading up to them. There was no electricity, and all I had for light was a large candle that Bram had gotten for me, which in those times was considered a prized possession. He had put some cellophane around the bottom of it to prevent dripping. That first evening in my new rooms, I heard a loud banging on the front door downstairs. Somebody yelled in German, "open up at once". My landlady wasn't home that evening, so I took my candle, and slowly descended the stairs, being careful not to spill the wax off the candle. The banging became louder and louder, and this time the German voice yelled, "open up or we'll break down the door". When I opened the door, somebody in an SS uniform pushed me, full force, against the wall across from the door. Another soldier followed him in and shut the door behind him.

A Tommy gun pushed my face up against the wall and I was asked in German, why a light was shining from my window. They yelled that I must be a spy trying to warn the allies. I was petrified, and tried to answer them in my best German.

"I am so sorry, I just moved to this address today, and I didn't know that the curtains weren't closed properly. You must know that all the people in Bloemendaal were evacuated, and that's why I just moved here".

The SS man who had pushed me against the wall said, "Why don't we just shoot her and get it over with, besides, it will be a good example for the others".

I heard a click from his gun and feared the worst. But then the other one said, "Wait a minute, maybe she's telling the truth. I believe her. She is young, and she is pretty, so let's give her a chance".

"No", said the first one, "I'm for shooting her. She could be a spy, after all".

The second man pushed the gun aside and said, "Let's go, we have a lot to do, so I'm for giving her a chance". He looked at me and said, "Make sure that your light can't be seen from the out-side".

And then he grabbed the candle from my hand with such force that all the molten wax on top of the candle flew around in a wide circle, thoroughly dowsing his uniform. He was furious, cursing and calling me names. By this time I was sure that he was going to end my life, but they both turned, pushed the door open and stamped out of the house, taking my candle with them.

When they reached the sidewalk, they turned around and yelled, "We'll be back". For a while I just stood there in the dark. I couldn't believe what had just happened. But then I blessed the soldier that had saved my life by preventing the other man from shooting me. I crawled up the narrow staircase, sat on a chair and stayed there for the longest time, trembling uncontrollably in the pitch dark. The next day my landlady asked me what had happened because the front door was scratched, and the neighbors had all heard the racket and were startled. Then she scolded me for not being more careful with my light. What made me mad by that time, was the loss of my precious candle, which was the only light that I had.

Fortunately, Bram gave me another small candle I could use. And the Germans never came back.

After I had been teaching for a year, I was offered an extra teaching job in another school in Amsterdam for two days each week. My salary was a meager F75.- per month. As a result my parents supplemented my salary with FL 25.-, so I could pay my bills and manage to stay out of debt. I knew that taking on a second position would be very tiring, but I really needed the money, so I accepted.

Teaching the whole week, plus my travel time, took all of my strength. My hours were long, from 7:45 AM to 5:30 PM which made for a very tiring day. Kieks Bakker's parents offered to let me stay at their house in Amsterdam during the week when I was teaching. One of their daughters had moved away, so I used her room, for which I was very grateful. They were a very nice family and enjoyable to be around. They had a live in maid whom I paid for keeping up my room also. Because food was so hard to come by, I made sure that I had my breakfast and early evening meals on my own. I got my so-called dinner meal from the schools. Even with this, I was always hungry, as the food situation grew worse by the day.

During the time that I spent at my girlfriend's home, I did talk quite a bit with Kieks. She told me that she had been engaged to a wonderful young man a few years earlier. But Kieks broke off the engagement because she was not ready to marry at such a young age. She was afraid that she was not able to be a married woman. But Kieks realized some years later that she had made a big mistake, and really regretted breaking off the engagement.

I felt very sad hearing this story, and I wondered if there was something I could do to help Kieks. Then a miracle happened. A short time later I was talking to Kieks' sister who told me something really remarkable. Toos had gone to a party a short while ago, where she met the very same young man, the one formerly engaged to Kieks. She found out that he was still single and he still felt terrible about losing Kieks. I could not believe what I heard. Sometimes I can not help it, when I put my nose into somebody's affairs, especially when it is meant to do some good.

A few days later I talked to Kieks and told her about what Toos, her sister, had found out about Kieks former fiancée, and about how he was still in love with Kieks. This all made me realize how stupid the situation was, where two people loved each other and did not have the courage to tell each other about it. Soon afterwards, I had a long talk with Kieks. I also wrote a note for her to copy and to give to her friend. Kieks copied over the note with some minor changes, and this was very difficult for her. Kieks was a proud person who opened up her soul only very rarely. Kieks sent the note to the address which Toos gave her.

This story has a very happy ending. Kieks' friend called her right after he got her note. Kieks met with him a few days later. I could guess what they talked about because Kieks told me later on, that she and her friend had decided to patch things up. Not too long afterwards they became engaged again, and two months later I became Kieks maid of honor at her wedding.

Their marriage was a happy one. They had two children, a girl, and a boy, and they both lived a long time. Her son became the Royal Dutch Librarian, a post he holds to this day. I was very happy about it, also because it gave me a "lift" in later years when I was mad at myself when I did something wrong and needed to feel good about something that I did well in my life.

Kieks' uncle, Dominee Bakker, her mother's brother, went through hell on earth in WW II. I wrote him a letter after the war, because I knew him well. He was my minister in Indonesia, who had baptized me there. He wrote me back, but his letter was terribly upsetting, because he wrote that he had left the ministry, because he did not believe anymore that there is a God who takes care of us. He lost some of his children and one of his sons was hanged in a concentration camp. I never dared to ask him more about it, but it shook my own faith a lot. When will it ever end in this world where people can be so utterly cruel, maybe also because they don't believe in anything any more?

Once a week you could get one loaf of bread made from potato flour, with a coupon. I would divide mine into small slices to make sure that I had a few each day. Once in awhile Bram gave me cheese spread, which he got at his workplace. It didn't taste very good, but it was food, after all, and I could spread it on a slice of bread. Quite often I would join my friend's parents at dinnertime, eating my own meager bread meal, while they had their own meal. The struggle to stay alive in those days was a matter of survival, and each person had to take care of himself. After a while, I just went straight to my room after saying, "Hello" to them, because I was so exhausted after coping with the noisy crowded classes. I had to rest and go to sleep early every evening. Sometimes I didn't have anything to eat and I didn't want the family to know. They had much more food, because they had friends who had a farm.

I never liked teaching in the second school. The principal was very strict and unfriendly. She treated me like an intruder, I guess because I only taught two days a week. I never got close to the other teachers at that school either, so at lunch time, after our hot meal, I would excuse myself under the pretext of having to prepare for the next class.

Something happened in that school that gave me a very bad impression of two of the teachers. During the summer, on nice days, we would go to the flat roof of the school after lunch, where one could enjoy a beautiful view of Amsterdam. Next to the school there was a lower building which we could look down on to see a table and several chairs placed around on the terrace next to the house. The table was placed for a meal, with food on the table, ready to be eaten, but there was nobody there at the moment. Since we were looking down at this peaceful scene and were always hungry and food conscious, we couldn't believe that anyone would let food just sit there, not to mention we dreamt about what kind of food there was in those dishes.

Before I realized what was happening, one of the teachers I was with tried to spit at the food dish in the distance. The other teachers joined her and they were all having fun trying to hit the dish with their spit. I couldn't believe what I was seeing. I started to yell at them to stop, but they ignored me until they hit their target a few times. I was so disgusted that I left, wondering if I should tell the principal. Regretfully, I kept my mouth shut because I didn't like the principal, and didn't think she would have believed me anyway. But I did make up my mind then and there, that I would leave this school as soon as possible.

I was exhausted, teaching the whole week in two different schools, without much food and feeling weak and hungry. Every two weeks I taught 786 students between the ages of 13 and 23, and with all that, my salary could hardly support me. I was cheated when I gave the school my food coupons because I could have gotten more food for those coupons at home. A few days later I went to the principal and told her that I was resigning. I told her that I couldn't handle it anymore. She was furious, but when she saw I was serious, she told me to go to the representative of all the schools, who lived in Rotterdam at the time. I wrote this person and made an appointment to see her. On Saturday, which was my day off, I traveled to Rotterdam and paid her a visit. I told her my story and asked her permission to leave as soon as possible. She was very nice and listened attentively to what I had to say. Then she looked at me intently and said, "I will allow you to quit because I know you are telling me the truth. You look like a ghost, but I would like you to work one more month because I have to find a replacement for you, and that's not going to be easy."

So I taught in the second school for one more month, and it was miserable because the principal resented me. Several times she tried to change my mind, even to the point of getting mad, but I kept on telling her that I was sure that I wanted to leave, even though it meant that my salary would be much less.

I stayed at the first school for quite a while. It was so nice compared to the other one. I got along well with everybody and the principal was a kind person and very supportive. But I felt sorry for most of the teachers, who were older spinsters. Some of them told me that they never had a chance to get married and have children. One of them got married when I was there though, and everybody envied her.

Life became more and more difficult. Several times when I went to the home of my friends where I stayed during the week, I would find that the house was locked, and I would end up sitting on the front stoop until their maid came back. This was especially miserable when the weather was bad. The time came though, that I couldn't go to Amsterdam anymore because the train service stopped and to make things worse, my bike had been stolen. I would have had to borrow my Mothers bike, and the trip from Haarlem to Amsterdam and back was almost forty miles, which was just too far to go for a few days a week. Luckily, the school still paid me because the circumstances were related to the war and therefore out of my control.

HIDING AND HUNGER IN 1942

Things got worse after I had to quit teaching. There was very little food available anymore, and Bram had to leave his job in Delft because the Germans were picking up more and more young men whom they sent to Germany to work in their factories. Bram, being a chemist, was particularly susceptible to these round-ups, called "Razzia's".

Very often a Razzia meant a death sentence for those inducted due to the fact that men were sent to German factories, which were later bombed by the Allied planes on a regular basis. I tried to help Bram find another temporary job, where he would be safe from the German persecution. By pure luck I managed to contact Bram's second cousin, who was the head of a cable factory in Amsterdam. He told me that he would give Bram a job, at least temporarily, until the war was over and then he could go back to his regular job. We were thankful, of course, because this meant that Bram would be safe for a while, and could take some days off to go with me on what we called a "hunger journey". Bram started working in Amsterdam and he found a place to live in Haarlem. He could take the electric train for a short 11 minute ride to work.

Since Boemendaal and Haarlem were only a ten minute bike ride apart, Bram and I could go foraging for food together in the northern Dutch countryside. On our "hunger journey", we would take our bikes and travel north, to where you could find farms sprinkled on the countryside. The northern part of Holland was still relatively safe during the first years of the war. Farmers were very important in those days, as they had extra food which they would trade for goods such as clothes, jewelry, household goods, and the like. We would take anything we could spare to buy food.

At first biking into the countryside wasn't too dangerous since the war wasn't near us at the time. But as we entered the third year of the war, everything started to fall apart. The last time Bram and I went north to forage for food was on a cold day in 1943. We stopped at different farms without any luck. Anything edible was so scarce that the farmers were getting particular about what they would trade for their produce. At the end of the day we were getting desperate as we approached a large farm. An elderly man called to us and told us that he could give us some flour to help us out, and he didn't even want anything from us in exchange. Of course, we were thrilled, especially when he asked us if we would like to stay overnight, just when we were going to ask him where we might be able to stay. Somehow we trusted him, even though we had been warned that there were traitors amongst the farmers. Around dinner time we were invited to join the farmer's family for their family meal, and we couldn't believe our luck. They were very hospitable and they were eating food that we had not had for a long time. We had a very pleasant conversation with our host and talked about our concerns of the war and how hard it was to deal with our lives. But when we started to talk about the war, the conversation took a frightening turn. The man who had invited us in, the uncle of the farmer, suddenly turned to us in the middle of the conversation and said "I have to warn you, before you say anything more, that I happen to be a member of the N.S.B. party. (National Social Bond, whose members were mostly Nazi sympathizers and therefore traitors). We were taken aback, as we were at the mercy of this man, and he could even deliver us to the Germans, which would be especially bad for Bram. The creation of this fear was what kept us on the move, hoping not to be in the wrong place at the wrong time. When the family saw how frightened we were, they assured us that they wouldn't turn us in to the Germans because they weren't mean people. In fact, they felt sorry for us and wanted to help us out. We felt we had no choice but to trust them, so we stayed overnight. When we got up the next morning we were fed a wonderful breakfast with eggs. We had nearly forgotten how good an egg could taste! We were also given some other food stuffs, like potatoes to go with our flour, for which we were truly thankful. We told them so over and over.

After the war was over, we received a letter from the government asking us if the elderly farmer and his family had treated us well. They were being investigated about their behavior during the war years, especially because the uncle had been an N.S.B. member. We wrote back that they had been good to us, and that the uncle hadn't turned us over to the Germans when he could have done so, easily. I'm sure our letter helped their case, as quite a few of the traitors were convicted after the war, for collaborating with the enemy. We thought maybe this farmer's family had treated us well on purpose, just in case the Germans lost the war. Who knows? In any case, we were grateful to them and hoped that they wouldn't be punished, though we never knew the outcome for this family.

Whatever food we could get, we shared with my parents and an older lady that was a close friend of Bram's mother, who couldn't fend for herself. This lady's name was Tannie, and Bram felt responsible for her, partly because she had only one leg, as the result of an accident, so he helped her whenever he could. Feeding the five of us made finding enough food even harder for us. The Germans were speeding up their efforts to pick up young men all over the country, and it was getting dangerous for Bram to be outside.

The second time we went north to the countryside was at the end of the summer. This time we decided to try to visit Bram's uncle, who lived some distance north of Amsterdam. The uncle and his charming wife were glad to see us. We had a short, but nice visit with them, as his uncle was quite sick, and wasn't expected to live much longer. When we left, we asked him if there was anything we could do for him. After some hesitation they told us that his uncle loved chocolate and would love to have just a little of it before he died. We promised to try to find some for them, although the chances of finding chocolate were very slim, indeed. We traveled further north, but we were warned that the Germans were rousting young men in yet another "Razzia", and this time they were trying to make a clean sweep for as many workers as they could.

Because of this Razzia, we had to be very careful, so we only went to isolated farms. Still, we were taking a big risk. Several times we heard shots in the distance, and a young man we met told us to stay as far away from the shots as we could to avoid getting caught. By that time we were getting pretty nervous, but we needed food so urgently that we kept on going. We managed to get some flour in the afternoon, but as the day faded, we had to think about where we would stay for the night. We knew we had to get off the streets before curfew, which was eight in the evening. We asked a woman that we met on the street if she knew of a place we could find lodgings, but when she asked us if we were married, and we said no, she said she couldn't help us because she only had one guest room available. This seemed so odd and so unimportant because the dangers of surviving took precedence, and the normal moral codes were the least of our worries.

As it got closer to curfew, our anxiety grew, and we decided to take the big risk of entering a hotel that we had passed. As soon as we entered we realized what a big mistake we had made. Sitting in the corner of the large foyer were several German soldiers. They had been active in a Razzia that day and were sitting there resting. Bram hesitated one moment, but then he did the only logical thing he could have done under the circumstances. He walked very calmly and slowly to the front desk and asked the hotel clerk if they could accommodate us for the night. When he was told there were no more rooms available, he walked back to the front door and together we left. It was a miracle that nobody asked Bram for his papers. Either they were very tired that day, or they thought that my friend Bram wasn't the kind of man they had been chasing all day. I was drenched in sweat from being so scared during this episode.

We were extremely lucky that time, but we were still in trouble because it was time for the curfew, and we hadn't found a place to stay. Staying out after curfew had some dire possible consequences. If Bram were caught out after curfew he would most likely be either shot by soldiers, or shipped off to the east to work in the munitions factories.

But luck was on our side that night. A man stopped us on the street and warned us that we shouldn't stay outside. When we told him that we were desperate, he invited us into his home. Of course, he could have been a traitor, a member of the NSB party (National Socialist Bond), but it turned out that he was working with the underground forces, and could help us. We stayed overnight, and the next morning our host gave us some potatoes before we left.

About a month later, we paid this man another visit to thank him again, and this time we brought him a box decorated for Christmas, which he liked very much. We never saw him again, but I'm sure he was one of those unsung heroes who helped in his own way to save our country. After the war, some of these people turned out to be NSB'ers who had mixed loyalties, especially towards the end of the war. Sometimes we had to vouch for these NSB'ers when their cases came up before the Dutch courts.

Because it was getting more and more dangerous for Bram to venture outside, we didn't travel together anymore. One day I went north to pay Bram's uncle and aunt a visit. This time I brought his uncle what he had wanted so much on our last visit, a bar of chocolate. He was so happy with this present. Bram had saved this bar for about two years, thinking he would use it for a very special occasion. When he heard his uncle's wish, he knew why he had saved this precious bar for such a long time.

About a month later I took another trip with a friend, whose husband also had to hide because of the Razzia's. Although it was winter time, the weather being interminably cold and miserable most of the time, we decided to go anyway because the food situation had become critical, and every little morsel that we could gather would be helpful. We started early in the morning and the weather wasn't too bad. Although it was cold, the roads were clear and bicycling was possible. This time we had more luck. There weren't too many people on the roads, so we went to some isolated farms in the countryside. I had some clothing with me, but not much, as there wasn't much left to spare. Around noon time we reached a farm where people were working. When we asked them if we could get some food for money or clothing, they invited us in for lunch. We were very pleased because they had eggs, bread, and large bowls of soup that had meat floating in it. Everybody took turns pouring the soup into their bowls with a large ladle.

There were a lot of children in the family and they seemed quite happy. One of the kids chewed on a tough piece of meat for a while, and then asked if he could throw it back in to the large soup bowl, which he did. And another child did the same thing with a piece of bone he found in his soup. By that time I had noticed how sloppy everyone was being with their food, and that practically all the children's faces were covered with an unhealthy rash, which was probably because they weren't very clean. Soap was very scarce in those days, and we decided that this farmers family didn't use much of it. My girlfriend and I noticed all of this and could hardly swallow our meal, even though we were very hungry. They were so nice and good to us that we realized that people can be dirty on the outside, but very clean inside. Most of the farmers whom we met were very clean though.

The weather was turning ugly, so we started back early in the afternoon. Gradually, the sky turned very dark and snow started to fall, making it difficult to handle our bikes. Between the snow and the weight of the potatoes, we were thrown off balance, not to mention I had taken off my only pair of woolen socks in exchange for a pound of potatoes. So this is what we had come to, warming our feet or filing our stomachs. A hard choice. In this case my feet were very uncomfortable, and they got stiff and painful from the cold.

After several hours of bicycling through the snow and cold, we were totally exhausted. My feet were frozen and several times we had to push our bikes. We reached the town where Bram's aunt and uncle lived. I knew that I couldn't go on and decided to ask if I could stay with them for awhile. My girlfriend was in much better shape than I, so she decided to go on, no matter what. When I found the house I was looking for, I got quite a shock. The aunt opened the door when I knocked, and I saw at once, that something awful had happened. She was crying, and when I asked her what was the matter, she told me that her husband had died that morning. I didn't know what to say, but at the same time I felt that maybe I could console her a little bit. She seemed to be glad to see me, so I stayed overnight with her. She insisted that I see her dead husband for the last time. He looked very peaceful, even though I knew he had suffered a lot. He had only one lung left and this had made it difficult for him to breathe. Death was a relief for him, and his release from suffering helped his wife accept his fate. When I returned home, Bram was very sad about his uncles death, but he was glad that he had been able to give his uncle a little pleasure in his last wish for chocolate.

Razzia's were held more and more often now. Bram didn't dare go outside, so that meant that he couldn't go to work anymore in Amsterdam, either. He was living in a boarding house where he rented a large room with a small bedroom. In the living room there was a large closet for hanging his clothes and coats. He was afraid that the Germans would inspect the boarding house, and not wanting to be found, he decided to make a hiding place somewhere, so he could disappear if they came. The closet turned out to be a possibility because the floor could be removed, and there was a small place between the walls big enough for his whole body to fit. He managed to make the closet floor removable, and this way he could pull the floor over the top of him after lowering him-self into the hiding space. He practiced several times going in and out of hiding. One evening when I was visiting, he asked me to watch him, to see if he could disappear fast enough, if necessary. He put a candle on the floor as he lowered himself into the hole and pulled the floor over him. There was no electricity, and we had the windows well covered, so candlelight was our only option. Just as Bram disappeared, there was a knock on the door and a mutual friend of ours entered. When he saw the open closet with the burn-ing candle on the floor, he asked me what I was doing and where Bram was. At that moment Bram lifted the floor slowly, being care-ful not to knock the candle over and said, "Here I am". This really startled our visitor. He thought there was a ghost in the room. We had a hearty laugh about the situation later on. We knew we could trust this person, and he told us that he thought we were very wise to make this concealed spot. He himself wasn't in danger of being picked up because he was old enough to be safe from Razzia's.

RAZZIA 1943

At any rate, we felt good that Bram had a place to hide if the Germans decided to ransack his boarding house, but luckily, they never did. We made another hiding place in my apartment, where I also had a closet. On the back side of the closet, we discovered that we could remove the wall, and behind that was a crawl space underneath the roof of the building. Not long after we had fixed the hiding place, there was an afternoon when we had some anxious moments. Bram was with me at the time, and we heard a lot of noise outside. When we looked out of my window we saw Germans blocking both ends of the street and placing machine guns in the middle of the street. Fearfully, we realized that a Razzia was in progress.

The Germans started to bang on the front doors of the houses, as they yelled "Open up". Bram disappeared quietly into the hiding place. I placed several boxes against the back of the closet, and just when I went to the window to see what was going on outside, somebody knocked on my door. Somebody was beckoning me in a frightened voice, "Please let me in". When I opened the door, a young woman came in. Without saying another word, she ran to the window and peered outside. She was looking across the street, toward a slanted roof above the porch. On this section of the roof two men were lying flat on their stomachs. These men had crawled onto the roof when they realized that the Germans were going to search every house. The young woman standing next to me, opened the window and yelled in Dutch to her husband, "William, lower your butt, it is still sticking up too much". "yes, that's perfect". She turned to me and said, "My husband and his friend were staying in a hiding place somewhere. Then they decided to pay me a visit, but soon realized they couldn't escape when the Germans put up the roadblocks. The roof was the only place we could think of to hide the men. Fortunately the Germans had been too busy entering houses to notice them crawling out there. Also, the Germans didn't understand Dutch, and there was so much yelling and protesting going on about the invasion of the enemy, making this woman's voice calling to her husband was just one of many.

The woman returned to her home, and a while later, I saw the Germans entering her home. I prayed for the safety of those poor men. It was bitter cold and they weren't wearing coats because they would have been too bulky. When the soldiers banged on the front door of my boarding house, the landlady opened the door immediately. I heard them ask her if there were any men in the house, and I was frightened because she knew that Bram was upstairs with me. But she said that she was alone downstairs, and that she only had a young woman upstairs. The soldiers believed her and left. Apparently the Germans knew who the occupants were beforehand, and therefore, mostly raided the houses where they knew male occupants might be. Later on we heard that several young men had been caught, but the ones who had been lying on the roof across the street, had not been discovered. Unfortunately, the woman's husband contracted pneumonia from being out there so long, and became very sick, but he did survive. After this episode, we breathed a deep sigh of relief, and later on, we had a big laugh about the woman yelling at her husband to "lower his butt".

Bram had another experience at his boarding house. The landlady had been married and divorced for quite some years, and she had a daughter about sixteen years old. She and her estranged husband were on friendly terms, but not together because this man was a religious fanatic. Nobody knew how he made a living, but it couldn't have been a very rewarding one, because he would take his meals with his ex-wife and daughter, and they would let him use one of their vacant rooms. Sometimes you could hear this man early in the morning, sitting by an open window, lamenting the fate of the world. He spoke in a plaintive voice, but loud enough that it disturbed anyone trying to sleep in the neighborhood, as he droned on, reproaching the Lord for letting the world be in such a state. He seemed quite normal, unless the subject of religion came up. When that happened, he seemed to lose all reason. In one such conversation, he mentioned the war and how he had asked God how the war was going to end, and how the world would be after the war. God's answer, in general terms, was that the world would be better after many people had died. He was a gentle man, moved to tears by the answers he perceived to have gotten straight from God. Then the conversation moved on to how a person should face the war. He told Bram that he was on the wrong track by trying to hide from the enemy, avoiding evil. He said, "You should act as Christ had done, facing the enemy, and say 'Here I am' ". This scared us because it wasn't unthinkable, that a man with his religious zeal, might take it upon himself to report Bram to the German authorities.

We voiced our concerns to the landlady, and she assured us that he would never betray anyone to the Germans, and that he was really a good man at heart. However, we didn't invite him anymore when the boarders all got together. We still felt insecure, and that was when Bram promptly started to build the hiding place in his apartment. Bram also decided to stop his tapping of tiny quantities of electricity. He had a small transformer that was shaped such that it would fit into the socket where a light bulb would go, and at the bottom of it was a three volt flashlight bulb that shed a rather faint light on the table below. It could be switched on and off by the wall switch, but that circuit was also connected to the other lights which served all the rooms, and he made all of them inactive by putting small discs of cardboard in the lamp sockets, all except the one in the kitchen, which he hesitated to put out of commission because there was always someone in the kitchen area. Bram didn't want anybody to know what he was doing, but keeping it a secret was difficult because most of the time the land-lady, or her daughter, or the other tenant were there having their meals in the kitchen.

Then one day a golden opportunity came, and Bram was ready for it. He always carried some of the cardboard discs in his pocket, in case he had a chance to use them. That day Bram was invited to join the other people in the boarding house for their meager meal in the kitchen. In the middle of the meal the landlady suddenly started to choke. It got so bad that everybody became alarmed. They started shaking her, and patting her on the back, but nothing seemed to help. The woman ran outside into the yard making horrible choking sounds. Until finally, she got rid of whatever was blocking her throat, and then sat quietly on a bench for a while, calming herself. This was the opportunity that Bram had been waiting for, so quickly, while all the commotion was going on, he fixed the kitchen light. From then on, he had a very small light in his room, which helped him tremendously. The lamp used so little current that it would be difficult to detect.

THE WOOD STOVE ADVENTURE 1943

I had noticed that Bram wasn't getting enough food from his coupons because his landlady was cheating him a little here and there, so I proposed that Bram do the cooking. It was very hard to cook though, because there was no electricity or gas, so we had only a wood stove made from an old tin can. We used tiny wood sticks to start the fire. This was very tedious work. I needed a better wood stove, but they were hard to come by. Then one day we received word that Bram's factory was offering wood stoves for their employees at a very reasonable price, but there was a limited number of them.

A wood stove was worth more than gold or diamonds to us because with a stove we would be able to cook more conveniently. However, there was a problem. Somebody had to go to Amsterdam to get the stove and transport it back to Haarlem, which meant a bike ride of nineteen miles each way. Not only that, we had to find some way to attach this cumbersome piece to the bike. I was the only one who could do this, and it seemed that it would be an onerous chore since we were all weak from lack of food. I made ready for the trip. My bike tires looked like a patchwork quilt from the countless times we had repaired the rubber, the chances of my getting a flat were pretty high.

On an overcast morning at 5 AM, I started my trip. It was bitterly cold, and soon it started snowing. By the time I reached the factory, everything had started to look like a Christmas picture card, but I didn't have any time to enjoy it because it took a long time and a lot of effort to attach the heavy stove to the carrier of my bike. It was getting later and later and I was pressed to get back before dark, which came early in the winter. An icy cold wind started to blow and drove the whirling snow into my face. I had promised to stop at my sister's apartment on the way back because my Father was visiting her, and had told me some days before, that he wanted to ride back with me. This delayed my trip, but it wasn't too far from the route I was taking.

I picked up my Father at around 5:00 PM. It was already dark when we both started back to Haarlem. Meadows and marshes stretched for miles on either side of the road, giving the fierce wind an unhampered chance to blow full force against us. It was difficult to stay upright on our bikes without falling. It is amazing how the struggle for survival can make a person strong, and how the will to live reigns over all living beings, especially when you have some hope left that someday everything in the world will be better. Our inner strength kept us peddling, on and on, for hours, slowly, but steadily.

Once in a while a German truck would pass, adding to our misery by throwing snow and slush against our frozen, but still moving legs. The German curfew laws prohibited the use of lights outside after dark, but our small bicycle lights in the middle of this snowstorm were too dim to be a threat, so the Germans left us alone. Most of the time, though, we moved through a cold dark blanket of snow. The only sounds were made by the whistle of the wind and our own heavy breathing. At nine in the evening we reached a village called "Halfweg", which was, of course, halfway between the two cities. The houses of the village were just dark shadows, since no lights were allowed to show. There wasn't a living soul in sight. It was such a temptation to stop, knock on a door, and rest for a while, but we decided to try to make it home as soon as possible. Soon after we had passed Halfway village, I lost my balance and crashed to the side of the road. I landed right between the tramway tracks next to us. Frantically, I tried to lift my bike up, while balancing the heavy stove on the carrier. Father helped, and together we managed to get the bike upright again.

Soon after this, I realized to my surprise, that my Father had disappeared. I couldn't see him anymore, and panicked, for fear that he had fallen off his bike and was lying in the snow somewhere. After all, he wasn't so young anymore. I went back to where I had seen him last, but he had vanished into thin air. The only thing I could do was start in the direction of home again, which I did. I didn't see him at all during the last part of my journey, but consoled myself with the thought that he had probably gone on ahead, and would be there when I got home.

Soon my body started to ache. My feet and hands were cold numb and lifeless. Gradually, a very sleepy feeling crawled up my body starting at my feet, and I had the strongest urge to stop bicycling, slide down to the ground, forget everything, and go to sleep. But my subconscious mind knew this was a danger, and giving in to the urge would be the end of me. The wind was so strong that I couldn't stay on my bike any longer, so I walked along beside it, pushing and balancing, and hoping that the blood in my veins would warm up. Walking helped for a while, but then my legs weakened and I stopped. The voice in my head kept repeating, "Don't give up miss, keep going, let's get it together." Outwardly, a voice was saying "Haarlem is in sight now, so don't give up please. Let's count our steps, one-two-three". I looked in the direction the voice came from and discovered there was a vague form of a woman in the darkness, who was also pushing a bike. She started talking again and I noticed that she was speaking Dutch with a heavy German accent. My first reaction was one of anger. The Germans were our enemy and you just didn't associate with them if you could help it. So I didn't say a word, but the woman began talking again and said, "I am a German woman, married to a Dutch man, and I know how you must feel about me. I find myself caught between

two countries in this cruel war, and I hate what my people are doing to yours. There's nothing I can do about that, but when I get
a chance to help someone, I try to help that one person at least".
Then I spoke to her for the first time, and in a bitter tone, I told her
about the unhappiness and miseries of our people, and myself at
the moment. "Go on", I said, "I don't need you. I will manage".

But she stayed with me, talking about her house, her family,
and her life. She must have sensed that I was on the brink of passing out, and her talking did help me to keep going for a while, but
only for a little while. Then the time came when I knew I couldn't go
any further. My legs folded under me. I remember pushing my bike
to the side of the road and sliding toward the ground, and after
that, nothing. I don't know how long I laid in the snow, but when I
came to, there were two men standing over me, lifting me up, and
taking the bike with us. In front of me I saw the familiar shape of
the German woman, pushing her own bike. The men carried me
to a nearby house. The German woman then turned around and
facing me, said "Miss, you will be all right now, remember what I
told you. Forgive me for being German, and God Bless You". Then
she vanished in the darkness. I never saw her face clearly, nor did I
know her name, but she saved my life by getting those men to help
me.

The kind people who took me in, gave me something hot to
drink, and told me later, that this woman had knocked frantically at their door and asked them to help her with an unconscious
woman who was lying in the snow alongside the road, who would
freeze to death if they didn't come soon. The two men volunteered
to come back with her to help. One of the men looked at me intently and commented about how peculiar it was that this woman
must have been German with such a strong accent. "Yes, I know",
I said. "Maybe it will help me in later years to forgive and forget". I
will never forget what this woman did for me and I hope God took
care of her.

When I was sitting on a chair in this good person's home, I remember being embarrassed because the snow on my clothes started to melt, forming puddles on their living room rug. Everybody assured me that it didn't matter to them, that they were more concerned about how I was doing. I stayed with them for at least an hour, and by that time I was feeling better. Next to me was a young girl sitting in a large chair. She asked me how bad the weather was outside, and I told her that it was just awful, and that she was lucky to be inside, not having to struggle through a snow storm in freezing temperatures. Her answer was disturbing. She said "I would give anything to trade places with you anytime. I'm a prisoner here because I can't walk. I had polio when I was a child and my legs are useless." Before I could say anything, she went on, "You see, there is always something to be thankful for. You still have the use of your legs, so you are better off than I am, after all". When I said good-bye to this wonderful family, I was feeling much better. At last I managed to reach Bram's apartment. It was close to midnight, and he was shocked to see me in such a stage of exhaustion. He helped me up the staircase and rubbed my hands and feet until they felt normal again. Then, at last, I went on to my own apartment, where I slept for a long time.

The weather cleared up the next day, which gave me a chance to find out if Father was safe. I was relieved when I saw him. He told me that he had gone on ahead when he couldn't see me anymore in the storm, thinking that I was somewhere ahead of him. Of course, he felt terrible, when he heard about my ordeal, but we were happy that both of us had survived. I never saw that family who saved my life again, for the simple reason that I couldn't find them. I knew it was somewhere on the outskirts of Haarlem, but which house it was, or even which street, I couldn't remember. I felt badly about this, as I would like to have thanked them. So every time later, that I could help somebody else, it made me feel good, like I was passing on the favor this family had done for me.

The wood stove was a God send. This simple convenience made it possible for me to cook for Bram and myself, and this way Bram could get full use of his food coupons, at least, to the extent that was possible.

MY SISTER META

My sister Meta had her problems too. Sometime before we evacuated our home in Bloemendaal she was in her last year of high school. It was then that she fell into a different situation. This incident could have ostracized her from the Dutch community altogether, but her naiveté didn't last long enough to hurt her, fortunately. On a sunny day she went to play tennis with some young people near our home. She met a young man who played tennis quite well, and she liked him right away. After they had played several games, they talked for a while and then they went to change from their tennis outfits. Meta was quite happy because this young man seemed to be nice, and she had ideas about them becoming very good friends. When this young man reappeared in his street clothes, Meta was shocked to see that he was dressed in a German officers uniform. Meta's heart fell as she asked him why he was wearing the hated uniform. He told her that he was German and therefore, had to serve in the German Army. "But how is it possible" Meta queried "that you speak fluent Dutch without any accent?". He told her that when he was a child he had stayed with a family in Holland during World War I, which was true, because it was a well known fact, that many children had come over to be protected at that time. These children had been starving, and badly needed to recuperate from malnutrition. That was why this young man spoke Dutch so well, but it was ironic that he came back to Holland, which had saved his life before, only this time he was the enemy. Now he was using his knowledge of Holland to serve his own country. Meta told him that she didn't want to see him because he represented the enemy forces, and she couldn't afford to be seen with him. She felt sorry about this, but it couldn't be helped.

Then something happened that frightened her. Just a few days after the episode with the German officer, as she was just about to leave her school in the afternoon, this young man showed up. Several girls saw him and wondered why he was there. They were curious to know who he was waiting for. Nobody seemed to know why he didn't leave, even when the school was almost empty, but Meta knew, and she hid in the school until it was completely empty. Then she slunk outside and told the German that she was upset with his being there after she had told him that she didn't want to see him anymore. He told her that he had just gotten word that he was to be transferred to the eastern front, and just wanted to see her once more to say good-bye. Meta never saw him again, but some time later the mailman brought a few letters from him, that were obviously from the German area. Mother managed to hide the letters, and she asked my opinion about what she should do with them, because she was frightened that my Father would find out. It would have killed him if he knew that German letters were coming into our home. Father hated anything to do with the Germans, because of what they had done to us and to the country. I told Mother she shouldn't give the letters to Meta, but destroy them, which she did. I felt like a criminal, but I knew that it was the only wise thing to do, because Meta would have felt sorry for the young man, because she knew he didn't want to be in the army, nor be caught up in the terrible war.

When the last letter came, Mother showed it to me. It was a very sad letter. Mother and I felt like crying because it was sent from a hospital in Poland, informing Meta that the young man had lost his right arm in a battle. He had loved to play tennis so much. This was the last letter he wrote, and we never heard from him again. I hope he survived the war and found some happiness in his later life. He was typical of the millions of victims of a cruel war, which was thrust upon everyone and didn't prove anything in the long run. Meta's brief interest in this young man put me in an awkward position for a while, because people would come up to me and ask if my sister was seeing a German soldier. I told them that it wasn't true, and that she had only talked to him once for a very short while. To compensate for the situation, Meta decided to join the underground forces. One of the reasons she joined this very dangerous group was because she worried about the gossip concerning her encounter with the German. Mostly, though, my sister wanted to do something for our country.

While Meta was in Amsterdam, she fell in love and lived with the son of a Dutch nobleman for about a year. She was quite happy during this period. This nobleman was also active in the underground, so they often worked together resisting the German occupation. Tragically, after about a year, this nobleman broke off his relationship with Meta, saying that her social status was too low for his noble blood. Meta took this very hard, and it took years for her to trust any man again.

The underground's support system was a big help to the allies. They served as couriers, transported goods, arms, and helped to hide downed pilots, not to mention people who were being sought by the Germans. Helping the Jews was a big job, helping them to find hiding places, and getting them enough food to survive this horrible ordeal. And last, but not least, they watched out for each other, capture meant torture or execution, or both.

Meta also participated in underground actions designed to enter an N.S.B. (National Social Bund) home illegally. The NSB houses were entered and the occupants tied to chairs in the cellars or basements. Then the underground forces would take everything they could find to help the cause. Food coupons and food were high on the priority list, as were things that could be sold on the black market. These operations allowed them to help many people that desperately needed their assistance. After they raided a house, they would call the police, and inform them about the people who had been left tied up. They did this because they didn't want those people to die, even though they were considered traitors to their own people. The underground forces were effective, toward helping the allies win the war, but unfortunately many of them were caught and killed by the Germans.

One of those who were caught and killed was my cousin, the son of my Father's sister. He was caught while walking on a platform at the rail station in Arnhem. He was carrying a gun and his captors found out that he was working for the underground which was considered a criminal act. He was transported to a concentration camp called Neuengamme near Hamburg, where he died on October 23,1944, one week after his arrival, supposedly from internal bleeding. He was tortured so much that his kidneys protruded out of his back. He was 23 years old, and I'll never forgive the Germans for what they did to him. What made it so tragic was the fact that my Aunt and Uncle had managed to get papers to free him, because he had already lost two sons, one from an accident, and the other from being killed fighting the Germans in1940. With the help of some important people they knew, he was to be granted the freedom of his third son. The papers arrived on the very same day he received word that his son had died in Neuengamme. I don't know how he was able to cope with all these terrible tragedies in his life, but he had a deep faith in God.

My sister experienced quite a few things when she was living in Amsterdam. There are too many for me to write about all of them, but I will relate a few of them to you. Meta was always on the lookout for something the underground could use. Early on one evening in 1944 she spotted a pile of something on the quay of the canal. She decided to investigate. Two sentries were guarding the mysterious pile, walking back and forth, crossing each others path at the middle of the pile. Meta watched them for awhile, and then, when they were far apart, she dove under the canvas to see what was hidden. It turned out to be barrels filled with molasses from a nearby factory. By now, it had started to rain, adding to the darkness of the night. Meta, dressed entirely in black, managed to roll a large barrel to the street, which was made of large round cobblestones, called "children's heads", in Holland. When Meta rolled the barrel over these cobblestones, it made quite a racket. Luckily the noise created by the pouring rain subdued the noise she was making. Just when Meta thought she had rolled the barrel almost far enough away from the sentries, a truckload of Germans approached. Meta did the only thing she could have done to prevent detection. She bent herself over the barrel, pulling her coat over her head, and stayed there, motionless, hoping that the Germans wouldn't see her. It was pure luck that they didn't. The truck passed by very closely, and then disappeared into the distance. She hid the barrel near a house and got help from one of her friends. The only problem was getting the barrel up to her apartment, but it was worth the effort because molasses was rare and a welcome commodity.

Meta had a lot of trouble keeping a bike in Amsterdam. Bikes were the only mode of transportation, especially at the end of the war. Most of the Dutch bikes had been confiscated by the Germans, so you had to be very careful, if you had a bike, to protect it from being stolen. Many people hid their bikes, sometimes even burying them under ground. Whole gangs of young people roamed the streets with tools that they used to cut the sturdiest of bicycle chains. Because of this, people would take the front wheel of the bike with them thinking this would stop anyone from taking their bikes. Of course, this was a nuisance, and even then, sometimes they would come back and the rest of their bike would have disappeared while they were gone. Meta lost several bikes, each time when she had gone into a shop for just a short time. She had locked her bikes, but lost them anyway. One time she had no choice but to start walking to her apartment. Luck was with her though, because she saw a German entering a building and he had left his bike outside, unguarded. Meta rushed to the bike and somehow managed to bend the lock and take off with the bike as fast as she could. When she reached her apartment, she hauled the bike up the staircase to her place. Then she discovered that there was a revolver attached to the bike. What she had done was very dangerous, of course, and she was lucky that she wasn't caught. The revolver was a bonus for the underground.

Meta was quite happy when she lived in Amsterdam. She was free at last, to be on her own, and she made many new friends. She had always wanted to have a dog, but my parents never gave her permission with the exception of one short period of time. Then they gave the dog away when she wasn't around because it was a wild dog. This was a cruel thing to do because Meta loved that dog even if it was unmanageable. So, now that she lived by herself, she collected several stray dogs. She was able to keep them because she could get food for them through the underground. They would have been destroyed if she hadn't taken them in, as most pets were eaten or done in during the war. One dog was Meta's favorite. She had gotten it from a friend who was a veterinarian. She requested that if he ever got a German shepherd, she would like to have it. After awhile, he let her know that a German soldier had brought him a shepherd, saying that he couldn't keep it anymore because Germany was losing the war and he had been called back to Germany. So the vet gave Meta the dog, and she was ecstatic. The German had named him "Kazan", so she decided to keep it that way. But it wasn't meant to be for Meta to keep this dog.

I happened to be with her in her apartment at that time because once in awhile she was able to get some loaves of bread, and I would share them with Bram, my parents, and the invalid friend who stayed with them. I was just about to leave when her doorbell rang. Because she lived on the third floor, she had attached a long rope to the banister, This rope hung down and was attached to the front door, so she could pull open the door, saving her a lot of steps. When she opened the door this time we saw a man standing there, looking up at us.

"Is this the place where Meta lives?" he asked.

"Yes, my name is Meta" my sister answered him. "What can I do to help you?"

Then the man said, "Do you have a German shepherd dog?, and if so may I see the dog please?' When he saw how puzzled Meta looked he added, "I think you have the dog that belonged to me before the Germans confiscated him. I have been trying to find my dog for two years. I could trace him most of the time, but had lost the trail of late, but somehow I found out that my dog was with a German officer who had kept the dog for himself. When he gave up the dog to the vet, I was able to trace him to your address. I trained that dog with his brother from the time they were puppies, and my wife and I loved those dogs. Both of them were taken by the Germans, and I lost the trail of the other dog right from the beginning, but this dog was easier to find. So may I see your dog please, to see if it is my dog?"

Meta had been listening to this story with growing anxiety because she realized she would lose the dog. She was wondering what proof he had, but the proof became clear very shortly. Kazan had been sitting behind her and listening intently when he heard the voice down at the bottom of the staircase. We could see that he had become very agitated, and just when the man stopped talking Kazan pushed his way past Meta and started down the stairs. The man called him by a different name, and the dog took such giant leaps to get down the stairs, we were afraid that he would break his legs. He landed right in front of the man, and jumped up against him, licking his face. The dog yelped, whined, and barked like a dog does when he sees a friend he loves. We didn't need any more proof that Kazan had been his dog two years before.

Meta invited the man upstairs and they talked for quite awhile.

"May I have my dog back?" he asked at last. "Can I pay you for what the dog cost you?".

"No, he's all yours" Meta told him.

But I could see that she was upset. She had loved that dog, but she knew that the dog should go back to his old master whom he obviously loved. All too soon the time came when Meta had to part with Kazan. His original owner and Meta were both sad. He was happy to get Kazan back after searching so long for him, but both of them knew they couldn't both have the dog, so he felt empathy for her loss. When they left, Kazan followed his old master willingly, but when they came to the corner of the street Kazan suddenly stopped and looked back at Meta. She was hanging out of her upstairs window watching, and when he looked at her, she called him "Kazan" for the last time. For a moment Kazan stood very still, deciding what he would do, and then he looked up at his owner, barked, and followed him around the corner.

THE LAST WINTER OF MISERY
1944 TO 1945

The winter of 1944 to 1945, was the last and the toughest of World War II. I was living in an apartment in Haarlem that Bram's sister, Cobi, had left vacant when she married Gerard van den Hoof. Cobi moved back into her childhood home in Amersfoort with Gerard. It was bitter cold and we had no heat. We made good use of the wood stove that I had brought home on my bicycle in 1943. To keep warm we put on many layers of clothing. This was cumbersome, and didn't help that much. Our hands, fingers, feet and toes were in the worst shape. Foraging trips that we had to take on our bikes were excruciating, but we had to keep going, even when we were exhausted and thought we couldn't go another inch. Food coupons were worthless, and even tulip bulbs were being sold at high prices. One afternoon, a woman came by, begging for food. She looked very hungry, so I offered her a few tulip bulbs, when we hardly had any left for ourselves. The woman looked at the bulbs and said, "Keep your filthy food for yourself". This left me speechless. I saw people who were walking skeletons, and you wondered how they managed to stay alive. Mothers with babies were selling some of their extra milk for very high prices.

Our daily routines were reduced to subsistence level activities. We were constantly trying to find fuel for the woodstove. At the same time we were trading anything we could for food, which at this point consisted mainly of tulip bulbs, and flour. For a time, a local baker would make bread for us from the flour, but in this last winter he was unable to continue that. Breakfast consisted of tulip bulbs and tea made from tree leaves. More tulip bulbs for lunch, and dinner consisted of some potato flour, and more tulip bulbs. From eating so many tulip bulbs during that last winter of the war, my intestines were permanently damaged so that now, even 55 years later I get periodic vitamin B injections to absorb food better. These foraging activities kept us busy most of the time. There was no radio, no newspapers that we could trust, only Nazi propaganda.

When you passed a restaurant, you would see a fat German officer eating huge meals, which created for us a consuming hatred towards them. But now, when groups of soldiers passed by, it was quite obvious that the kind of soldiers had changed. They were now the very young and the very old ones with gray hair. They were the leftovers because the rest were fighting on several fronts.

The final winter from September 1944 to May, 1945 brought us new hope of being liberated by the approaching Allied armies. The first days in September 1944 we heard that Belgium was being liberated and the southern part of Holland fell in Allied hands. In the remaining months of the war, the Germans were facing now an ever more hostile Dutch population. This resulted in drastic measures whenever possible. Dutch men of military age were drafted or arrested primarily out of fear that they might assist the approaching Allied forces.

Bram described this period of the war in the next few paragraphs:

It was September of 1944; the Allies had landed in Normandy on June 6, 1944, and had pushed the German army back to the east, and to the north to the river Rhine that separated the northern 7 provinces of Holland from the 4 provinces in the south. Although the 4 provinces to the south had been liberated, the remaining 7 northern provinces were still in German hands.

On the 17th of September, 1944, Allied Troops were ready to cross the Rhine at Arnhem to start the liberation of the rest of Holland. A large part of the Dutch population in these 7 northern provinces were elated and were counting on liberation from the hated German yoke by the Allies in just a few short days. They started to celebrate early by consuming the remainder of their precious small reserves of food and delicacies that they had guarded for the past five years. They also started to round up the hated NSB'ers (that sympathized with the Germans) who were all scrambling to escape into Germany. In addition, the Dutch in the north became overtly critical of the Germans, and those young Dutch men that had been in hiding from the Razzia's came out to chide the German soldiers. The 5th of September, 1944 became known as "Dolle Dinsdag" – "Crazy Tuesday". But then, disaster struck.

The Allies had underestimated the strength of the German forces near Arnhem, and had no knowledge of the presence of one of the crack Panzer Divisions that had been pulled back to the northern provinces of Holland for some rest and recuperation, and reinforcement. Also, the Allied crossing of the Rhine was poorly prepared, lacking the necessary equipment, and even being incapable of communication between the British and American Divisions because of a difference in radio frequencies. These Allied forces ran into an overwhelming, well trained army and suffered an embarrassing total defeat with the loss of much equipment, and thousands of lives.

For the Dutch, the consequences were immeasurably worse. Those who had used up their reserves were desperate. Those who had participated in anti-German or anti-NSB activities were rounded up and either sent to German Labor camps or simply shot.

Next, the Dutch Government in exile in London had ordered the Dutch railroads to strike, in order to prevent transportation of essential materials and manpower to the front. This order was strictly obeyed by all railroad personnel, and all rail movement came to a standstill. For the Dutch citizens, this meant no more commuting between cities, like from Haarlem to Amsterdam, and worst of all, no more transport of food from the farms into the cities.

Our only remaining form of transportation were bicycles, but the best of these had already been confiscated by the German Occupational Forces. So what was left were many mostly defective bicycles. Some ran with old tires with many patches that needed frequent repairs. Some bicycles had old garden hoses in place of tires, and still others had no tires at all. The few reasonable good bicycles became enormously valuable, and it was at this time that my bicycle was stolen. Johanna had to borrow her mother's bicycle, which was much older, but stood up remarkably well. Although neither Johanna nor I could go to work any more, the Dutch companies and institutions continued to pay us our salaries so as to keep us alive. Everyone expected the war to end soon. However, before the end of the war, the entire Dutch population was to go through an ordeal of deprivation, starvation, and suffering during the long winter months of the winter of 1944 to 1945. It is hard to imagine now how difficult these times were.

There was very little food to buy. The allocations were very small, and food available on the black market carried astronomical prices. In the big cities, the people suffered the most. Some of these set out on foot with a pushcart or just a rucksack to the farmlands in search of food. Since transport by rail or even by truck had stopped, farmers were willing to sell some of their produce to individuals who would come by on these "hunger trips".

The defeat of the Allies at Arnhem meant that the Dutch population of the Northern Provinces had to cope with another winter under German occupation, and under even worse conditions than ever before.

A 50 pound bag of potatoes sold for as much as 600 to 800 guilders. A guilder at that time was equivalent to an American Dollar. Some additional prices on the back market:

One pound bag of sugar	fl	250
One egg	fl	25
One loaf of bread	fl	55

Only the very rich (often collaborators) could afford to pay such prices regularly. What saved us was that we were able to purchase a couple of 80 pound bags of tulip bulbs at the beginning of the winter when the growers first started to recommend them for food. Tulip bulbs can be very nourishing if properly prepared. We obtained the bulbs by the end of November 1944, and they were edible until the beginning of March of the next year. Then these tulip bulbs began to sprout, and that made them unfit for human consumption.

By this time, March, 1945, the needs of the Dutch Population had at-
tracted the attention of the International Red Cross, which organized sev-
eral distributions of wheat bread with the grudging consent of the German
Occupational Forces. This bread tasted like a gift from heaven and did much
to help us to persevere.

In the last year of the war, food was so scarce that we were eating tulip bulbs as a last resort, although we were happy to get them. Somehow, when the International Red Cross gave out loaves of wheat bread, Meta managed to get some extra loaves from time to time and shared them with us. For months I went once a week to Amsterdam to get the bread from Meta. We shared the five loaves of bread we got with my parents and Tannie. These loaves helped keep us alive. On the "black market" you could get some food for very high prices. In later years, I discovered that a lot of things were missing from our home, like jewelry, my prized doll, clothing, and other things. My Mother had exchanged everything for food. What hurt me was not the fact that she had sold these things, but that she didn't ask me before she did it. I never would have parted with the doll, which was given to me by my maternal Grandmother. I felt that the doll was a part of me. I had made a huge outfit of clothes for that doll, all handmade. I had thought that I would save it for my own children in later years. But I did understand how Mother thought it was the right thing to do. We were all so hungry that all we could think about was how we would obtain food for the next meal to stay alive. Most of the time I was wearing a belt with my shirt and pants. I had two pairs of each and because I was losing weight, I kept cinching up the belt, notch by notch, until I had to create a hole that wasn't originally even there, as my waist had shrunk at a startling rate. Tightening your belt, helped to reduce stomach cramps. I didn't have too worry about being overweight.

During that time, Bram got word that his aunt, one of his Mother's sisters, had passed away, and Bram had promised her that he would be her executor when she was gone. In her will, she left a few possessions to Bram, Bram's sister Cobi, and his cousin, John. It was Bram's task to divide everything in three parts. Bram couldn't go to Amersfoort, where his aunt had lived, because he was still in hiding from the Razzia's. I offered to go in his place.

Bram's friend "Louis DeBont" offered to come with me because he wanted to see one of his relatives who lived in that area. Bram gave me instructions on how to try to divide the goods as fairly as I saw fit. It made me nervous because I was an outsider, after all. But it was the only way Bram could do it, and he trusted me to be fair.

DeBont and I started at daybreak the next morning. The weather was fine, which allowed us to pump our bikes at a steady pace. We talked about the war and enjoyed each others company.

Four hours later, I felt miserable. My stomach was acting up again and pretty soon I felt so sick that I told DeBont I had to take a break, so I could throw up at the side of the road. I was embarrassed, but when you feel sick, you can't help it. DeBont felt sorry for me, but there wasn't much he could do to help. By the time we reached Hilversum, the town where my uncle Bert lived, I decided to stop and ask for help. DeBont thought that was a wise choice, and he wished me luck and went on his way. I hated to stop at my uncle's place because I didn't want to invade his privacy at this time of mourning. He had been through such agony and turmoil, what with losing his three sons, and now his second wife, who had just died of a brain tumor. It wasn't a favorable time to bother him but I was desperate and I had to find a doctor. My paternal Grandmother was still living with my uncle, and I knew she would be there for him. I had always loved her, but I knew she was suffering the loss of her daughter, my aunt Lies.

When I reached my uncle Bert's house, I didn't know what to say, at first. But he looked at me, and with a surprised expression on his face he asked me what I was doing at this hell house? I told him "I'm so sorry, but I'm so sick, would it be possible for me to see your family doctor?".

My uncle looked at me, turned around and yelled, "My God, I can't take any more misery, do you hear me?" He held his head in both of his hands, pacing back and forth in the hallway, with tears streaming down his face. After a while he saw me still standing in the doorway, and said

"I can't help you, I'm sorry, but the doctor's house is down the street on the left, you will see the sign".

Just then my Grandmother came out of her room. I told her how awful I felt physically and spiritually, but she hardly listened, staring at me with a far away expression on her face.

"Did you know that my daughter is gone?" she asked.

I answered that I knew and felt terrible about it, but that I knew that God would help her if she had enough faith. She said, "God Bless you child", and then turned and went back to her room. I stood there all alone in that big hall thinking to myself that hell is a place that can also be found here on earth.

The only thing I could do was to go down the street to find the doctor's house. The doctor's wife answered the door and let me in because she could see that I was on the verge of fainting. She told me that the doctor wasn't home, but she told me to sit down in a chair and tell her how I felt. I told her, but she couldn't tell me exactly what the problem was, although she thought I was suffering from food poisoning.

"Can you remember what you ate since yesterday?", she asked.

When I told her that I had eaten some tulip bulbs, she said,

"I'll bet you ate a hyacinth bulb, by mistake, because they look like tulip bulbs, but are poisonous."

I remembered vaguely that there was a suspicious looking bulb between the tulip bulbs that I had eaten. So I told her about that, and she gave me some charcoal tablets, telling me that sometimes they helped with this condition. I couldn't keep them down, and gave up trying to swallow them. We talked for a little while and I told her about my uncle, who had sent me to this doctor. She agreed that my uncle's story was unbelievably horrible.

The Germans had hurt her family too, and she was wondering if we would ever get rid of them. Talking to her helped me and I started to feel a little better, although I was far from feeling normal again. I decided to bicycle to Amersfoort. It was really the best thing I could do under the circumstances. I thanked the kind doctor's wife and went on my way. I forced my legs to move on and on, hardly seeing where I was going because my eyes weren't focusing well, and my head felt as if an elephant had stepped on it. I was pretty near the end of my endurance.

I did reach Cobi's house. It turned out that she wasn't home, but her husband's brother lived upstairs, and he let me in. He knew me, so it was all right. When he saw how sick I looked, he put me on a sofa in Cobi's family room, and covered me with a blanket, telling me to get some sleep. I slept till the afternoon of the next day. When I woke up, Willy was standing next to me, and asked what on earth had happened to me. When she had come home and found me she said I looked as if I were dying, but she had decided to let me sleep. Luckily, I was feeling much better, and I even asked for some food, if possible. After two days, I felt good enough to go with Cobi to her aunt's home to decide what to do with all the inherited goods. It took several days to sort things out and put them in piles. Cobi's cousin came over and we tried to work out a fair deal for everybody. There wasn't very much of any worth though, only two rugs, and only one of those was in good shape. Then they started to argue about the rugs, each saying that they had been promised the good rug by the Aunt. Cobi insisted that she had to have the rug because she lived near the Aunt. Watching both of them, I wished for the wisdom of Solomon. Cobi ended the quarrel by packing one of the piles of goods into some boxes and telling her cousin to take those boxes, and by all means, take the older rug with him. "That's all you will get", she told her cousin when he left. I was disgusted with both of them, and decided I didn't want to have anything to do with this selfish quarrel. It reminded me of a famous Dutch poem:

> "When a rich uncle is dying then everyone comes who
> had to inherit.
> With a handkerchief in front of their faces.
> Everybody peeks where the safe is standing.
> And then there are fights and arguments.
> Then we all enjoy the show."

Cobi gathered up her things and put them in a corner to be picked up the next day. I was left with a smaller pile, but I didn't care, because I knew Bram wouldn't mind. Bram and I weren't greedy and what he inherited wasn't worth any fight. Cobi and her cousin never talked to each other again. What struck me as ironic was the fact that neither of them considered Bram and what he was getting, nor would they in the future. Greed is such an ugly side of human nature. People don't seem to understand that material goods will never bring them happiness, nor will they really have peace of mind. Altogether, it took a week before I felt well enough to return home. Louis DeBont, who also rented along with Bram, was already back when I saw him again. He was relieved when he saw me. I could have died from the poisonous hyacinth bulb I had ingested. It turned out that I was lucky this time.

Finding fuel for the small stove became more and more difficult. Most of the time I used sticks and small branches whenever I could find them. Everybody was chopping down trees and shrubs, which were disappearing from the streets and parks at an alarming rate. One time I was running low on wood and had to get some. Even though nobody was allowed to go back to our town of Bloemendaal, my mind kept going back to a horse chestnut tree, that had been standing in front of our house. I knew it could supply us with enough wood to last a long time, however it was very dangerous to go to Bloemendaal. Nobody but the Germans were allowed there. Somebody told me that there weren't too many soldiers patrolling the streets there, so if you were careful, they could be avoided.

Bram couldn't help me because he had to stay in hiding. By day, the Germans were looking for young men everywhere, and if anyone got caught cutting wood, could be punished by jail, or worse, by concentration camps. You had a better chance at night, hiding in the dark, especially when there was no moon, and it was possible to hide more easily. On one dark evening when there was no moon I took my bike and a small hand saw and went to Bloemendaal. Nobody was out in the streets, not even a patrol. When I reached our house, in the Dr. Bakkerlaan, I stopped in front of it, and grabbed in the dark for the chestnut tree. It was still there and as I touched it I got a sickening feeling, because it was larger than I had remembered. But I had come this far and just had to try to get at least some branches from it. The branches the size I wanted were too high for me to reach, so I decided to cut down the whole tree. I started to saw, which seemed like it would take forever. I thought if I cut the tree a certain way, it would fall towards me, so I watched closely, and when it started trembling, I planned to run to the side, so I wouldn't get hit by the falling tree. But I had miscalculated, and as the tree went crashing down, it fell in the opposite direction, into the street. This was one of the scariest moments of my life because if a German patrol came by and saw the tree, they would be looking for me. Frantically, I started to saw off branches. Luckily, most of the trunk had fallen on the sidewalk.

Just as I was progressing with removing the top branches that were in the street, I heard a truck approaching. I had to choose between hiding and trying to prevent the truck from hitting part of the tree. The dimmed lights of the truck came to a halt because I was standing in the middle of the street, waving. A soldier came over to me and asked what in the world I was doing. I explained to him that I was trying to get some fire wood, so I could fix something to eat, because I was very hungry. I also tried to explain, in my very best German, that I had misjudged the direction in which the tree would fall. I was so afraid that he would kill me. But, to my surprise, he suddenly laughed and told me that he should arrest me, but instead he ordered me to get rid of the top of the tree within an hour, because that's when he would be back. Sometimes I had the feeling that a lot of the Germans weren't too happy about the war and were really good people. They were caught up in the huge net of terror that Hitler had created.

I still don't know how I did it, but I managed to clear the street, sawing like mad in the darkness. Within an hour, I was racing back to my apartment, thanking God for sparing me. I don't know if the German patrol came back, but I hope that the soldier who talked to me survived the war. I did sneak back to Bloemendaal the next morning to get some of the wood I had left. But when I approached our house, there wasn't even one stick of the tree left. Everything was gone, the whole tree. Other people had helped themselves and all my hard work had been for nothing.

A few days after I lost my tree, a horse drawn wagon rumbled down our street, loaded with tiny coal pellets which spilled onto the street every time the wagon jumped a little. I saw small piles of coal here and there, which I quickly gathered up for fuel to use in the stove. I was bustling around with my dustpan and broom, gathering up some coal, which had some horse manure mixed in with it, but this didn't seem to matter in those days, as we had to compromise in so many ways. For a short while it gave me fuel to cook my tulip bulbs, which was our daily fare now. But soon I had to get something else to use in our stove, so I decided to try the dunes, which weren't very far away. Of course, they were forbidden and it was dangerous to go there. Ever so many people went there though, and tried to get dried branches from the shrubs and trees. I did find a nice heap of gnarled dried roots. I tied them with a string and started to walk back to the road where I had left my bike hidden in some bushes. So far I had been lucky, but when I was half way back to the road, I heard several shots behind me in the distance. I felt something whistle past my head and shoulders. I looked behind me, and saw soldiers aiming their guns at me. I managed to run down the slope, grab my bike, and get out. This could have cost me my life. In wartime you never knew what might happen. You just learned to take one day at a time, hoping for the best, which was for the war to end. I never went back to that spot in the dunes again. I was convinced though, that the soldiers didn't really want to kill me, they just wanted to frighten me, which they surely did! And it did give me a better understanding of how an animal that is being hunted must feel trying to escape its killers.

One evening there was a knock on my door, and when I opened it, a young man quickly stepped inside and whispered,

"Close the door fast. I hope nobody followed me". I recognized him as a close friend of my sister Meta. Jan was his name, and I asked him to sit down. He was looking terribly upset, shaking all over from fright and chill from the rain that was pouring down outside. Looking at me, he tried to explain what had happened. I knew he was a member of the underground forces, so I knew that it had to do with the war.

"I just killed several German soldiers", Jan said. "I hope God will forgive me. It was awful".

The underground had found out that a patrol of German soldiers were on their way to perform an execution, and they would be taking this particular road. Jan and the others were told to kill them, if possible, because this was the only way to save the prisoners. The underground had ordered him to hide in a ditch along side a country road with several other fighters. The soldiers did travel that country road and when they passed the hidden fighters, they opened fire and killed all the Germans. I asked Jan how many had been killed, but he didn't know. He just looked at me and said, "I will never be the same again". I knew he was a religious person and I could only guess how badly he must be feeling. I tried to console him, and gave him something to drink and eat. After awhile he left. He didn't want to stay for protection because he was afraid somebody might have seen him come in, and he didn't want to cause any trouble for me. I saw him some time later, and he told me that he had learned to live with what he had done because he had helped save the lives of young Dutch men, and he had to choose between his own people and the enemy. In later years, when the war was over, everybody realized what an awful waste of resources and time, and how much human suffering had occurred, and for what?

My parents' healths were failing, and this was heart breaking. They were suffering from hunger edema, which caused badly swollen legs. The people in whose house they were placed weren't very nice. They never shared any food with my parents, even though it was a medical doctor's home. They had much more food than anybody else because they had friends who owned a farm. It was understandable though, because everyone was on their own to survive. My Father did help me a few times when I was gathering wood, but he could hardly walk anymore. The war news we heard was scarce and obviously censured in the Germans' favor. It didn't give us much hope. According to them, they were winning the war, but this wasn't what we heard from the underground. The word was that the war had taken a turn, and the Germans had lost on several fronts. We heard that the Allies were winning more and more. The underground news kept us going and gave us new hope. But the bad news that reached us was about the murders in the concentration camps. It was so gruesome that we didn't want to believe it, at first. Once in Haarlem, I had gotten a glimpse of a train filled with people en route to the so called work camps, which were really extermination camps. All the people in that train were holding out their hands, begging for water or food. The trains would pass by slowly, and all one could do was watch and feel helpless, for there was nothing we could do to help them. More and more friends and other people we knew of were being killed, executed like my cousin. You never knew if you would be alive the next day, so you lived day by day with some hope for a better future.

The only people who had any food now were the farmers and the wealthy, who could buy food on the black market. One of the most difficult things for us to deal with was keeping our faith. Where was

God to help all of us? Why did He allow this war to happen? Why were so many innocent people slaughtered? It wasn't until years later that I came to the conclusion that people do it to themselves, and that God helps those who help themselves.

LIBERATION AND MARRIAGE

The Allies lost the famous battle of Arnhem in September of 1944, just when we thought our ordeal would be over. We felt that we had been left to the wolves. If the war had lasted another year, we would have all been dead. Somehow, winter passed, and spring brought a ray of hope. And then it happened! The war was really over.

At first we didn't dare believe it, after the drama we had been through on Crazy Tuesday. We heard many rumors from neighbors with secret radios and these rumors raised our expectations. My landlady told me one day that Holland had been liberated by the Canadians. By now, it was the 21st of May, 1945, and I went to Haarlem to see with my own two eyes, the large Canadian trucks roll by. It was one of the happiest, most wonderful moments in all our lives. Everybody was crying and waving at the Canadians. Candies and chocolates were handed out, to the children especially. There was dancing and music on all the streets.

Within a few days, everybody received loaves of bread and large cookies, which were sent to us from Sweden. We had to be very careful with those cookies when we ate them because they swelled to twice their size in our stomachs. Most of the people could only eat small amounts of food because their stomachs had shrunk so much. A lot of people tried to eat too much too fast and became very ill. A few of them even died from burst stomachs. Soon the

Germans left. Long columns of soldiers marched out of town. They looked quite different from the proud ones who entered our country in 1940, five long years ago, five years of pure hell. I could not feel sorry for them after all they had done to us. It was beyond comprehension how they could have murdered, tortured, maimed, and starved such an enormous number of innocent people. How was it possible that they had followed the crazy rulings of the totally insane German, named Hitler?

After the liberation, life became better, although it was far from normal. Food was still rationed and scarce, but now you could get something for your coupons. Our country had been plundered, and it would be quite a while before we would have plenty of food again. I didn't go back to my job, as school was closed for summer vacation. Bram and I decided to get married, so I turned in my resignation. The principal of the school pleaded with me, not to give up my position, but Bram didn't want me to teach when it meant so much hard work for a low salary. Several of our friends were getting married too, and all of us were a bit older than most couples who had been married before the war. Five years had been wasted, after all, and all of us had gone through times of starvation, terror, and persecution. This had proved to be a good test of our commitment to each other. When you got along under those circumstances, you could be pretty well assured that your marriage would last, and all of them did.

Bram went back to his job in Delft. We rented rooms from a woman who had a large house in Haarlem. We didn't have much furniture, or anything else, for that matter, so moving in wasn't any problem. On September 28, 1945, Bram and I were married in Bloemendaal. For transportation, we rented a carriage. We wanted to get married in bridal outfits, but they were hard to get. Materials weren't available, so all we could do was to rent the outfits. I wasn't happy about it, but I guess it wasn't so important, after all. The only bridal dress I could get was one that was falling apart from ten years' of use on different occasions. I couldn't get the dress until the day before we were to be married, so I spent the night before mending the dress. Unfortunately, my sister, Meta couldn't attend the wedding because she developed a sudden case of appendicitis, and was operated on to have it taken out. The wedding was a very simple, but happy one, because we couldn't afford much, and getting food for our guests was nearly impossible. The minister who conducted the service was the father of one of my girlfriends. It was a nice happy wedding and we were grateful for the better times we knew were ahead. Bram and I spent a few days on our honeymoon in a hotel near Hilversum, which had beautiful natural surroundings. We had money problems though because the government was taking back all of the paper currency, and for a short while, everybody had to do business in coins only. We had saved quite a pile of coins, but that wouldn't get us very far money-wise. This made it impossible for us to go to a fancy restaurant or anywhere else, for that matter. So we walked a lot, rented bicycles, and spent many afternoons on the dunes, which at this time of the year, were covered with purple heather. I remember one evening in our small hotel when there was a farmer's wedding party. It made us feel good, watching the party from a distance. The bridegroom was deformed from being hunchbacked, so he walked awkwardly, but he had the handsomest happy face one could wish for, and his bride was pretty and happy. This was real love which didn't look at the beauty on the outside, but saw the inside of a worthwhile person.

One day we paid my parental Grandmother a visit. She was living in a nursing home nearby. She had not met Bram before, but she was delighted when she saw and talked to him. Grandmother was a proud Friesian, coming from one of the most northern provinces of Holland. Bram's father also came from there, which made grandma feel close to him, right away. I was happy that they got along so well, especially since, not long after that, grandmother passed away. She had been a beautiful woman, and we were sorry that she had to go through the rough times of the war.

When we came back from our short honeymoon, we moved

into our rented rooms,where we stayed for about six months. The landlady was very peculiar, and she made our lives more difficult than it needed to be. We shared a kitchen, which wasn't easy, being that it was small and there was no place for me to put my kitchen wares. The landlady's time for cooking took priority, so I was forever asking her what her schedule was, so I would know when I would be allowed to use the kitchen. Bram wasn't home during the day. He had to travel each day between Haarlem and Delft. He would come home early in the evening and want to eat a prepared meal. Often, when I wanted to prepare Bram's evening meal, the landlady decided she wanted to use the kitchen, so it took a lot of patience and cooperation for me not to get mad at her.

Her small, but fierce fox terrier practically ruled the household, and each time I went to the kitchen, the dog tried to bite me. His food dish was placed right in front of the stove. When I asked permission to move the dish to another spot, the landlady told me that he was used to having it there, and so I would have to make the best of the situation. Then I noticed that someone had been in our room when we were out because things weren't where I had left them. To prove my suspicions, I left a string in front of the door to our room when I left. If you didn't know the string was there, it wouldn't have been noticed. I did this several times, and on each occasion, when I returned I noticed that the string had been broken, and so I knew that somebody had been in our space. I asked the landlady for a key, telling her that I had heard that there had been several burglaries in the neighborhood of late. At first she didn't want to give me the keys, but Bram told her that we wouldn't pay the rent unless we were given the keys, and of course, then she gave them to us immediately. She obviously didn't trust us, and this was sad because we weren't the type of people to go through others' things, but I was upset about the idea of someone going through our private things.

Our unhappiness about dealing with this woman escalated. Several times she left the house for the weekend, and she would lock the cellar door. In those days we used the cellar like a refrigerator, and when she was gone, and I wanted to get to some food that I had in the cellar, it would be locked. Not only that, but by the time she got home, whatever I had down there, would be spoiled, and I would have to throw it out. When I asked her not to lock the cellar door, she would say she was sorry, but the next time she was gone, she would lock the cellar again, so I gave up the use of the cellar. Food coupons were valuable. Sugar was especially hard to get. A few times I left my sugar in the kitchen, and each time, when I returned, it would be gone. I asked the landlady if she knew what happened to the sugar, and she retorted that the maid must have taken it. Another time we picked up some pears that had fallen to the ground to keep them from rotting or from being attacked by wasps. We put them in a basket in the kitchen, thinking we were doing her a favor, but when she returned, she accused us of stealing her pears. She told us that it was none of our business picking up the pears. We were getting desperate, knowing that we couldn't take much more of this woman's attitude, impossible lady that she was! We had even taken care of her once, when she had the flu, and she never thanked us. We tried to find a house or an apartment in Delft, but nothing was available. We kept looking, knowing that sooner or later, luck would be with us. We took pride in the fact that we didn't ever lose our tempers, quarrel, or try to get back at this woman.

Another winter came and it seemed as if we were always cold. I wanted more than anything else, to have a fur coat to keep me warm. Just before the war, I had been able to buy an old rabbit coat, but it was falling apart at the seams. I took it to the furrier for repair, but by the time I was supposed to pick it up, the war had broken out. It wasn't until much later that I went back to the store to retrieve the coat, but the former owners weren't there anymore. They were Jewish and nobody knew what happened to them. The coat had been repaired, but there was no bill with it, and the person who was at the store told me that all the customers could take their coats without paying for them. I felt this was rather tragic, so to help me feel better, I gave some money to the underground movement, instead. The coat didn't last very long because I sold it to get extra food. But I always remembered how warm it had been, and made up my mind that I would have another fur coat somehow sometime.

Bram, being a chemist, told me that he could cure and prepare fur skins by using a chemical bath. It would be a tremendous amount of work, but it could be done. This gave me bright idea because I knew a poultry man who also sold rabbits for food.

"Oh", he said, "most of the time I sell the rabbit fur pelts to the furrier. But I don't get much for them because the rabbits fur isn't unique. It isn't my best seller."

I asked him if I could buy thirty two skins from him, and he said that he would have them within two weeks. Sure enough, two weeks later, I came home with the skins, some of which still had the rabbit ears attached. I asked Mother's permission to use her bathtub, and she agreed, although she wasn't thrilled about having rabbit skins floating around in her bathtub. Nevertheless, we were all curious how this would turn out, so the skins got a chemical bath and when they came out and were dried, I dyed them gray. They came out very well. Then we stretched the skins over boards to dry, and when that was finished, we removed the inner skins, which was a terribly strenuous job.

After all this work, we had a pile of soft gray skins. Then I drew a pattern for a winter coat, cut skins with a razor blade in straight pieces, and sewed them together by hand, having learned the process from a furrier. At last, I had a fur coat. It was perfect, and I was proud of it. I also made matching accessories, such as a pocketbook, mittens, and hat from the left over pieces. For the first time I felt nice and warm when the weather was freezing. Knowing that my efforts had paid off, that I had made this coat myself from start to finish, made me feel even better. Since I had been so successful with the rabbit skins, I decided to buy a goat skin from the same man. A local person learned of my rabbit fur coat and taught me more about leatherworking. This knowledge came in very handy to make and sell things after the war. Mother wasn't happy because she didn't want to have her bathtub used again for curing, and made me promise that this would be the last skin to come to her house. She said: "If I let you, you will bring a cow or a giraffe skin, and that would be just too much." The goat skin came out just fine. I made belts, pocketbooks, and mitten cuffs, which I sold.

I had quite an ordeal when Bram and I had only been at our landlady's a month. I went to the dentist for a regular checkup and he told me that I had a serious problem. It turned out that I had an abscess on my upper jaw above the roots of my front teeth. He said he would have to either pull my front teeth, or cut my jaw to be able to reach the abscess. It was important that I had the operation as soon as possible, he said, otherwise my eyes could be affected. I chose to have my jaw cut, even though it would be quite an ordeal, but at least, it would save my teeth.

An appointment was made and a few days later I went to a hospital in Haarlem. Just before the operation the dentist asked me if I would allow three medical students to observe the operation, so they could learn how to deal with this problem that was caused by malnutrition. (I was one of many that this had happened to from the war.) I gave permission for them to watch. There was one problem though, a shortage of medical supplies, and one of them was anesthesia. Even though that meant I had to endure a lot of pain, I was determined that I wasn't going to lose my teeth, no matter what!

My gums were cut, as well as my jaw, and the abscess was taken out. I fainted twice during the operation, and when it was over, I was very shaky, and in a lot of pain. My mouth was swollen, I had stitches in my mouth, stitches in my gums, and there was blood on my dress. I didn't want to go back on the bus, in this state, so I walked all the way home, which took about an hour. Nobody had gone with me because Bram had to go to work, and I didn't want to ask anyone else. I thought I could handle it by myself. My parents, were very upset when they found out what happened to me. My dentist took an x-ray of my jaw a year later, and it showed no hole where the abscess had been. New bone growth filled the cavity.

DELFT 1946

When Bram and I had been with the landlady about six months a miracle happened. One of Bram's colleagues, who was living in Delft, warned us that he was changing jobs and his rented apartment-house would be coming on the market. We applied for the house, and to our amazement, we got it. At first we couldn't believe our luck. At last we would be free to have our own house. Moving our possessions was easy, not only because we didn't have much, but because the thought of having our own privacy was something we looked forward to eagerly. We cleaned our rooms thoroughly and much to our surprise, the landlady told us that she thought we were the nicest renters she had ever had. Unfortunately, we couldn't say the same about her, after all the mental abuse she had dealt us, but we felt good about our behavior, which had been a real test of how to make the best of an unpleasant situation.

Our new house in Delft overlooked a street, beyond which was a wide canal. In the back was a tiny garden enclosed by a wooden wall. A door in this wall opened to reveal an open space of beautiful green meadows. It was a delight to walk in these peaceful surroundings. Watching all the different boats passing by in front of our house was a real treat too. People on the boats would wave to us as we watched them sailing by our front room. We were so happy to have this house, as there was always something to observe, like a movie, that was constantly changing scenes. Although we didn't have any worthwhile furniture, to speak of, we did buy an old table and chairs, and a chest with drawers, but that was all. For curtains, we used rugs. What really made us happy was the fact that there was progress everywhere. We were still using coupons, as was the case, especially on the coastal towns, but all in all, our first year in Delft was a happy one.

We were enjoying our freedom, and it was nice to be able to decorate our place the way we wanted with curtains, and other personal items. The tiny garden in back was a nice challenge to landscape. The previous owners had used it as a playground for their children, and it was a mess to clean up. We had to be careful with our money though, so there were a lot of things we couldn't get, either because they just weren't available, or the cost was exorbitant. We made do with what was possible. I saved money by sewing and knitting all our sweaters for winter. I bought a spinning wheel and learned how to make my own yarn from the wool of a sheep. Some farmers in the country sold their wool to anybody who wanted it, and it gave us a lot of satisfaction, making our own things. Although we had little money, and were struggling to make a go of it, these were happy times for Bram and me. The war was over, we relied on each other, and the future looked positive once again.

After a year, we settled down to a daily routine and were happy with our lives. But then a visitor from Denmark, a Mr. Zeeman, came to see us. He was a friend of Bram's family and Bram had known him for quite awhile and liked him. When Bram graduated from the university, he had stayed with Mr. Zeeman for awhile in Denmark. When our guest asked Bram if he would like to pay him a visit in Denmark, Bram was happy to accept the invitation. We both thought it would be nice to spend a vacation in another country, for a change. A few weeks later we took the train to Denmark. It turned out to be a long trip because the railroad went through Holland, then Germany, and finally to Denmark.

It was now 1946, and a year since the war had ended. Holland had recuperated somewhat, but what we saw in Germany was different. The devastation of whole cities was visible. There were ruins everywhere and the people we saw were dressed poorly, and looked depressed. As we passed through we seldom saw a smile on a face. And for the first time, it dawned on us that our enemies had also suffered. We started to feel sorry for the many innocent people who had been caught up in this mess of a war.

We were very tired when we arrived in Denmark, not only because it took so long to get there, but also because there were some unpleasant fellow passengers on the train with us. One family was Dutch, and they had a deformed, undisciplined and dirty child with them. The mother was apparently of Danish descent, and they were going to see her parents in Denmark to show them their first born child. This little one was possibly also an indirect victim of the war, expressed through his deformities. The situation was uncomfortable for everyone, and it seemed like such tragedy that this child was so deformed.

Unfortunately, our stay in Denmark was a disappointment for me. Our hostess, especially, resented us, and even told me outright, that her husband was always inviting everybody, and then she had to cope with unwanted guests. This abrupt declaration shocked me, and I asked Bram if we could please go home as soon as possible, but Bram insisted that it would be impolite for us to leave so soon after we had gotten there. The children of the family didn't speak a word of Dutch, and their English was bad. Most of the people around us could only speak Danish, which was foreign to us.

Bram and I did a lot of walking in Denmark, and thoroughly enjoyed the scenery, with its beautiful rolling hills, and vast flat areas between the farms sprinkled here and there. We went to Copenhagen once, a beautiful city with many historical sites. Denmark seemed to have escaped most of the suffering of the war, because Denmark surrendered as soon as the Germans invaded. The Danish people had plenty of food throughout the war, and their cities weren't bombarded. This was really the reason that Mr. Zeeman had invited us. He'd felt guilty when he saw how little we had, and how devastated our country was.

After a few weeks, at last, we could leave. Mr. Zeeman wanted us to stay longer, but we told him we had to get back. We thanked him several times for his hospitality. It was sad to see the unhappiness in that family. One of the reasons that Mr. Zeeman had been unhappy was that Mrs. Zeeman's father was a high ranking military officer, who had always controlled his family, and this trait had passed down to her. She was dictatorial in her management of her family, and it caused the children to rebel against her by cheating their parents in several ways. I felt the unhappy atmosphere throughout our stay, and I promised myself that I would create a better relationship and rapport in our home.

During our stay in Denmark, I tried to be friendly, offering to help with the household, but to no avail, as there was nothing I could do to please our hostess. The only time she was friendlier was the day we left. I couldn't resist telling her as we left,

"You're probably happy we are leaving, at last." I could see that she was embarrassed then, and she said

"It wasn't so bad having you as guests." I guess this was the best she could do to console me, but still remember our visit as an unhappy time. I never went back to Denmark, as it was the only time in our lives that we felt unwelcome. And to top all this off, we flew home, and it was a very shaky flight. I had never flown in an airplane before and the thought of flying terrified me. The plane went right through a storm and I got air sick, this made me even more anxious to be back home. At one point in the flight, I asked the stewardesses when she would hand out the parachutes. The stewardesses started laughing, not realizing that I was dead serious.

Two happy years went by, and the economy of Holland was getting better. More and more goods became available, and once in a while we even got some chicken parts to add to our soup, which was pure luxury for us. For a while we had two cute pets. They were hedgehogs that we had caught in the meadow behind our house. We built a cage for them in the backyard, and they became so tame, that we were able to pick them up without getting hurt by their quills. In the wild, a hedgehog rolls up into a ball when it is alarmed, with its quills sticking out in all directions. This protects the animal from its predators. Hedgehogs are nocturnal and it was fun to watch them at night when they become active. After a while we let them go because it was kinder to let them run wild in the meadow.

At the end of 1947 I became pregnant. This made us happy because we had wanted a family and had lost so many years due to the war, when it was impossible to even think of having children.

Several of the couples our age had married and started families. None of us were very young any more, so everyone was trying to catch up with their lives. In later years, all the babies that were born right after the war were called baby boomers. The doctor I had chosen during my pregnancy was a general practitioner, who hadn't delivered many babies. This turned out to be a bad choice on my part. On the third of August, 1948, I went into labor and a taxi took me to a hospital in Delft. I knew delivering a child would be painful, but I hadn't counted on just how bad it could be. I struggled through the night, and on the morning of the fourth of August, my doctor was sure that the baby would be delivered early in the morning, but it was a slow process. I remember being put in a small room on a high hospital bed. The nurse who stood next to me for a while was a Catholic nun. She told me that I had to be brave and that childbirth was a very common, natural thing. I remember thinking that she would never have to go through this, as she preached to me.

I was left alone for quite awhile after the nun left. I stared at a statue of Mary that was hanging on the wall at the foot of my bed, and as I looked at it, I wondered if my frantic prayers for strength would be heard. Hours of agony went by. What frightened me was that I wasn't making any progress, whatsoever. Then the doctor came, took one look at me, and told the nurse to call a specialist quickly. My baby was going to be a breach delivery. My doctor couldn't handle this type of case. Then, about ten minutes later, I saw a young man enter the room, clad in tennis clothes, holding his racket. He threw the racket in the corner, yelled for a sterile gown, and started to wash his hands in the sink. Then he turned to me, and told me that he was Dr. Fish, and that he was going to put me to sleep. He told me not to worry, and that everything would be all right. The last words I heard him say to the nurse were, "For god's sake, why didn't anybody call me any sooner? Now there's a chance we will lose both the mother and the baby."

INGRID: AUGUST 4, 1948

Luckily, Dr. Fish did a good job with my delivery, otherwise you wouldn't be reading this story. When I woke up, I was lying in another room, with a nurse sitting next to my bed. She looked at me and said "Mrs. Boonstra, you have a beautiful baby daughter." Later, the specialist told me that it had been a miracle that the baby and I had survived. It had nearly been too late, and when he had delivered the baby, it was blue and lifeless, but the hospital's team had been able to revive her. Bram had been waiting for quite a long time, but when he was called to see his daughter, he was thrilled, as everyone told him that this baby was the prettiest newborn they had ever seen. I knew they meant it. Of course, I was happy and grateful. It was one of the happiest moments of my life, but I was mad at the doctor who had been so negligent, nearly costing both of us our lives. I changed to another doctor when I came home. Because of the difficult birth, Ingrid had to wear leg braces for about a year.

My mother came over to see her first grandchild, and was so happy. I will never forget the look on her face when she looked at me and said, "This baby will be happy in her life, I just know it." In later years, I often thought of her, and how she must have known somehow. We named our daughter Ingrid Maria Boonstra. We didn't name her after any family member, on purpose, so there wouldn't be any hurt feelings from anyone, not to mention causing any more rifts in the family. Luckily, there was bottle feeding available at the time, so we knew that Ingrid was getting the amount of milk she needed to grow, since I needed to be treated for a breast infection I had gotten from trying to nurse the baby.

It turned out that all the mothers in our area who had given birth about the same time came up with the same complications. Perhaps it had something to do with the problems we faced during the war. Who knows? We made a crib from plywood, on which I painted fairy tale figures, hoping it would become a piece of heirloom art. All the baby clothes and diapers we made by hand. In this way we managed to save a lot of money. We enjoyed our daughter tremendously. Everybody called her "the Boonstra doll" because she had the perfect face of a doll.

My mother came over every Thursday to spend the day with me. It took her quite awhile to travel from Bloemendaal to Delft, but she loved doing it. She took a small ferry near our house; otherwise she would have had to walk a long way along the canal. An old man worked the ferry and people paid him for the use of it. He was very nice, enjoying chatting with people as he did his work. Mother's visits were very dear to me.

Father came over once in a while but I knew he didn't care much about small children, so I was resigned to that fact. He was a lonely and bitter man. Before the war, he worked as a stevedore in the harbor of Amsterdam. He had to check all the cargo of the ships when they docked. It wasn't an easy job, especially as the winter set in, with his having to be outdoors in the inclement weather. But some extra money was always welcome since Father's pension was small and my Mother's sister and her three daughters also lived with them. In later years, I realized how hard it had been for my Father, and I felt badly that we hadn't appreciated him more. He did have a good sense of humor though, and once in a while he would laugh heartily at funny things that had happened.

Some of the things that happened in our neighborhood in Delft were sad and funny at the same time, befitting a soap opera. The neighbors above us had a student boarder, who had a nasty habit. The landlord served him porridge that he didn't like for breakfast, so he would get rid of it by tossing it out the upstairs window when they weren't looking, and it would land on the roof and sides of our tool house. It was an awful mess to clean up, and when we complained to our neighbor, she said that it was impossible that her precious boarder could have done such a stupid thing. Our complaint did help because the porridge suddenly stopped coming in our direction.

Some of our neighbors were at war with each other. They would yell back and forth, and sometimes they would even throw things like rotten tomatoes at each other. The rest of the neighborhood took sides between these combatants. Some were laughing, and some were angry. Bram and I managed to stay out of these fights, and had a hard time understanding how people could be so nasty to each other, especially after having been through the war together.

Another neighbor had two sons. The older boy was six and a holy terror. The whole neighborhood gave him space so they wouldn't get involved with him. At that time, we had a milkman coming to our door everyday, and sometimes he would have his four year old daughter with him. This boy would attack the little girl, and one day he bit right through the girl's earlobe. The milkman refused to service that family from then on.

One morning we witnessed a real drama. Besides the milkman, we also had a baker and a vegetable man coming to our door. They delivered several times a week. The vegetable man had a horse and wagon, and he loved to feed his horse carrots, and as the animal munched happily on the carrots, his owner would be selling his goods. On that fateful morning, I was standing in the front of the house with Bram, when we saw the vegetable man right across the canal with his horse and wagon. Suddenly we heard several people yell and scream because the horse had pulled the wagon too close to the embankment of the canal. The wagon was very heavy and started to fall backwards into the canal. Before anyone could do

anything about it, the wagon tilted on its side and slid into the water, with a big splash, pulling the horse with it. The horse couldn't
free itself and frantically tried to keep its head above the water.
Several times it managed to surface, screeching in a horrible death
scream, which brought tears to the eyes of those who were watching. It would have been impossible for anyone to free the horse's
harness under the water, and after what seemed like more than just
a few minutes, the horse drowned. The vegetable man was beside
himself, sobbing, as he ran back and forth watching the circles in
the canal where his horse and wagon had disappeared. He must
have felt terribly guilty, because he was to blame, after all. We had
nightmares about this incident long afterwards.

Bram and I decided that we wanted more children so we tried
again a year after Ingrid was born. I did manage to get pregnant
a second time, and was looking forward to our second child, but
then, still early in the pregnancy, we lost the baby. I had a miscarriage. Bleeding started early in the pregnancy, and by the time I got
to the hospital, I had lost the baby. Our doctor said he thought it
may have been caused by a severe head cold that I had during this
time.

When Ingrid was about two and a half years old she gave us
quite a scare. I had put her out in the yard, where I thought she
would be safe because it was completely enclosed by the high
wooden fence. But there was the door in the back, which led to
the meadow beyond. There was a path that ran along behind all
the houses, where the children often played. I had taken Ingrid for
walks there often to watch the other children, so she knew what
was beyond the door would be fun. I was always careful that the
door was locked, so she wouldn't get lost or be in danger from
wandering off. At the end of the path was a branch of the canal
coming from the main one in front of the house. It was dangerous for children to walk near the canals and too often children in
Holland were drowned in the many Dutch waterways.

On this particular afternoon, I went in the house for a while because I was sure that Ingrid would be safe playing outside. But when I looked outside, I didn't see Ingrid and the yard door was wide open. I ran outside and down the path, calling Ingrid's name over and over again. But there was no answer and I didn't see Ingrid anywhere. I ran along the branch canal to the front of our house, where our milkman was busy serving his customers. "Have you seen Ingrid?" I yelled. He shook his head and said that he would help look for her too. By this time I was petrified, and ran back the same way I had come, hoping I had missed Ingrid somewhere. When I turned the corner, I saw Ingrid, in the distance, running towards me. Since she had heard me calling her, she had started back and was looking for me. Words can't describe what went through my head. I was so relieved and happy to have Ingrid back that I was in a state of shock.

I picked up Ingrid and carried her home, put her down on the dining room rug, and then I fainted. When I came to, Ingrid was sitting next to me, calling "Mama, Mama", as she sensed that something was wrong with me. Luckily, I was only unconscious for a few moments, but then I was all right. I think I had fainted partially because I had suffered a miscarriage a short time before, and was still weak from that trauma. Bram and I were sad about the miscarriage, but the doctor told us that it was a blessing in disguise because something was wrong with the fetus. So we resigned ourselves to losing this child, and trying for another healthy baby. Bram and I noted that Ingrid was a happy and cheerful child, and we took her on hikes to many beautiful places where nature abounded. Delft didn't have much to offer in this respect, just the canals and some meadows. We missed the scenic places that Bloemendaal and Haarlem had to offer, but even so, we were happy with what we had. Occasionally, we would visit my parents, especially at Christmas time, and we would visit old friends there too.

When Ingrid was almost three years old, I became pregnant again. Soon after that we had another scare. A close friend and her son paid us a visit. Her son was one year older than Ingrid, and we had a wonderful time together. We had been close friends throughout the war, which had created a lifetime bond between us. A few days after she had left, I got a letter from her, telling me that her son had contracted German measles. She was concerned for me, and hoped that I wouldn't get that dreaded illness. We were very conscious of the fact that contracting German measles early in a pregnancy could cause much harm to the unborn child. The youngest child of Queen Juliana was born partially blind because of this.

I went straight to the doctor, to ask if he could help me ensure the safety of the unborn child. He said he would give me a shot, but he wasn't sure it would help. I had to just wait and see if the baby would be all right. But there was something that gave us hope. I vaguely remember that I was sick for a short while when I was ten years old. I remembered having tiny red spots on my body, but it couldn't have been the regular measles, because I had that when I was thirteen years old. My Mother couldn't remember if I had the German measles or not when we lived in Boeloe Blanc Ara. At that time there weren't doctors readily available, so if and when the doctor came, the illness had come and gone. So all I could do was to hope for the best, and luckily, I didn't get sick, for which we were very grateful.

In 1950, our lives changed drastically. It's interesting that one never knows what lies ahead. Bram's job wasn't as promising for the future as we thought it would be.

When Indonesia became independent in 1949, and was no longer under Dutch rule, the Rubber Foundation was funded by Indonesia, which made Bram's job, as a researcher of the rubber products, insecure because everybody seemed to know that sooner or later the company would fold. And if that happened, everybody would be looking for new jobs, and this close to the end of the war, jobs were hard to come by, especially research work. The country was still in a stage of recovery, and would be, for quite some time, due to the widespread devastation of the war. The distribution of major foods, even with coupons, lasted until 1948, three years after the war was over. The good news was that we could see progress as the country slowly inched back to normal, even though it seemed that reconstruction happened at a snail's pace for all that needed to be done.

In 1950, Bram was asked to go with the directors of the Rubber Foundation to the United States to attend and present a lecture at the International Rubber convention in Cleveland, Ohio. At that time, Ohio was the rubber capital of the world. The convention was combined with a series of meetings with French and English delegations of the I.S.O., the International Standards Organization, also with visits to large rubber and tire manufacturers, like Goodyear, Firestone, Goodrich, and DuPont. Bram's lecture and discussions made a good impression, and he was approached by several of the businesses, asking him if he would be willing to move to the United States, and go to work for an American company. He was told about the enormous size and potential of the U.S., where prosperity seemed to reign.

PART 3: NEW LIFE IN AMERICA

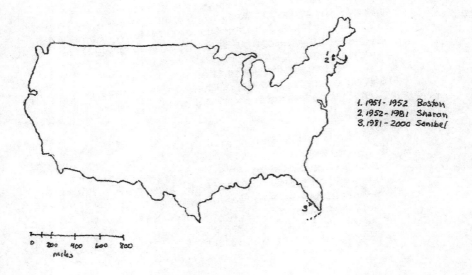

1. 1951 - 1952   Boston
2. 1952 - 1981   Sharon
3. 1981 - 2000   Senibel

A NEW LIFE IN AMERICA

After the war, Bram had tried, without success, to find another job in the Netherlands. He even applied to South Africa, Australia, and New Zealand, but there didn't seem to be any requirements for a professional scientist. Bram hadn't applied to any of the companies in the United States for various reasons, such as long waiting lists for immigration, and the concept that the U.S. was noted to be a very materialistic country. But after Bram's visit to the U.S., he knew differently. The Directors of the Rubber Foundation had, on previous visits to America, made contact with the Cabot Corporation, a leading company in the manufacturing of carbon black. The main application for this material was in tires, using about one part black to two parts of rubber. It improved the resistance of wear on tires considerably. Cabot Corporation and the Rubber Foundation made an agreement to develop special rubbers and carbon black. Bram was the contact man. So when he went to the U.S., one of his first visits was to the offices and laboratory of Godfrey L. Cabot (later Cabot Corp.) in Boston. He gave a presentation about the testing of tire rubber in the laboratory that was favorably received.

Back in Holland, Bram received several offers from American companies to come and work for them in the U.S., and one of these was from Cabot. After some difficulty weighing the pro's and con's of the situation, he decided that we should go to the U.S., where he would go to work for the Cabot Corporation. Bram felt that Boston was most like the European cities that we were used to, and would require the least adjustment for us. Even so, it was a big decision for us. In a way, it was heartbreaking, because it meant leaving family and friends, to start all over again, in a new country with new surroundings, with a different language and new customs.

I never really liked Holland, with its cold and wet climate, and the often narrow minded attitudes of its people. People who had lived in the Dutch East Indies were much more broad minded and companionable. Of course, there were exceptions to this, and we did have wonderful Dutch friends. Shortly after Bram accepted working for Cabot, he was sent to England for a few months, where Cabot had a factory, and besides, we had to wait for our visas to enter the United States.

To receive our visas, we had to submit to several tests, one of which was a blood test. When my blood was poured into a tube, Bram discovered just in time, that the blood was poured into the wrong tube, which was marked for a young Hungarian man. Fortunately, it was corrected immediately. We laughed about it, because it would have been tough for the Hungarian man to explain why his blood showed that he was pregnant.

It was quite a shock for my parents when we told them we were going to live in America. I could see that my Mother took it especially hard, but she told me that she and my Father had done the same thing to her parents when they married and moved to the Dutch East Indies. She did understand that this was Bram's big chance for advancement in his field, his chance to be able to make a better future for his family. I was grateful that my parents took it this way, but the pain of separation was there and always would be. The look on Mothers face will haunt me for the rest of my life.

When all this happened we received a letter from the U.S. A lady named Ruth Hamburg had befriended Bram, so when he came back from America, she came also, to bring the ashes of her deceased husband back to his native Denmark. Bram had tried to console her a little, which she appreciated. After going to Denmark, she stopped to pay us a visit in Delft. Ruth seemed to like us, and when she heard that we were planning to move to her country, she invited us to stay with her for a short while when we arrived in New York. Her home was on Long Island, not far away from our port of entry. We wrote and told her that we would be happy to accept her invitation.

When Bram came back from England, we had a lot to do. Since we were only allowed to take part of our furniture and personal belongs with us, so we hired a professional mover that had been recommended to us. Everything was placed in huge crates for passage to America. We sold the rest. People were coming and going, seeing if there was anything they wanted to buy. And as soon as we told the landlord that we were moving, the owner instantly had a new renter, which was somewhat inconvenient because they would come at the oddest hours to measure windows and rooms. It was like living in a mad house, and to top all that off, I wasn't feeling very well from morning sickness, so I had to keep faith in God that I could manage all these vacillations we were going through.

I believe that everything that happens to us in life has a purpose, and it's up to us how we handle it. In October, 1951, we received our visas and it was time to leave. I was glad when the boat left Holland, and the sad farewells were behind us. A large bouquet of flowers was placed in our cabin with a note from my parents, wishing us "Good Luck.", which made me cry. Suddenly I wasn't so sure that we had done the right thing. My Mother had always called me her "sunshine", and now I was taking that sunshine away from her.

Most of the time, the fall season is stormy in the Atlantic ocean, so it wasn't surprising that our ship rocked and rolled every which way. This was difficult for me because I became quite seasick, which only added to the morning sickness. When I asked the ship's doctor if he could help me out in some way, he told me that I just had to hang in there because I was pregnant. Any medicine that he could give me, wouldn't be good for the baby.

I was more than happy when we arrived at the harbor in New York. Going through customs took quite a while. I had an orange with me, and to my astonishment, it was confiscated right away. There was another family from eastern Europe, with two children, standing near us. They had brought a large crate filled with chinaware with them. The crate had been damaged, and you could see a lot of broken pieces of china showing through the cracks of the crate. I felt so sorry for those people, as they were very upset and crying. I hoped that they would be able to adjust to the loss of their family heirloom, but in any case, they were better off being in America in the long run. When we came out of customs, we saw Ruth, and it was so nice to see a familiar face. It was just wonderful of her to sponsor us and to make our first few weeks in this new country more pleasant. Bram stayed with us for the first few days, but then he had to go to Boston to start his new job. I stayed three weeks with Ruth, and she was very nice to Ingrid and me, but at the same time, it was difficult for us to adjust to her way of living, which was very different from what we were used to.

The radio was on the whole day, every day, from morning until late at night. The loud constant noise gave me headaches, but Ruth told me that she couldn't stand silence around her, so I tried to endure the noise. Ruth had some very nice neighbors, who invited me over to watch some television with them. I had never seen a television before, so I enjoyed it tremendously. Going outside for a walk every day helped me to find some peace and quiet. Ruth wasn't used to children, so she became irritated several times when Ingrid played around the house and tried to talk to her in Dutch. One time, Ingrid touched one of the lamps in Ruth's living room, and Ruth started to yell at Ingrid in such a way that Ingrid was frightened and burst into tears. It was then that I decided that we should leave. I called Bram and pleaded with him to let us come to Boston. We had stayed long enough with Ruth and, after all, it wasn't fair to her either. I had wanted to go by train to Boston, but Ruth insisted on driving us in her car, which would take at least five hours.

Bram told me that he would arrange for us to stay in a hotel in Boston, until we could find a house near his work. It was such a relief for me to leave, because I didn't want to quarrel with Ruth, and so far, we had managed to keep the peace between us. Ruth was some "character" though. She drove very fast, and cursed at everyone that got in her way. When we arrived in Boston, she nearly hit a taxi cab. It was her fault, but even so, she yelled at the taxi driver, calling him all kinds of names. Most of the names were foreign to me, but I could guess what they meant.

Bram had reserved a large room for the three of us in the Parker House Hotel of Boston. We stayed there for three weeks. Bram was gone in the daytime during those weeks, and I had to take care of Ingrid and keep us busy. On the sunny days, Ingrid and I would walk for hours in the Boston Common Park, where we had fun feeding the squirrels and pigeons. Sometimes we would go window shopping near the hotel, and I marveled at the wealth of all the stores, which was quite different from Holland. Because I had been so cooped up in one room every day, Bram told me to go see a movie one evening. After enjoying the movie, I left the theater and was walking down the street towards the hotel when a car stopped next to me, and two men asked if I would like to go "party" with them. I said "no" and started to run, being frightened at their boldness, especially since it was obvious that I was quite pregnant. When I told Bram about it later, he wondered what kind of country America was, where even pregnant women were bothered.

While we stayed at Parker House, we visited several towns that surrounded Boston, trying to find a suitable place to live. Ruth had also helped us the day she had dropped me off in Boston. It wasn't easy to find a decent house to rent. One of Bram's colleagues Mr. Lamon Gilbert, suggested that we look around the area of Sharon, where he lived with his family. To our surprise, we found a new development, which was only half finished. Most of the homes were already bought, but there was one street where you could rent a house. It was a simple house, but it was within our financial reach, so we took it. But then we had to wait for our crate with our possessions to arrive in Boston. A few weeks later, it was delivered to our house. Now, at last, we could settle down. But when we opened our crate, much to our chagrin, we discovered that a lot of our furniture was damaged. A radio was smashed, but a large mirror was still intact. Still, it was so much better having our own peace and quiet in our own home that we made do with fixing a few broken items.

At first, we were the only family on the street. The road was still a muddy country road, and there were no trees or vegetation. The houses looked like forlorn pieces of wood plopped down on the land. But soon there were more houses being built, and trees and shrubs were planted. As more people moved in around us we didn't feel so isolated any more. Bram's colleague lived in the same development with his wife and two children. At that time, we didn't have a car, and there was only one store that I could walk to. So when I had to buy food, we went shopping in the nearby town of Norwood with the Gilberts. The Gilberts took us with them once a week to do all of our shopping, which was very nice. Jane was expecting her third child about the same time that I would have my baby, so we had a lot in common. What made my life difficult in those days was the fact that I had trouble making myself understood. Even though I had taken English in High School, I had trouble deciphering the Bostonian accent, which made it difficult to communicate. Especially I couldn't understand slang expressions that were frequently used. When I went shopping, for instance, I found that I had never learned the names of grocery items, and so I would ask the butcher for "pig's meat", which was directly translated from the Dutch language. The butcher didn't understand me until I drew a picture of a pig on a piece of paper. "Oh", he said, "you mean that you want some pork". Many words were pronounced wrong by me, resulting in a lot of misunderstandings.

Ingrid was having the same problem. Nobody could understand her when she spoke Dutch, poor child. But somehow, she managed to play with the Gilbert children, using sign language. Several of the children in the neighborhood made fun of her though, telling each other that Ingrid was obviously retarded. One afternoon Ingrid was playing outside when she was joined by a group of children, who made fun of her when she tried to talk to them. One girl, who was about two years older, who seemed to be the leader of the group, in particular was very mean to Ingrid, taunting her when she tried to communicate. Ingrid started to cry and I lost my patience. I ran outside, yelling bad names in Dutch at the girl, on purpose. Of course, the girl was frightened because she could see how mad I was, but couldn't understand a word I was saying. Then I switched to English, and said

"Do you understand me?" The girl shook her head and I continued,

"You are a mean and nasty girl. Where did you learn to be so mean as to torture a girl smaller than yourself? Would you dare to treat me like that?"

By this time she was crying because of my tirade. I told her that Ingrid was a totally normal girl, but that she was speaking another language, and the girl apologized, as she sobbed.

I turned around and said to Ingrid that the girl was sorry for her behavior in Dutch, whereupon Ingrid answered me, saying

"Mama, I want to play with the kids and make new friends."
"What is she saying?", a few of the children asked.

I told them what Ingrid had said and then I had an idea.

"Why don't you kids try to teach Ingrid English, and you can learn some Dutch from her?" From then on the children had fun with the two languages. Soon, Ingrid started to speak English words and the Americans were proud to show off what little of the Dutch language they had learned. When Ingrid entered nursery school, she was able to make herself understood quite well.

ERIC: FEBRUARY 5, 1952

When I was eight months pregnant, I went to see the doctor in Boston every week. He was an obstetrician by the name of Dr. Baker. Bram couldn't come with me most of the time, so I took a taxi to the Sharon station, then a train to Boston, and finally a subway to my destination. I took Ingrid with me because I didn't know anybody who could take care of her. On one of the last visits I had a very hard time dealing with the freezing cold weather. The snow was falling, covering everything with a thick blanket of snow. When we stepped off the train in Sharon, coming back from Boston, I saw only one taxi, and before I could catch it, I was pushed aside by a man who jumped in, instructing the driver about his destination. The taxi driver saw me standing there, with a little girl beside me in the snow, but he decided that he couldn't help me for the time being. Even so, he leaned out of his window, and yelled that he would be back as soon as he possibly could, and then rushed away. By this time there were no passengers around anymore, and we were left standing there in the storm, all by ourselves. Ingrid started to cry because she was so cold, and I will never forget the long hour we waited there for the taxi to return. When the taxi finally did come, I was totally exasperated. When we came home, I told Bram that I wanted to crawl back to Holland. I pleaded with him to leave this "terrible" country.

A week later, Bram went with me to visit Dr. Baker for the last time. I knew the baby was about due, and Dr. Baker said that he thought it would only be a few more days until I delivered. I looked at him and asked if he would have me admitted to the Lying-in Hospital in Boston, right then?.

"I'm not going back home because I think the baby will be born sooner than you think". At first, Dr. Baker didn't believe me, and he shook his head saying,

"Who's the specialist here, you or me?" But I didn't give in, and seeing how serious I was, he made the arrangements for me to go to the hospital. Bram settled me in, but when he left with Ingrid, it was heartbreaking to see how upset Ingrid was. Bram told me later that she had cried all the way home, and he'd had a hard time consoling her. I went into labor that night, and Eric was born the next morning.

Dr. Baker gave me anesthesia at the end of my labor because he didn't want me to have the same problem I had had with Ingrid's birth. As it turned out though, Eric's birth was normal, and when I woke up from the anesthesia, I saw a nurse sitting next to me, and she told me that I had a son. I was so happy because now we had a child of each sex. What was funny was that the nurse said I was talking all during the time I was asleep, in Dutch.

Bram, having left the hospital, didn't find out that we'd had a son until later. I was in the hospital for a week, and nobody but Bram visited me, so some of the nurses felt sorry for the poor new foreign mother. I didn't mind it too much though, even though I did miss my parents and my friends from Holland. Next door, at the hospital, there was a well known actress, who received so many flowers that there was no more room left for them in her room. She had a baby also, and there were so many visitors that I couldn't sleep from all the noise I heard. The actress heard about the fact that I had no flowers or visitors and so she had a beautiful bouquet of flowers sent to me, which made me happy, because I knew that at least one person was thinking about me.

Ingrid and our newborn, Eric, kept me very busy. I loved my

children dearly, and I always had the feeling that God specifically gave me those wonderful kids to take care of for Him for awhile. That's why I tried never to own them, but to give them enough freedom to develop in their own precious ways, so they would become happy adults.

OUR FIRST HOME IN SHARON 1952

We had lived in our rented home in Sharon for a year when Bram decided that it was time for us to buy a car. He used to take his bike to the station, even in the winter when it was snowing, and he became known as" the flying Dutchman". Our lives became easier when Bram bought the Chevrolet. I took driver's lessons until my instructor decided that I was ready to take the exam. I remember one of the first times I sat behind the wheel of our car, as I tried to drive past the lake in Sharon. I made a beeline for the lake at one point, and I didn't know what to do. My instructor told me very calmly,

"It is your choice whether you want to drown or use your brains."

So I turned the steering wheel frantically and managed to avoid plunging into the lake. I flunked my first driver's test because I drove right into a root at the bottom of a steep embankment, and then I had to back up to get past it. Finally, I passed the driver's test. I was not a great driver, but I managed to avoid getting into accidents.

From then on, I took Bram to the Sharon station to go to Boston, always with the children in-tow, as they were too small to be left alone. Sometimes Bram would take the car and leave it at the station. In the summer of 1952, we decided to do some exploring around Massachusetts. We drove to the summit of some mountains at the northwest corner of Massachusetts. At first, we couldn't find a place to stay overnight, but then we were told there was a lady that rented some cabins at the Whitcomb Summit near North Adams. We were lucky because we got the last cabin available, which had a beautiful view over the mountainous terrain, and there were trails everywhere that we could explore to our hearts' desire. Once a year, for many years, we went back to this same place, known as Moore's cabins, run by Marjorie Moore, and it gave us all many happy memories. We called it going to the Mohawk Trail and the children loved it as much as we did. Marjorie would often tell us of her adventures during the very cold winters there in the Berkshire Mountains.

Soon after we had settled in Sharon, we got some new neighbors. A whole family moved into the five houses that were still available. They were all related, a grandmother, her four grown children and numerous grandchildren. This changed our quiet neighborhood into a noisy one. We had mixed feelings about it, especially when we had problems with them. I had planted some flowers in the front yard, and built a small pond in the back yard. But some of the children on our street came into the yard, pulled up the flowers and tried to catch the goldfish in the pond. I asked the children nicely not to bother these things, but they paid no attention, so when they came back, I yelled at them "to get the hell out of there", which proved to be much more effective. But then some dogs got into my pond, making a terrible mess. Most of the time, however, we were able to enjoy the yard.

Two boys came over to my house to show me some creatures they had caught, like turtles, lizards, and beetles. They had discovered that I loved nature, and they were happy when I showed some interest in them. I enjoyed their company, but after a while I didn't see them anymore. Then one day I was walking down the street, and I happened onto one of them. I asked him why he didn't come to visit anymore, and he told me that his priest had told him that he thought it would be better if he didn't see me anymore because I was a heathen. It turned out that all the families on the street were Catholic and we were Protestants. I felt badly about this because we had been raised with all ethnic backgrounds and many religions, and my parents always told me to respect all mankind, whatever their beliefs were or how they differed from mine.

Not long after the incident with the boys, I had a chance to meet and talk with the Catholic priest. I asked him if it was right to forbid a Catholic child from talking to a Protestant. He was appalled, and assured me that this was not the teachings of his church. It reminded me of the situation in Northern Ireland. I wondered what Christ would say, if he came back to earth and saw how his followers were practicing what he had taught them. So we were more or less the outcasts in our street in Sharon. It made me feel even more homesick for my own country. To make things worse, I had a negative experience with another religion.

I had found a pediatrician in Sharon, who turned out to be Dutch. His family had left Europe just before World War II broke out. Because he was Jewish, he was one of the lucky ones. When I needed a dentist, I found one, who was also Jewish. I liked both of these men and their families. I wanted to make some new friends, so I invited them and their families over for dinner and they all accepted my invitation. I was thinking that I would make some new friends now and spent days preparing a special meal, and was looking forward to having a happy evening with all of them. But then I got a call from the dentist, saying that they wouldn't be able to come because they didn't have a baby-sitter for their children. Shortly after that, the other couple arrived. We had some drinks, and we chatted, and then I started to serve dinner.

The doctor's wife looked at my table and asked me if the food was "Kosher". I looked at her and didn't understand what she was asking. "What does kosher mean?" I asked. So she explained that kosher food had to be prepared in a certain way, and that she couldn't eat anything that wasn't prepared in that manner. So to make a long story short, our guests ate practically nothing, left soon thereafter, making me feel confused, and very unhappy. For days, we tried to finish the many left over dishes. This experience was so disheartening, that my homesickness came back, tenfold. I felt like crawling back to Holland again.

Some time later I met a Rabbi at a friend's home. This gave me a chance to ask him about "kosher" food. When I told him about the Jewish guests I'd had over and how they refused to eat my food, he told me that this was inexcusably rude, and that these people should have known better when they were dining with gentiles. But soon after that, our lives started to change for the better. For a while, we went to a Christian Science Church, where we met and made new friends. Bram's mother had started with the Christian Science Church after her stroke, in the hope that the healing teachings of Mary Baker Eddy would help her.

A wonderful lady came to my door, introduced herself as Madeleine MacMaster, and told me that one of her friends had told her about me, and how lonely I had been. She became one of my dearest and best friends for many years. Her friend was a friend of my uncle John in Chicago, and had been sent at my uncle's request. I was grateful to my uncle, of course, but I saw very little of him over the years, which was too bad, because he was the only relative I had in America. Through Madeleine, our friend, we met and befriended the Bussewitz's, a couple that lived in a part of Sharon that was a preserve called the Moose Hill bird sanctuary. This sanctuary covered miles of beautiful meadows and woodlands, with a wealth of wildlife. We went there often after Eric was old enough to be pushed in a stroller.

When Ingrid reached Kindergarten age, at first I took her to school in our car, even though there was a school bus available which would pick her up, not far from our home. Eventually I let her use it, but it made me a little anxious at first because we didn't have anything like that in Holland. In fact, there weren't any school buses at all in Holland, and the children used to walk to school, sometimes up to an hour's hike, which was especially difficult in the winter. Now, we had to get used to New England's weather, which was colder, with much more snow and ice. Ingrid and Eric enjoyed making snow men in the front yard when they were a bit older. We bought a sled, and they had fun taking turns whisking down the hill near our house.

At Christmas we went shopping in Boston. On one of these trips, Eric was about two and a half years old, and not very talkative, probably due to the fact that two languages confused him a little. In the train we were sitting across from an elderly gentleman, chewing gum as we traveled. Eric watched him intently, and when the fellow passenger started to talk to us, Eric suddenly spoke up,

"Excuse me Sir, have you any gum?" We were surprised to hear Eric voicing his first sentence. Somewhere he had picked up the words for bubble gum.

Gradually, we started to get used to our new life, with all the new impressions we were collecting of this totally new country. With the help of our new friends we appreciated more of the good things around us.

There were a lot of young children, who often played in the middle of the street. We had asked the neighbor across the street to keep an eye on them, but it didn't help very much. I always felt that I had to be doubly careful when I backed out of the driveway, looking for any children that might be around. One afternoon I had an appointment with my physician. I was a bit late as I rushed out of the house, looking around to see if it would be safe to back out of the driveway. But when I started the car, driving slowly, I felt uneasy somehow, which made me stop sooner than I normally would have. Suddenly. I heard a woman who lived across the street, screaming, and when I looked behind me, I saw her running towards my car. Quickly, I got out of my car to see what was the matter. Then I saw her three year old son, lying directly behind my car on the street, not an inch away from my left rear tire.

I thought I would have a heart attack. The woman picked up her son, crying, and screaming at me. The child had a lump on his forehead, where the rear bumper had hit him, but otherwise he seemed all right. It turned out that he had been playing behind some of the parked cars on the street, and when he saw my car moving, he thought his Father was coming home. He started to run towards my car, and I never saw him; nor could I have seen him because he was so small. Some angel must have been watching over all of us, making me stop the car prematurely. I offered to take the woman and her son to the nearby hospital, but she said she wanted to do it herself. So I went to my physician all shaken up. When I told him what had happened, he said that indeed, we were very lucky, but that he felt I wasn't to blame. Coming home, I saw the neighbor's car come back and went to ask if the boy was okay. Thank God, the only thing wrong was the bump on his head. A few days later, an insurance man came by to ask me for my version of what had happened, and I told him the whole story. When I finished, he shook his head and said, "Mrs. Boonstra, we know the families on your street, and they are the ones who should be blamed because they don't keep an eye on their children and they let them play in the street. But, if you had killed a child, you could have gotten a prison term for manslaughter." Our insurance company had to pay one hundred and ten dollars for the x-rays, which was not too bad after all. Ever since that happened, I was even more careful. Ironically, the same boy was in another accident a year later. This time it was serious. His Mother's car was hit by a drunk driver, and several of the kids in the car were hurt, including him, but they all survived.

Another accident happened shortly afterwards at the end of our street, which I couldn't forget. The town of Sharon was placing large cast iron pipes along the sides of the road to be used for new water lines. These pipes were stacked up high, like a pyramid. When I saw them piled like this, I knew it was very dangerous, because when we were in Delft, a girl was killed while trying to climb up a similar pile of pipes. She was killed instantly as the pipes rolled over her. As I was coming home from taking Bram to the railroad station one morning, I saw several of the kids from our block climbing on the pyramid, like the girl in Delft had done, It scared me because the pipes moved a little each time the kids jumped on them. So I stopped the car and told them to get off the pile, explaining how dangerous it was for them. They got off, but as I drove up the street I could see them starting to climb again.

I recognized one of the girls as one who lived in a large house at the end of our street, so I decided to warn her family, but when I knocked on the door, the Mother answered and when I told her what was happening, she told me to mind my own business. This gave me such a defeated feeling, because I thought I had done my best to warn them of the impending danger. Later on, I realized that I should have gone to the police. Even now, many years later, I still feel badly about not having done that in the first place. As it turned out, the little girl was actually killed a few weeks later, when one of those pipes crushed her to death. I never saw the mother again, but I shudder to think about what must have gone through her head after having been warned of what might happen.

It seemed like quite a few unpleasant things happened around us the first few years we lived in Sharon, because another incident befell us right after the pipe accident with the little girl. Late one night, one of our friends, who lived nearby, called us and asked if we would baby-sit because their son, who was Eric's age, and still a baby, suddenly became very ill. They wanted to take him to the hospital because they were worried about him. I volunteered to go because Bram had to go to work early the next morning. When I went to our friends home, I knew right away the situation was serious. They were both crying, and holding their baby son in their arms, who was also very upset and crying. Everyone was so upset because of the fact that the baby's right arm was paralyzed, hanging down like a rag doll. "We are afraid that our son has polio", said the baby's father.

For a period of time around 1953, polio was still very dangerous and the Salk vaccine had not been introduced. I stayed up most of the night with the other two children, wondering and praying that the child would be all right. When my friend came back from the hospital without their son and looking very upset, I knew that the news wasn't good. They said that their son did have polio, and that they didn't know how serious it was, and that they would just have to wait and see how serious a case he had. When I left and came home, I hoped that I would not come down with the same dreadful disease. Bram and I were quite worried for some time afterwards, especially because Eric had played with the sick boy the day before he had become ill, so there was a chance that Eric would have contracted the illness. It turned out that none of the rest of us, from our family or theirs, caught the dreaded polio. What seemed such a shame was the fact that this boy was one of the last cases before the cure was available. It was ironic that years later, Eric fell victim to being handicapped also. Nobody knows how life unfolds.

All this didn't help with my homesickness. There was another thing that bothered me a lot. One of Bram's colleagues told us that he hated black people and wanted to become a member of the Klu Klux Klan. This was the second time I had experienced racial prejudice. The first time was during the war in Holland, when the Jews were murdered by the millions. Such hatred is frightening. It makes you wonder if we will ever lift up our thinking about the human race to a higher standard. I think it will happen eventually, but it will take quite a long time, maybe in the next century.

In the summer of 1955, Bram had to travel to Europe to give a lecture for his company. He decided this was an opportunity for him to take the kids and me with him to see my parents and Bram's sister. We flew to Quebec, where we stayed for two days in a motel before we embarked on a Dutch ship named "de Groote Beer" (the Big Bear). When we arrived at the harbor and saw our ship, we noticed a lot of people hanging over the railing of the ship, watching us come up the stairway. They all looked like farmers to us, and Bram looked at them and said "We are dressed much too neat and fancy for these people." He said it in Dutch, and I realized that "those people" were Dutch and could understand everything we said, so told Bram "to shut up." because I could see that some of the people were laughing and some were angry. We were embarrassed and it taught us to be careful what we were saying.

It took us five days to reach the harbor in Rotterdam. The trip was not very pleasant because the weather was stormy, and I was the only one who was not seasick. My doctor had given me some seasick pills, which helped, even though I felt and moved like a zombie. One night Eric climbed out of his cot, walked to the cabin door, tried to open the door, and said "I am going to leave this boat because I don't like it." It took some time to quiet him down, but we didn't blame him for the way he felt.

It was a very happy moment when we docked at the harbor in Rotterdam, seeing my parents in the distance, waving at us. My parents saw their grandson for the first time, since he had been born in America. Especially my mother loved the children. My Father was more distant, but he thought his grandchildren were cute. Our stay in Holland was wonderful. We visited a lot of our old friends, Bram's sister Cobi, her husband Geraard, and their daughter Willike. It was lucky that our children could understand and speak Dutch. Ingrid was amazed that everyone around her seem too understand the Dutch she was speaking. For the first time, it dawned on her that more people spoke Dutch than just her parents. In the three and a half years that we had been gone from Holland, there had been an immense change in the commerce of Holland. There was more luxury everywhere. The stores were filled with merchandise, and food was much more available than there had been when we left.

For the first time since we'd moved to America, we saw how small Holland was, and how crowded the streets were everywhere. On the other hand, we enjoyed the coziness and warmth of the people we knew and loved. If we had been able to go back to Holland for good, I would have loved it at that time. But we had started a new life in another country and we couldn't go back again. When we were on the ship coming over, we only met one couple that was returning to Holland for good because they couldn't cope with living in Canada, where they had been for two years. All the other people were only visiting because they were happy living in Canada or America. I guess something happens to you when you immigrate to another country. You start to compare the countries with each other, and you find that each country has something different to offer, so you have to make a choice about which one suits your needs the best. It was heartbreaking for my parents when we left Holland.

My Mother was just wonderful to me, telling me that she, her sister, and three brothers did the same thing many years ago. All of them lived outside the Netherlands. Four of them lived in Indonesia, and the youngest brother moved to America. When my grandmother died in 1927, none of her children were there for her, so mother felt that she had no right to complain about her daughter building her life somewhere else. I was so grateful to her for telling me this, as it helped to cope with the guilt feelings I had about keeping family from her. I wrote my parents every week for years, never missing one week. My parents had done the same thing for their parents when they were living in Indonesia. In those years, it took about eight weeks for a letter to arrive at its destination.

My Mother's youngest brother served in the Dutch navy for awhile before he settled in America, and he didn't write his parents very often. After awhile, he didn't write them at all, and they didn't know if he was alive or dead. Then one day he suddenly arrived at their door in Holland, which nearly caused my Grandmother to have a heart attack. He stayed with them for about a week, and then one day he went to the store to get something, and never returned because he didn't like good byes. Before he went to the store, he put his suitcase in the yard, so he could retrieve it undetected. Some weeks later he wrote his parents, explaining that this was his way of not confronting tearful good byes. His parents had been sick with worry when he didn't return from the store, but then they realized what had happened. How selfish and gutless some people can be! In later years, my uncle paid his parents a few visits, and by this time they had gotten used to his sudden disappearances when he left. I hardly knew this uncle, but I'm afraid his actions gave me a bad impression of him.

Our First American Home

Morning Assembly at Moose Hill Day Camp

Butterfly Hunting at Moose Hill Day Camp

Moore's Cabins at the Mohawk Trail

THE NEW HOUSE 1955

When we got back to America after five weeks in Holland, we stayed several more years in our rented house in Sharon. Every month we would put a few dollars in our bank account, and gradually we had saved about six thousand dollars over a period of six years, which we could use as a down payment for a house of our own. We started to shop around for a "suitable house" in Sharon. But we couldn't find anything that we liked that was within our means, and just when we were thinking of looking in a different town, something surprising happened. We had often gone to the bird sanctuary in Sharon, where we had originally befriended the Bussewtiz's. They took care of the museum in the sanctuary, and they lived there, in a house that was owned by the Audubon Society. The Bussewtiz's had become close friends when we helped them clear trails in the sanctuary after we had quite a bad storm, resulting in most of the paths being blocked by obstructions. Even Ingrid and Eric helped us, and we all had a good time doing this work. It was good exercise, and at the same time we were helping the Bussewtiz's.

Our friends were very happy with the help we had given them, and they told one of their wealthy friends how we had helped at the sanctuary. This friend, Mr. Kendall, was a real nature lover. He had given quite a large piece of his land to the sanctuary, and then on one beautiful day, Bram and I, and the children met this man. He turned out to be quite a nice person. We chatted about the sanctuary, and then he turned to the children and asked them some questions. I wasn't surprised when Eric answered him in a very polite way. Eric was about three, at the time, and he answered Mr. Kendall with a "Yes Sir" and a "No Sir", which impressed Mr. Kendall. I had taught the children to be polite to everyone, wherever they were, and this time it really paid off, because the Bussewtiz's told Mr. Kendall that we were looking for a home in Sharon or possibly another town. Mr. Kendall liked us and wanted to help us find something in Sharon. Soon thereafter, we received an offer of a piece of land in Sharon that belonged to Mr. Kendall on Maskwonicut Street, and he was asking a very low price. This was such a good opportunity that it was impossible for us to refuse, so Bram and I made a deal with Mr. Kendall. Of course, we were excited and happy, because now we could stay in Sharon, and build a home to our own specifications, which thrilled us. It took a while though, before the official papers were drawn and signed, and a contractor was found to build our house.

We decided to have a split level house, partly built against a hill on our land. We encountered some trouble with the surveying of the land we had bought. Bram had checked the borderline of our property with Eric, who was then just 3 years old, and was disturbed by the fact that the surveyor and Mr. Kendall came up with a different property line. Luckily, Bram found the marker, half hidden under an old stone wall, indicating where Mr. Kendall's land started. From there it wasn't difficult to figure out how the lines ran, and they agreed with the map at the town hall. Mr. Kendall wasn't happy with his surveyor when Bram told him that a mistake had been made. This was especially embarrassing when Bram reported that he had discovered the marker with the assistance of his 3 year old son! It was a good thing that Bram discovered the mistake, because then Mr. Kendall would have sold us a piece of land that didn't even belong to him. To correct the mistake, we had to sell the land back to Mr. Kendall, and then buy the land back again with the right title and property lines.

When our house was only half finished, Bram discovered, to his horror, that the foundation of the house had been built on fill land, which wasn't very sturdy and could cause us major problems. The walls of the basement started to show cracks which were widening each day as the foundation settled. Bram was very worried about this. He had a chance though, to ask some of the engineers where he worked for help and advice on how to correct the settling of our foundation. They came up with a solution which was to jack up the house with eight lolly columns which had to be placed in the basement, under the floor. It was a tremendous job, and we didn't know if it would be successful. But after Bram showed that the sagging part of the house could be held with four heavy jacks put at an angle against notches in the heavy house wall, we obtained the help of a very able contractor who was willing to take on the challenge. In the end, it turned out all right, thank God. The cracks in the basement wall closed up again, giving us faith that the building was straightened out and would hold.

In the meantime, my sister, Meta, paid us a visit in our rented home. After working as a stewardess for the KLM for several years, she had married a Dutch mining engineer who worked in America and she wanted us to meet him. We liked him a lot and I was glad for Meta, but her marriage was hard for my parents. Now their whole family lived in America. It turned out that it would be years before I would see my sister again.

Early in the year of 1958, our house was finished, at last. The landscaping around the house was simply a strip of grass and some shrubs. We knew it would take years before we would be able to finish the rest to our liking, but we were so happy to have a new home for the first time, and to our own taste. This gave us such a rich feeling. We sold the large crate in which we had transported our furniture from Holland. We had been using it for a tool shed in the yard. The people who bought it were happy because it was built so sturdily. Moving our things from the rented house to our new home didn't take that long. Moving was a happy chore.

The people on the street where we had lived for six years were much nicer to us when they found out that we were moving. I was glad that we had managed to make the best of our relationships with the neighbors, but we certainly weren't sorry to leave that area behind. There was so much space inside our new home and our land was ideal for the kids to play in the hundreds of large trees and the small shallow brook that ran behind our house. Altogether, we had three and one half acres in which to enjoy nature. Way back in the woods, there was a small pond that was tucked between two large hills. It was fun to catch frogs in the spring and summer, and in the winter, we could skate on its frozen surface. We didn't have much furniture at the beginning, but it was fun, over the years, to gradually collect pieces that we really liked. A school bus came by to take Ingrid to elementary school, where she met children in our new neighborhood, and in no time at all, we felt at home. We were so much happier than we had ever been before. Our house was near the town, and there was close access to the highway that went to Boston, and the other suburbs. The railroad station was also closer, making it easier for Bram to get to work, but our house had so many trees that we were never bothered by the noises of the community.

When we had lived in America for five years, we started the process of becoming American citizens. At first, I was concerned about passing the exam, but to my surprise, all they asked me was "Who is the President of the United States?". I answered that Dwight D. Eisenhower was president at the time, and that was it. Two of our closest friends came with us for the ceremony, and then we celebrated being fellow countrymen. I did have some sad feelings about losing my Dutch citizenship, but I also realized that we would be staying in this large wonderful country, so we felt we owed America our love and support.

In August of 1958, my parents decided to come over from Holland to pay us a visit. We took our car and went to the dock in New York to meet them. We were thrilled to see them, of course, but I noticed that they had both aged considerably, and especially my Mother. She wasn't the person that I remembered so dearly. Father had written me some time before that she was getting more and more forgetful, which was dangerous when you were running a household, and don't keep an eye on the stove, for instance. So I knew that she would be different, but I didn't realize how bad the situation had gotten. As we drove back to Sharon, Mother was talking constantly, repeating sentences over and over again. Father would look at me and shake his head slightly. Later, he told me that it had been very hard for him to cope with Mother's behavior, and he didn't know what to do about it. At first we thought it was just old age creeping up on Mother, but a few years later she was diagnosed as having Addison's disease, which, among other things, attacks the brain. Bram, the children and I tried to make the best of things during the time my parents stayed with us. Ingrid was disappointed about her tenth birthday party because we felt we could only have a few of her friends over for a party, as more would have been too trying for my parents.

We took my parents to Vermont to visit some friends for a few days, and we had a wonderful time. It was fall and they couldn't believe how bright and colorful the trees and falling leaves were. On the way back, we took the route of the famous Mohawk trail, in northwest Massachusetts. For years, we went there because it was one of the most beautiful spots in New England. Throughout the trip, we had gorgeous weather which made it worthwhile. I was so happy that I had given my parents this memorable experience. After several weeks with us, they flew to my sister's in Oklahoma, where they stayed for several more weeks. They had a good time there too, but Meta also had trouble keeping her patience in check when dealing with Mother.

When my parents came back to our house after a few weeks, we had quite a difficult time because Ingrid became very ill. First she had the measles, and just when she was getting over that, she came down with scarlet fever, and was so sick that we feared for her life.

Although she did get over that, she developed a bad ear infection, which took another four days to heal. Our pediatrician was debating whether to send her to a Children's hospital, but luckily she felt better before we had to make the decision. Amazingly, this was the only time in her childhood that she was very ill. It was a difficult time, dividing my time between my sick child and taking care of my parents. But with God's help, we all managed to have a good time, and even got in another small trip to New Hampshire.

Then the time came for them to go back to Holland. We drove them back to the ship in New York, and it was even harder to say good-bye. They were in the twilight of their years, and we didn't know if we would ever see them again. They couldn't stay in America because they needed Father's pension to survive, and we didn't have enough income to support them. They also had their ties to the old country, and it would have been emotionally devastating, at their age, to start all over again. Mother's sister had stayed in their house while they were with us, which was a nice arrangement for everyone at the time. We were very grateful that they had good times with us. Even though Ingrid was ill part of the time, we were glad to have had the time with them.

THE JOY OF ALL GOD'S CREATURES

The next few years were happy ones in Sharon. The children grew up rapidly, and we all enjoyed the quiet life of being together in our rural town. It was such a bonus to have the bird sanctuary nearby. We hiked many miles along the woodland trails all four seasons. Even in the winter it was beautiful to see the bright snow on the trees and the imprints of different animal tracks pressing the snow to the ground. Friends would often come over to play with Ingrid and Eric, and they would join us in our walks through the bird sanctuary. When Ingrid was eight years old, she was able to go to day camp at a facility in the bird sanctuary. At first, Eric was too young to go to the camp, but I did take him with me to help the counselors here and there. When Eric was old enough to go to camp also, I became a counselor and enjoyed sharing my knowledge of art and nature with the children.

I became interested in insects, and helped collect and preserve them. I also learned of a place where I could send for butterflies and moths from all over the world. They were captivatingly beautiful, so I started quite a collection that I placed on Ryker mounts, under glass. After I had enough display boxes, I gave talks about insects to the scouting groups, schools, and one day a Rotary Club. At first, the Rotarians snickered at me giving a talk about this species, but when I was done with my presentation, they came up to me and told me how much they had enjoyed it, and they admired all the work I had done too, preparing the display cases. So, I did a lot of good with this hobby, and besides, it gave me a good excuse to go butterfly hunting with the children, which kept them alert and interested.

In the nature camp, there were a lot of animals for the kids to take care of and study. We had baby raccoons, snakes, turtles, salamanders, rabbits, squirrels, and a large owl. We even had a calf and two baby goats. The counselors went on long hikes with their groups, teaching the campers everything about nature. We taught them how to make butterfly nets, catch the insects themselves, then carefully dispatch and mount them. Sometimes I would buy cocoons to show the kids how fantastic it was to see a moth coming out of a cocoon, spreading its wings to their full size. We also taught them which insects were beneficial and which ones were detrimental, or even dangerous.

We did the same with other animals, especially snakes. The owl was a permanent fixture at the sanctuary, impressing everyone with its ability to swivel its head without apparently moving a bone of its body. The baby raccoons were also nocturnal and they were so adorable, until they reached maturity Then we had to let them loose because if they grew too tame, they would become victims in the wild. Some knowledge of plants that were edible was also important. I was grateful, and wished I'd had some of this information during World War II.

The Moose Hill Bird Sanctuary was the pride of the Audubon society, and there was even a moose head ("Wilbur") hanging over the barn doors, which served as a gathering place for all of us to meet, several times a day. We would work on projects or listen to lectures there, or if it rained, we would move inside the barn, where it was cozy and dry. At the end of each session, the counselors would cook a meal made with some edible plant, which tasted fairly good. Many friendships were made, which lasted a lifetime. For me, it was a good way to be with my children, having a good time and knowing what they were doing at the same time. This created more precious memories, to keep in my "memory treasure chest".

I remember having lunch with the counselors on a nice sunny day, sitting on the lawn across from the barn. One counselor was telling us about the research he was doing for his thesis in college.

He had decided to study and write about Tarantulas. I looked at him and asked if he was really serious about it, and he said that he would give anything to be able to have one of these spiders for a subject to study. I told him that I would try to get him one, and he laughed, thinking that I was kidding. Then he realized that I was serious, and I confirmed that I was intending to follow through. So, when I came home that day, I called Meta in Oklahoma to see if she could get me a tarantula. There was a pet store near her house, which I knew sold these spiders, and she told me that she would get me one, not even questioning why I had asked, because she was used to my peculiar hobbies. So, a few days later the mailman came up the driveway, and handed me a sturdy cardboard box, telling me that the box was damaged and had several holes in it. I told him that the box was intended to have holes in it, so the tarantula spider could breath. He listened patiently, and then turned and started down the driveway, and I watched and waited for him to absorb the information. He was halfway down the driveway, when he suddenly stopped, turned around and came back, asking me if what I had said was really true.

"Mrs. Boonstra, did you say tarantula? You mean one of those large spiders? Is it alive?"

I nodded my head, that yes, it was alive, and would he like to see it? He wanted to see it because his curiosity had gotten the best of him, but from a safe distance.

I slowly started to open the box, not knowing if the spider was loose inside, or contained somehow. It turned out that there were two old coffee cans inside, each with a spider in it. I told the mailman that my sister had sent me two spiders, and that it was safe for him to come closer to have a look at them. One spider was dead, not surviving the trip, but the other one was very much alive, pacing around in its can. It was very beautiful, with it's shiny fur coat, and legs, which he moved slowly and gracefully. By this time, the mailman was thrilled, and said,

"Wait till my wife hears about this. She won't believe me. Are you going to keep these spiders?". He seemed a little relieved when I told him that I had ordered them for one of the counselors at camp.

Ingrid was petrified of the spiders. When she came home, however, both she and Eric were fascinated by the spiders, even though neither of them wanted to touch the creatures. The next day, I took the spiders to the counselor, and told Billy that one was dead, but the other was ready to be observed. He was really dumfounded that I had actually gotten them. Later, he put the dead spider in a jar with Formaldehyde, and the other one in a terrarium, where the campers could watch and admire this hairy creature. It was a big success at camp, and later the camp counselor took it home where he studied it, and then gave it to the science museum in Boston, where it was gratefully accepted. Our family always loved animals, and I have so many stories that I can only relate a few of our adventures here.

One day, just after a storm. I found a squirrel's nest in our yard with three naked babies in it. Their Mother was probably killed, and they were left to fend for themselves. Only one of the three was still alive, bald, blind and quivering, and I wondered if we could save its life. Eric suggested we try the vet, so I called him. He said that he had never taken care of a squirrel before, but if we wanted to bring it in, he would try to help. The vet said that the animal had a large hole in its body filled with maggots, so he gave us some medicine, which miraculously killed the maggots and healed the wound. So we took it home and used a doll's milk bottle, filled with diluted milk, to feed the tiny baby. To our surprise, the squirrel survived, and grew into a beautiful specimen. We named him "Perry" after one of the characters in a Walt Disney movie. It was fun to watch him perform his graceful acrobatic movements, and as he became mature, we noted that he didn't like to deal with males, of any species. But Ingrid or I could handle him easily. He even bit Bram and Eric without reason. When he was little, we kept him in a cage, and as he matured, he roamed the yard, but hadn't discovered that climbing trees was something natural to his breed.

Eric decided to show him how it was done. At first he was afraid, but then he got the idea, and climbed higher and higher, up the trees, and soon he was outside all the time, and would come to pay us visits. Several times he surprised people, like our baker, for instance, who came to deliver one morning and just as he rang the doorbell, Perry ran out of the woods, ran up his leg, and sat on his shoulder. When I opened the door, the baker was making frantic motions in the direction of his shoulder, and asking me what was on him. I told him not to be afraid, that it was just Perry Boonstra, our tame squirrel, paying him a visit. He breathed a deep sigh of relief, and after a while, got used to seeing Perry around, but Perry had other plans, as he ventured further and further into the woods, and before long we didn't see him very often.

One morning I was working in the yard, near the street, when Perry suddenly appeared out of the woods, climbed up my back, and settled on top of my hat. He was contentedly chewing on an acorn when a sports car came by and the young man who was driving it, glanced at me and was so startled to see the squirrel perched on top of my head, that he nearly lost control of his car and came to a screeching halt to confirm what he had seen. The last time we saw Perry, he was chasing another squirrel, probably a female, so we felt that he had found himself a mate and was happily creating his own family.

About this time we had a bright green Iguana, which was given to Eric by someone who didn't want it anymore. Eric kept it in his room, and it stayed in the terrarium most of the time, but sometimes it would roam about his bedroom. Eric named him "Iggie". This fellow particularly liked to hang on the curtains, not moving for hours. The Iguana loved to eat lettuce and fruits, which it gulped down in chunks. As winter came on, we were afraid that the Iguana would get cold, since it was a tropical animal, so I decided to make it a coat. I had a piece of furry red material that I thought would make a suitable coat, so I made a pattern and cut out the material, placing a zipper along the back of the outfit. This was a hard piece to make, since it was so tiny, and as for the Iguana, he wasn't pleased at all, as I tried to put his legs into the snug fitting sleeves. At first, the Iguana was very agitated with his winter wear, but became resigned to it after awhile, and as it got colder, he actually seemed to enjoy the warmth. Of course, everyone laughed when they saw it, as there was such a contrast between the green of his body and the red outfit, not to mention that this was a rather eccentric notion – dressing a reptile. Iggie wore it with pride and warmth all winter.

Then spring and summer came, and the whole family went to the beach at Cape Cod. We took the Iguana with us, still in his coat, as it was still a little chilly outside, and we put him in the back window well, where he could run back and forth, as he pleased. The only trouble was that, this was totally distracting to drivers of other cars, wondering what could possibly be green and red, going back and forth, from one side of the car to the other. People were sticking their heads out of their cars, and craning their necks to see what the moving object was, as some of them tooted their horns, wondering if they should alert us. As we settled on the beach, the situation escalated, as Eric took Iggie for a walk down the beach on its leash. Eric soon discovered that these animals can run very fast when it saw a stretch of land out in front of it. Eric could hardly keep up, running his fastest. The folks at the beach became curious about this spectacle, and they came from all directions, to see what it was. Then the lifeguard saw a group of people all in one spot, and hurried over thinking that someone might need his help. There wasn't a dull moment at the beach that day. After a while, Eric got tired of this pet, and we started looking around for somebody who would like to have it. Then I met a gentleman at the sanctuary, who was a scientist studying reptiles, who had a whole room of his home devoted to this species, so we knew the iguana would be happy there.

Not long after that, we found a baby Blue Jay in the woods. We tried to find where the nest had fallen from, but to no avail. There were foxes and raccoons in the woods, and any bird that couldn't fly, didn't have much chance of surviving, so we decided to take it home with us. Eric knew exactly what to feed it. Raw hamburger with dirt and worms mixed in, was a gourmet dish for the bird. It looked very unappetizing to us, but the bird thrived on it, and to our delight, grew fast. Eric named it Hubert in honor of the vice president of the United States at the time. Studying this bird was educational. It was smart and considered us its parents. When it started to flap its wings, Eric decided it was time to teach it to fly. He placed the bird on the grass and stood in front of it flapping his arms up and down, hoping the bird would get the idea and emulate him. This was quite a sight, with Eric looking like a giant standing in front of this little heap of feathers, making strange gestures. But surprisingly enough, the bird did get the idea and soon he was off the ground and winging his way through the woods. He was so tame that once a neighbor was visiting, and Hubert landed on the shoulder of the person I was talking to, so I introduced him as Hubert Boonstra, one of our pets. I enjoyed Hubert for the whole summer. He would come by when I was working in the yard, and I would throw a worm over my shoulder, which was a tasty treat for him. Eventually, Hubert joined the other Jays, and off they went into the wilds to find their own way of living.

I built a small pond in our back yard, next to the porch, where we could enjoy watching the carp languidly swimming in its cool environment. The pond had a waterfall at one end that kept the water circulating and clean most of the time, and some water greenery, which gave the goldfish more oxygen and created attractive scenery for us to observe. The fish grew fast, and the largest one was about eight inches long after a year's time. We were proud that it was doing so well, and Eric named it Gertrude, a name he felt befitted the fish.

Early one morning I was sitting on our porch, admiring the surrounding woods, when I glanced in the direction of the pond and was mortified to see that a large snake had Gertrude's tail gripped in its jaws, and was trying to pull the wriggling fish out of the pond. I got up quickly and ran towards the snake, and picking it up by the head, I pried its jaws open until it released Gertrude. Gertrude plunged back into the pool, and seemed to be all right, even though its tail had been torn. Still holding the snake, I went to the garage, where I found an empty coffee can to put the snake in, because I didn't want to release him in the yard, for fear that he would try for a fish dinner again. Later that day, I took the snake to the sanctuary where I hoped he couldn't find his way to the back yard again. Amazingly, Gertrude survived this ordeal, and soon after that, her tail mended itself.

In later years, I told my children that you don't have to be rich or famous to enjoy nature, it's around for everybody to enjoy and study. When you are upset or unhappy, it's good to sit quietly and take in a sunset, a beautiful sky, or possibly the pouring rain of a storm, from which we get a new perspective from the transference of freshly renewed colors. Watching the interesting behaviors of animals or closely observing flowers can give a person great peace of mind. The human race will suffer greatly if all this disappears in the name of "progress". Hopefully, it won't come to that, but at any rate, there is enough undeveloped territory for generations to come. This is why I have encouraged not only my own children, but everybody that I've known over the years, to use their eyes and ears to enjoy God's beauty.

Once, I unintentionally made a mistake, which even upset the balance of nature. Bram and I took the children to Vermont for a few days in the fall, to enjoy the colorful season. We stayed with some dear friends there, and all of us spent days amusing ourselves at a nearby river. The children enjoyed building dams in the river, while I took long walks along the water's edge, looking for plants I could use in my garden. It was always a challenge for me to find a new type of plant, and try to cultivate it in my yard. Our host was busily casting for river trout, but not very successfully. I was walking in his direction, with a butterfly net in my hand, which had become an integral part of my outdoor gear, when suddenly I saw a trout in a small pond, that had been pushed there by the fast moving current. So I scooped up the fish with my net, and it was gorgeous. Only a few yards away, our friend was patiently waiting to get his first bite. As I approached him, I asked, "Is this what you are trying to catch?" He looked at it, as his mouth fell open, and said, "That's it, I quit. I've been standing here for hours, and you show up with the fish in a butterfly net!". Then we both burst out laughing, and decided to throw the trout back into the river because it was too beautiful to eat, and besides, the one trout couldn't feed all of us anyway.

As I started to walk back, I noticed that there were a lot of toads along the shoreline, so I decided to try to catch some to put in my yard because they are beneficial when it comes to eating harmful insects. I asked our friends if they had a bucket I could borrow, and asked the kids if they would help me gather up some of the toads. Toads aren't as difficult to catch as frogs because they don't hop like a frog, nor are they as fast, so when we left for home, we took about sixty toads with us. At home, we released them in the yard, and I was curious to know whether they would make the difference in the preservation of my best plants. It definitely made a difference, and I was proud that I had come up with this solution for my insect problem.

But when the next spring and summer came, something evolved, which I hadn't counted on. We noticed that there was quite an abundance of snakes of every size and description in our yard. This had never happened before, and when I mentioned this to our friends, they giggled and said there wasn't really any mystery about it, because snakes loved to eat toads, so if I had this type of animal, I would have the other too, until the snakes were through feasting.

In the fall we took another trip to North Pond, along the famous Mohawk trail again, enjoying another weekend getaway. We had a mission to collect salamanders, which were in abundance in that area. It seemed that there used to be quite a few salamanders in Sharon, and over the years, they had vanished. So I decided to restock the brook near our house. We brought back many of these beautiful creatures and released them in the brook. Soon the neighbors mentioned that it was strange that there seemed to be a sudden influx of salamanders in all the waterways of Sharon. This time I kept my mouth shut about the phenomena, but I felt good about knowing the answer to the puzzle of the salamanders.

I left our house early one morning to do some shopping in town, and as I passed a neighbor's house, which was up on a hill, an object fell down right in front of the car, and of course, I wasn't able to stop fast enough to avoid hitting it altogether, so I got out of the car to see what had come tumbling down. It was a large box turtle, and I felt badly because it was severely injured. It had cracks in its shield in the shape of a star, and it was bleeding. The sharp edges of its shell were cutting into the flesh, and as I picked it up, the turtle was angry and hissed at me. I turned around and went back to the house, thinking about a way I could help the turtle mend. I found some strong tape, with which I wrapped the turtle's back, making sure that the star shape was aligned such that his flesh wasn't pinched any more. Then I took him to my studio and painted a pattern over the tape, copying the natural pattern of the turtles back. The end result wasn't bad at all. The turtle looked like new again, so I let him go in the woods behind the house wishing him well, and wondering if I would ever see him again. A year later, I saw a turtle in our woods that had a star shaped tear on its back, and it made me happy that he had survived his ordeal.

Another time on Maskwonicut Street I had an encounter with a large snapping turtle. A car driving down our street hit a large turtle, but they didn't stop to help it. About this time, I was getting the mail from our box, when I noticed the injured creature, slowly trying to edge its way to the swamp at the far side of the road. It was impressively large, with a long neck, which told me that it was a snapping turtle, making it quite dangerous because their strong jaws can bite right through the arm of an adult, when they are fully grown. I knew I had to be very careful if I wanted to help it, so I headed back to our garage to get a trash barrel and a broom. Luckily, the barrel was large enough, and I was able to entice the turtle into it with the broom. But now what could I do without getting bitten, as he was hissing at me, as he tried to climb out of the trash barrel? The turtle didn't seem to be hurt very badly. It only had a slight crack in it's shell, and I could have let it go, but before I did that, I decided to do something beneficial as a show and tell for the children, so I called the principal of the grade school and asked if she would be interested in me showing the animal to the classes. She seemed very enthusiastic and asked if I could come over right away. So I managed to get the can in my car, and took the broom too, so the children could watch the strong the jaws of the turtle bite right through the handle, which did make quite an impression. The teachers were glad the children had a chance to see this creature, so they would be careful if they saw one, and not try to pick one up. Eric told me later, that he was a little embarrassed when I showed up in his class, but later he thought it was "cool" that his mother showed the turtle to everyone. So I let the turtle go and hopefully it never tried to cross another busy street.

As I told you, Eric had his collection of harmless snakes in a terrarium in his room. One evening we had company, and Eric came down the stairs with one of his pet snakes rolled around his arm. It caused quite a stir among our friends because most people want to kill any snake they see out of fear. But what they don't think of is that snakes are very beneficial to the balance of nature, and without them we would encounter a serious infestation of rats and mice. One time I gave a talk about insects to some children from the city, who had never been to the country. I felt sorry for them, as one little girl asked me if the mounted butterfly I was showing her was real. Imagine never having seen a butterfly!

Then there were the unwelcome animals who visited us, such as the ambitious groundhog that dug large holes in our yard. We tried to discourage it by throwing smoke bombs in the holes, hoping that the groundhog would find another place more amenable to tunnel. But this was a stubborn creature that decided our yard was the nicest place for its headquarters, and we would quite often see it resting on our lawn. But when we tried to close in on it, the groundhog would disappear down a hole. Then one morning when I was ready to go to the sanctuary, I saw him in front of the kitchen window, munching away on some clover in the grass. He didn't seem to notice me, so I went to the garage and got two butterfly nets, came back, and quietly opened the kitchen door. By this time he saw me and headed for the nearest tree. He didn't seem to be in any hurry, which surprised me, and just as he started to climb up the tree, I saw my chance to get him. I placed one net below him and the other above him, which was confusing to the animal, and he stopped just long enough for me to tap him on the nose with the upper net, making him drop right into the lower net. He couldn't bite his way out because the material of the net was too supple for him to get between his teeth, so I closed the nets together, and had him trapped, but now what? I remembered that I had kept a live animal cage for just such a purpose, but getting him into it was tricky. Our dog, Amber, came to investigate, barking and growling. She discovered what was going on, as the groundhog hissed and snarled, trying to get at the dog through the bars of the cage. What a noisy scene this was! When it was time to go to summer camp, Eric helped me to get the cage into the car. Everybody at camp was surprised to see that I caught the little digger alive, not to mention using butterfly nets.

Eric had a gray rabbit when he was 10. When it matured, it was quite large, and sometimes Eric would let it out of it's cage to hop around the yard, eating clover. One day it wandered off into the woods, Luckily Amber sniffed it out and we got it back. But the second time the rabbit got loose, we didn't find it. Then, a few months later, we were talking to a neighbor, who was a hunter, and his wife, and she told me that a few days before her husband had shot the biggest gray rabbit they had ever seen in the wilds, and then she added that the family had enjoyed the best rabbit stew they had eaten in years. When her husband had picked up the rabbit, he had suspected that it wasn't a native rabbit because it didn't look like any of the rabbits he had seen in the wild, but he had already killed it. I was almost sure that this was our rabbit they had eaten, so I didn't say anything to them. They would have felt as badly as I did if they knew they had eaten our pet for their dinner. And besides, they didn't have a lot of money, so the dinner was a real treat for them and there was nothing we could do to get the rabbit back anyway. Later, I told Eric what I thought had happened to his rabbit and he took it very well.

When Eric and Ingrid were still quite young, I reluctantly agreed to give a lecture about Dutch and Indonesian art for a group of people. I made native Dutch costumes for the children to wear, and took quite a few pieces of art with me also. My program was a big success, and the children's costumes were of great interest, even though the children had a hard time balancing themselves in the wooden clogs they wore. By the time we got home, Eric was so tired that he collapsed on his bed, and fell fast asleep. I took a picture of him, which is one of my favorites. I call it the "the Sleeping Dutchman". My former teaching made it easy for me to give lectures to people, and it made me feel good, doing something useful for the community.

When Eric was older he also worked as the nature counselor at a different day camp. One summer he was told to get a baby goat from a farm that was close to Sharon. There is nothing more adorable to watch than a kid – a baby goat kid. They are so full of life and curious about everything around them. The children enjoyed this animal immensely, and when the camp was closed, Eric brought the goat home. One Saturday morning, Eric asked us if we would watch it for him. I needed to be home anyway because a serviceman was due, so I had the goat in the kitchen with me, as this was the safest place to have it. When the man arrived to work on our kitchen, he was startled to see the goat, but assumed it was our pet. When he leaned over his tool chest, the goat saw his chance to do a little climbing, and he jumped up on top of the man's back, scaring him out of his wits. But then he smiled and asked if I would remove the jumper, commenting that the animal would be better off on a farm. I took the goat and put it in the garage. This was a big mistake. Later, we discovered that to amuse himself, he had chewed the insulation off the wiring for our outside spotlight, and the next time we plugged it in, there was a fountain of sparks, and the circuit breaker cut out. Goats are hard to keep outside a pen because they will eat almost anything from material to plants. We were glad when the goat went back to camp, and then to a farm after that.

The next year, Eric got another baby goat for the campers to enjoy. This one was so cute that everyone wanted to play with it. It was pure white with startling blue eyes, and when we had it for the weekends, it would sit on our laps and go to sleep like a kitten. It was remarkable that this animal considered Eric his parent, and would follow him everywhere, taking every opportunity to hop on Eric's back when he leaned over. We really enjoyed these adventures.

Our New House on Maskwonicut Street

Amber Our Dog of 17 Years

*My Daughter Ingrid
and Baby Goat*

Summer at Our House in Sharon

"Iggi" Our Pet Iguana in Beach Attire

AMBER

I must tell you about the dog we had for almost seventeen years. We had lived in our new home for about two years, when we started talking about getting a dog, but there weren't any pet stores nearby, so we would have to take the train into Boston to look for a pet. One time, I took Eric and Ingrid with me when they needed new shoes. On the way back to the train station we passed by a pet store, and stopped to look at some adorable puppies in the window. There was a sign that said they were a cross breed of German shepherd and a medium sized collie. Someone had told me that this mix was a very compatible type of dog to have for children, and one of the best family dogs we could wish to own. We watched them for awhile, and decided we wanted one. There was one, especially, that kept running towards us, wagging its tail, and looking intently at us, so this was our pick of the litter. So home we came with a large cardboard box, and when we showed it to Bram, he was surprised, but accepted the puppy right away. After some deliberation, we named her Amber because that was the color of her coat. We decided that her full name should be Amberina, and she seemed to take pride in that name. We bonded with her quickly and enjoyed her thoroughly. Amberina wandered around the woods close to our home, which didn't disturb the neighbors because their home wasn't that close. Amberina preferred to stay fairly close to home anyway, so we didn't have to worry about her.

In 1959 we took a trip to Florida. This was the first time I had seen tropical scenery in many years, and I loved it. I felt as if I was coming home to a climate where I really belonged. The children loved it too. They enjoyed the beaches, swam a lot and got a nice tan. The next year we went to Florida again, and visited the tropical gardens and the zoo and had a great time. In later years, though, it made me shudder to think that we had made those trips to Florida in our old green Chevrolet without seat belts. Luckily, we never had an accident, although the roads in those days weren't as good or as fast as they are now.

In 1961 we went to Holland to see my parents once again. Eric and Ingrid stayed with Bram's sister because my parents weren't well, and it wouldn't have been good to put any strain on them with kids around. Bram rented a car and we took my parents on a couple of sightseeing tours, which they really enjoyed. We also contracted a Dutch scoutmaster to take Eric under his wing, and since Eric was a scout too, he could participate in their activities. It turned out to be quite an enjoyable exchange for both of them, as Eric's uniform was different from the one used in Holland. They went camping and shared other differences in their cultures. The Dutch were very surprised at the size of our house, as it was more common for Europeans to live in smaller spaces. It was then that we realized how luxurious our life had become.

Eric had a rather unpleasant experience with a boy that was living in my parents' neighborhood, even though he was only there for a short visit. The boy was a bully and called Eric names and tried to start a fight with him. I was mad when Eric told me about it, and went to see the parents of the boy, telling them what had happened, confiding that I was disappointed at the very unpleasant image my son was getting of the Dutch youth. Luckily, this man was a good father. He punished his son and made him apologize to Eric for his behavior.

Ingrid didn't have as a good time with Bram's family as we had wished. Her aunt and uncle were nice, but her cousin, who was a couple of years older than Ingrid, didn't pay any attention to her. She would have girlfriends over, and ignore Ingrid, making her feel unwanted. I felt badly about this and it made me count our blessings about what we had at home in the states. By now, we had adapted to a different lifestyle in America, which was more open, and we had much more space for ourselves than we would have had, if we had stayed in Holland. So many people came to Holland to live though, from Indonesia, the West Indies, and other places where they could no longer live. There wasn't enough housing for everyone, so a lot of them ended up living in cramped quarters and had a difficult time finding a job.

Before World War II, Holland was quite a respectable country, without much crime. It survived the recession of the thirties, and was headed for better times when the war broke out in 1940. World War II ruined the country in many ways. It didn't totally destroy it, but it never came back to the era of wealth it had known in times past.

The loss of our colonies was a tremendous set-back, because most of the Dutch wealth came from there. Of course, we have problems in America too, but there are so many more opportunities of living a decent life. Bram and I were glad that we had given our children the opportunity of a better future. So many Dutch people left their country after the war, and they are now spread all over the world, especially in the areas of Canada, America, New Zealand, and Australia. On our return trip to America, Bram continued his business in Chester and London, England, so we were able to visit in England for several weeks to show the children the British culture.

HEALTH OR ELSE 1962

In 1962, I had a personal hurdle to overcome. I hadn't felt well for some time, and in November of that year, I had some alarming symptoms, which made me hurry into the doctor. Within one day after the doctors consulted, I was admitted to a nearby hospital for a hysterectomy. A large benign tumor was also removed, and fortunately, it wasn't cancerous. I stayed in the hospital for two weeks, and shared the room with two other patients. I learned another valuable lesson in human behavior between the two of them. They were both waiting for the results of their tests for breast cancer, and of course, both were quite anxious but they behaved quite differently. One was difficult, always demanding, complaining and wanting constant attention. The other was an older lady, about seventy, and she was the opposite, calm, elegant and quietly nice. On the day of their biopsies, the complainer was taken out first, and then the nice lady went for her test. I prayed for both of them, hoping that they would be healthy. Not long after that, the first patient came back, and her test had turned out negative, so she was all right, but she was still complaining that she didn't believe the doctors and that she was sure she was going to die. The second patient came back later that evening, and she was all doped up and was bandaged across her chest. She had obviously had a mastectomy, and I felt sorry for her, but when she woke up the next morning, she wished me a "good morning", and said that she was grateful because she knew she would be all right with God's help. The first patient was still complaining as the nurse wheeled her out to go home, and she didn't even say good-bye. Later in the day I was talking with the nurse, and she told me that the unpleasant lady probably wouldn't live as long as the woman who was nice because a person's mental attitude definitely made a difference in their longevity. I strongly believe that God helps those who help themselves, and it made a definite impression on me how these two women behaved under stress.

Just before I was due to be released from the hospital, I went into shock. I didn't know what was happening to me, but I was shivering violently and felt icy cold. Several nurses came running and wrapped blankets around me, which helped a lot. Later I heard that I was in critical condition, but luck was with me. My specialist kept asking me if my legs hurt, and I knew he was asking me because I had told him about the problem of my mother developing thrombosis in both legs when she had the same operation. I told the doctor that my legs weren't bothering me, but my back was hurting. The doctor didn't take any notice of my complaint, and later that caused me big problems.

While I was in the hospital, I was very worried about how my family would be able to cope with running the household. Ingrid had learned how to cook a little, so she could take care of the meals. Both she and Eric were a big help to Bram and we had some friends that had them over for dinner. At the beginning of December I came home, but I had been through enough pain that in was in a weakened condition, and had to stay in bed for several days. Bram had to go back to work and the children to school, and we had no offers of help then. I had assured the family that I would be all right just staying alone in bed. On the third day I had to crawl out of bed to go to the bathroom, and I fainted. When I became conscious again, I managed to go to the bathroom and get back to my bed. I wasn't even worried because I thought the fainting was caused from weakness, but the next night I started to have terrible pains in my lungs when I took a breath. I didn't wake Bram that night, but by the next morning the pain was unbearable. He called the family doctor, who came to our house right away. It didn't take long to discover the problem. When I was thirteen years old I had double pneumonia, and this was the same pain that I had experienced before, so Bram took me to the hospital and I was treated for pulmonary thrombosis. I felt badly about being such a nuisance, but I had to try to stay alive for my family. After a few days, I hadn't improved, and everyone was worried, so Bram asked the Director of the hospital, whom he knew personally, to take a look at me. Thanks to him, I was treated by a specialist, who was much better than his predecessor. From the x-rays of my lungs, they could tell that a large blood clot had passed through my heart, which had caused the fainting spell, but now the clot had settled in one of my lungs.

The specialist said he thought I might need another operation, but just to make sure, he wanted to wait a few hours to see what developed. By this time, I was frantic. I needed to stay alive for my family. I remember looking out the window of my room, it seemed so dark outside, with lights moving in the distance from the highway, and I wondered if the people in those cars were happy. At any rate, they were alive, and that's what I wanted too – to be alive and well again.

We had a friend that was a Christian Science practitioner, and whose faith was remarkable. Bram and I couldn't accept the level of her faith, but we were impressed by her convictions. In my moment of despair I decided to ask for help, so I crawled out of bed, and headed for the telephone in the corridor. Nobody was around because it was the middle of the night. I called Bram and asked him to call this friend and ask her to pray for me. As I crawled back into bed, my roommate woke and asked if I was all right, and when I told her what I had done, I could see an expression of doubt on her face. Some time later that night, I was wheeled in for another x-ray. Early the next morning, the specialist came in to see me and said,

"Mrs. Boonstra, I have good news for you. We don't need to operate after all, because your body has taken care of the blood clot, and you're going to be all right".

I improved greatly in the next few days, and even my roommate was sure that the prayers of my friend must have helped. I stayed a little longer in the hospital, where they treated me to prevent more blood clots. By this time, Christmas was upon us, and it was a lonely one. Bram and Ingrid came to see me as much as they could, but Eric was too young to be allowed to visit. Our friends had the family over to spend Christmas with them and I was thankful for that, but I really missed being with my family. Early in the New Year I was able to go home at last, but this time I recovered slowly. It was rather difficult without any help. After a while, a friend found a woman for us, who could come twice a week to help with the household.

Before I went into the hospital, I wrote some predated letters to my parents because I didn't want them to know I was sick. I felt it would have put more stress on them if they knew I was ill. I was able to complete these letters and send them as I was recuperating, but by this time it was too late for my mother. Between the Addison's and the dementia that had taken her mental capabilities away completely, my Father had placed her in a nursing home, and after only a few months, she died in May of 1963. I was distraught that I couldn't go to Holland, but I was still too weak to travel from my ordeal, and my Father told me not to feel guilty because her mind was gone a long time ago anyway. Her passing was a blessing in disguise. She had died without much suffering. Of course, I will always miss her, but I hope to meet her soul somewhere, somehow, after this life.

TEACHING MY LOVE OF ART

In September of 1963, someone asked me if I would teach art to a few young girls, as they had heard that I taught in Holland. At first, I was reluctant, but then I remembered how much I had enjoyed my classes in Holland. A few years before, Bram had given me an art correspondence course as a birthday present to help update and improve my talent. It took me three years to complete the course, but I did it, and got my diploma, which allowed me to teach art at my home. I remember that I had to ask permission from the instructors to take an extra six months to finish the course because of my illness, and that was all right because they considered me a good student, as long as I finished the whole course within three years.

So I decided to accept a few students, and this was the beginning of many years of teaching. I enjoyed it, and it gave me some extra income, which was welcome to meet some expenses we had incurred. I gave art lessons in the afternoons, after school for two hours, two or three days per week. Gradually, more and more students came to my classes, but where was I going to have room to teach them? For a while we had Eric's train layout in a room in the basement, and he loved playing with it. But after a while, he got tired of this hobby, so he decided to sell the set and use the money to buy his first car.

After the train was gone, I had more room to make a studio

for teaching. Bram made built in wall cabinets, and a show case for art objects I wanted to store or show off. A large ping pong table and a smaller one were put up, where the students worked on their projects. At first I only taught children, but later on, I took on some adults. Some of these people were very talented, and went on to art studies. A few became teachers themselves, which was fun for me to watch. It made me feel like I was doing something very worthwhile with my life.

Most of my students were enjoyable, and some of them stayed with me for years. I rarely had trouble with my students, but once I had a young boy whose Mother wanted him to take lessons. But I realized after a few sessions that he really didn't have any talent in art, and so it was hard for him to compete with the other students. Then one day, the boy started to play the piano that I had in the basement, and it amazed me how well he played for a child so young. When I got a chance, I told his Mother that he would be much better off taking music lessons, as art wasn't his forte. She got mad at me and told me that her son did have talent in art and that she would find another teacher. I felt badly about this, until some time later, I found out that the other art teacher had also refused to teach the boy. I think it's cruel to force a child to take lessons in a subject where they have no talent. Each person has his own talents, and it's better to let them apply themselves where their interests are, than to force them to fit into a preordained mold that isn't meant for them.

Another young boy in my class, kept wanting to draw fighting scenes, with people hurting each other with guns and knives, with bloody crosses drawn in the background. It bothered me because obviously the boy was unhappy and his anger and resentment were manifested through his paintings. I found out that the boy's Father was cruel and abused his son, so I spoke to his Mother, but she said that she couldn't do much about it. The boy left my classes soon after that, and I felt sorry for him, and wondered how his life was going, even though I was relieved that he wasn't with us any more. Years later, when he was a adult, he ended up in jail, and when they released him, he killed himself.

Another boy told me that he watched horror movies almost every night. Sometimes he was so sleepy in class that he could barely draw or paint. I decided to talk to his Mother, but when I discussed her son's problem, she told me outright to mind my own business. It turned out that she was hardly ever home, and the boy had to take care of himself. I tried to help the boy by paying more attention to him in class, which was easy because he loved art and did have a talent for it. Soon after that the family moved out of town, but I prayed that this boy grew up with a strong spirit.

Most of my students were happy kids though, and they kept me busy and young. The bonus was some extra money coming in, and the fact that I was home when my children came back from school. I also enjoyed my adult students, and some of them became good friends. There was an art teacher in Sharon, who was a well known portrait painter. I started to take lessons in her studio. For several years, about seven of us enjoyed her class and learned to do portrait painting from live models. All of these students were very talented. The models were mostly women, but sometimes a male model would pose. Each new model was drawn from a different position, so we could get the experience of creating the human body from all angles. Our teacher was not only a good friend, but also the best talent we could have wished for. It was also interesting to see the different styles and what each person saw through their eyes as they created their art. It was good for me, because I learned from the students that were better than I, and also saw that I had progressed further than some others, who were struggling to produce a likeness in their portraits.

One time, I felt good about the likeness I had created of our model, but when the teacher looked at my work, she told me that although I had painted the eyes and the nose well, the distance between the eyes was all wrong. Then she left it up to me whether I changed the painting or not. Those are very humbling moments when you get frustrated at your own shortcomings. On the other hand, I was so happy in those art classes, that later I missed going to them. I did learn how to capture the subjects most of the time. In later years, my portrait teacher moved to New Hampshire, and then I was on my own, because I never found another teacher that equaled the lady who had moved. We did keep in touch though, which was nice, even though she stopped painting after a few years.

In 1965, something frightening happened. Bram was building an enclosure onto our porch area, which had been open on three sides until now, the fourth side being the house wall, a door leading out from the dining room, and awnings used as windows. This gave us a nice place to be in all the seasons except winter, when it was too cold. Bram took special care in building this, to prevent leakage or rotting of the wood sections. To achieve this, he soaked both ends of the two by fours in molten paraffin, which had been heated to a temperature that was so high that when the supports were dipped about six inches into the wax, water boiled out of the end of the wood. This seemed to work very well, and when the studs were all treated, Bram turned off the stove of molten wax and went to the basement to cut the wood to the right size for the porch.

But the switches on the stove were made such that when a person turned them just a little bit further than "off", it became "high" again, and visually we were unaware of this peculiarity. The positive side of this dial location was that the children couldn't reach the dials at the back of the stove. I was busy ironing in the front room, when I caught a glimpse of a strange light out of the corner of my eye. I turned my head and was shocked to see the kitchen was on fire, and a huge flame was coming from the stove and licking at the ceiling. I unplugged the iron, and ran to the kitchen, where a towering flame was mushrooming from the can of paraffin. I screamed and yelled "fire", while running towards the basement stairs. Bram came running up the stairs, and grabbed the fire extinguisher that

I threw at him. He took it to the kitchen and aimed the spray at the stove, but it only succeeded in creating a dense black cloud of smoke, which made us cough. Then our attention was drawn to the wooden trim on the adjacent window, which had fiberglass curtains. Bram dowsed them thoroughly with water. More billowing black smoke rose up, but reduced the flame to the extent that Bram could grab one of my best cushions, and put it over the top of the can of paraffin, smothering the flame. I opened the back door, so Bram could take the can and throw it out on the grass, which would have been good, except some of the grass was dry and it caught fire too, which we hosed down immediately. Bram discovered later, that he had burned his fingers. Meanwhile, the heart of the fire wasn't out yet. We had always thought that the hood over the stove was made of stainless steel, but silvery streams of metal were running down on the stove, counter, and floor, where each spill started another small fire. By then, I had called the fire department, and was running upstairs to get the children out of their beds, hustling them out of the house. We also took our parakeet outside before he got asphyxiated.

Bram finally managed to get the fire under control before it became a real threat to the house. All this happened in about eight minutes, but it seemed much longer. As we stood outside coughing from all the smoke and gas we had inhaled, the fire engines came screaming up the driveway with sirens blaring. Several firemen ran into the house, and then placed fans in the hall that sucked the black smoke out of the house. They were surprised that Bram was able to put out the fire. The whole interior of the house was black from the smoke. When Ingrid came out, she noticed that one of the firemen was a boy she knew, so she covered her head with her hands, because she didn't want him to see her with curlers in her hair. Later, we all laughed about it, because it was so silly to be worried about your appearance when your house was on fire. The fire chief wanted to chop down the wall cabinets above the stove, because he was worried that some fire might be smoldering in there, but Bram convinced him that there was nothing behind the cabinets that could smolder and that the fire was definitely out and he said he would keep a close eye on that area, just to make sure.

What saved the kitchen and probably the whole house, was that fact that the cabinets were made of Formica instead of wood, so they charred, but they didn't burn. Our neighbors came running over to see if we were all right and asked if we would like to come and stay with them for the night. It wasn't really necessary, since the smoke had been sucked out, and it was mostly the kitchen that was damaged. The ceiling and walls were all black, not to mention the light, which was hardly visible. It took a professional team of three men ten days to get us back to the original condition. Luckily, we were well covered by insurance. They even wanted to give us more than we had claimed, since there was a lot of damage. What had been so scary was that the fire had spread so fast, and we couldn't turn the burner off, because the switch was at the back. Only when Bram choked the flame with the pillow, were we able to get things under control. We got a new stove, and this one had the controls at the front and which couldn't be switched directly from low to high heat.

Secondary to my love of teaching art, when the children were at school, I spent time caring for the house and working in the yard. I had always loved gardening, so I joined the Sharon Garden Club. We met once a month, except in the summer, had a lecture from a professional horticulturist, and enjoyed exchanging information on our favorite gardening topic. Twice we had a gardener over, who worked with the famous Arnold Arboretum in Boston, and he showed us how to prune small shrubs and trees.

Once every four years we would participate in the South Shore Flower Show near Boston. We were told to build small theme gardens, for instance, a rock garden, or a sunny garden, or a garden in a pond. Our club was successful at these shows and won several awards. Once in a while we would have "open house exhibits", which some people call garden tours, to raise money for the club.

Plant sales also helped our budget. It was quite an honor if your garden was selected for a garden tour, even though it was a lot of work. After a few years, I became chairman of the conservation for the club, and then vice president and finally president of the group. This gave me a lot to do, but I enjoyed it, although I did have some odd experiences. There were only Caucasian women in our club, not by design, but because there weren't many African Americans living in the area who wanted to belong to a garden club.

There was one African American family, though, who was very interested in gardening, and their yard was a showpiece. Our club gave a money prize once a year to the owners of the nicest garden in Sharon, and one year we decided that the African-American home had the nicest landscaping and that they should get the award. I proposed that we let this woman join our club at one of the meetings, and everyone agreed, so I approached her and asked if she would like to join us, and to my utter amazement, she looked at me angrily and told me that she wouldn't even think of joining our club, with quite an adamant tone in her voice. If she had slapped me in the face, I couldn't have been more hurt. This made me realize that we still had a long way to go with the problem of discrimination. The end result was that the woman never did join our garden club.

Meta, my sister, also had a problem with discrimination when she first came to America in the fifties. Shortly after she had settled in Houston, Texas, she went shopping one morning. As she was waiting for the traffic on a street corner, a black man came up to her and asked if she knew where a certain street was, and so she directed him on which way to go. Later, her husband got a call from his boss, telling him that he'd better keep on eye on his wife because white women weren't supposed to talk to black men. Meta was so upset, she was ready to move back to Holland, as she didn't want to stay in a country that was so narrow minded. Meta and I had been brought up in a area where there were mixed races, and we had been taught that you should treat everyone equally well, as you would your own friends.

Sometimes I wished that my Dutch accent wasn't so noticeable though, as some people had a hard time understanding everything I said, and I never managed to lose that accent. Bram spoke English with very little accent, but he was a born linguist, so it wasn't hard for him. Both of our children went through the stage where they protested, and were just a little embarrassed that their parents were a bit different from the average American, or more accurately, their friends' parents. I wanted to keep up our language, and so I would speak Dutch to the children, but I didn't want them to pick up on my Indonesian-Dutch accent. I taught Ingrid how to read and write Dutch when she was about eight years old. When we first came to America, Ingrid was only three and a half, and it was difficult for her, but the young absorb information so quickly when they are surrounded with a new culture that she learned the new language quickly from the other children.

I always thought it was a bonus for a person to be bilingual, even if they didn't use it every day. You can never tell when it will come in handy, and I've always been very happy that I taught Eric Dutch also, even though Ingrid got more lessons than Eric. But Eric is very smart and from the Dutch conversations we had at home, he picked up enough of the language that when he became an Eagle scout, he was chosen to become a host corps translator at the Idaho Jamboree in 1967. At the Jamboree he got a chance to exercise what he knew as a interpreter for the Dutch scouts. I was so proud of him, and later, he told me that he was glad, after all, that we had kept up with speaking Dutch at home. Several times, over the years, we went to Holland, and our family and friends were pleasantly surprised that the children spoke Dutch as well as they did. It makes me feel sad when I meet Dutch people here in the states, and their children don't understand their native tongue, but at the same time, I believe that people living here in America should learn English, and not be expected to communicate with foreigners in their language. It would always amaze Eric and Ingrid, when we went to Holland, that everyone there spoke Dutch, and English was the exception. This way they truly knew they were in a different country that spoke the language of their parents. The Dutch have to learn English, German, and French because they live in such a small country, and are surrounded by these other cultures within a short distance, so Dutch children learn four languages to make them functional in their surroundings.

When I started to teach art in my house again, some of the children decided to mimic my Dutch accent, which was rude, but it made the other students laugh. My solution for the problem was to give the critiques and instructions in Dutch, which they couldn't understand, of course. So I asked them if they understood me, everyone shook their heads, and then I told them that they had a choice of what language I would speak. Would it be Dutch without an accent, or English with a Dutch accent? From then on, I didn't have any more problems.

Of course, we had all kinds of ups and downs as the children grew. When Eric was still quite young, he was hit in the eye with a branch when we were on a hike in the woods. His eyeball looked all bloody, so we took him to an optometrist we knew quite well. After examining Eric's eye, he told us that if the branch had hit him one millimeter closer, he would have been blind in that eye. Another time, Eric was helping me get ready for summer camp, when he grabbed a thermos bottle I had filled, which didn't have the stopper in yet, and he spilled the hot liquid all over himself. I rushed him to our family doctor, who assured me that he hadn't burned himself too badly, but we were all more careful with handling hot fluids from then on.

Bram and I were very happy with the children's progress. They did well in school, most of the time. We hit a snag with Eric when he was in elementary school. He seemed to be slacking off with his studies, so we hired a special consulting teacher, and he told us that Eric was very intelligent and had a high IQ, but he wasn't applying himself because he was bored. He felt that we should put

Eric into accelerated classes, which we did, and it turned out to be the right solution, as Eric blossomed where there was more competition and he had to work harder.

Eric was always a risk-taker, and sometimes it turned out to be a blessing in disguise, and then there were also the times it was a disaster in later years. I was very proud of Eric when he helped to save one of his friends' lives. Eric had gone skating with his three friends, Jeff, Jon and Charlie. The lake in Sharon was frozen over well enough to skate, but the boys knew there were still dangerous spots where the ice was thin, and they needed to watch out for thin spots. At one time they were approaching one of those areas. Eric, who was in the lead, spotted a weak spot, and swerved to the right, He warned Jon to do the same, but Jon was watching some birds sitting on the ice, and he didn't hear Eric's warning, and a few seconds later, Jon fell through the ice. He tried desperately to get out, but the edges he grabbed for, kept breaking off, so he had nothing to hold onto. For some reason, Eric took some extra clothes in a small knapsack with him that day, and when I asked him why he had it with him, he just answered that "It was just a precaution, you never know if someone might need it".

When Jon fell through the ice, Eric asked Jeff to hold his feet while he crawled towards Jon, flat out lying on the ice to distribute the weight. Eric used his knapsack as an extension, and still holding on to one of the straps, threw it towards Jon. At that time Jon was only 3 to 4 feet away from Eric. Jon was just able to reach it. This all happened in only a few minutes. Jon's clothes were soaking wet, but Eric had brought along an extra sweater and woolen hat, and the boys quickly shared their other dry woolens. After this rescue, Eric just wanted to continue skating, as if nothing had happened. At first, Jon agreed, but then the shock of Jon's cold plunge sunk in, and they all agreed to return home and get Jon warmed up. It wasn't until much later that Eric told me what had happened, because he was afraid that I would have been upset, and he was right. When I asked him how he had known what to do, he answered that in the Boy Scouts he had received training for ice rescues. As for Jon, his parents were both overjoyed that Jon was safe, and angry with Eric for having put Jon in that situation in the first place.

Ingrid did quite well in school, and she had a lot of friends that kept her busy with a lot of activities. The schools in Sharon were highly rated, and had excellent teachers. When Ingrid was in the fifth grade, her teacher asked to have a meeting with me, as there was something happening that disturbed him. So I went to see him, and he told me that Ingrid had befriended a girl that was having a bad moral influence on Ingrid. I talked to Ingrid and she agreed to stay away from this girl, but I felt badly because the girl was a problem child, and it was my duty to protect my daughter from unhealthy influences. But I was glad that the teacher was alert enough, and had high enough standards, that he stuck his neck out to speak to me.

One day, years ago, I went shopping in Boston, and as the afternoon faded, and the shops began to close, I remembered an item I had forgotten to buy. I rushed to the counter and the salesgirl got snippy when I couldn't decide which product I wanted, her impatience repulsed me. But I looked into her face, and noticed how tired she was, and commented, "You must be very tired", and then added, "I really don't need this item right away, so I'll come back for it another time. Why don't you go home and take a nice rest?". Just as I turned around to leave, she started to cry, telling me that I was the first person that day, who had been kind to her, and she thanked me. We parted as friends, and each time I went shopping in Boston, I made sure that I went by her counter, to say "Hello".

I had another encounter with a woman which turned out unhappily. Over the years, I've tried to forget the experience, but I still feel hurt when I think of it. I was asked by a member of our church, to give a demonstration of my needlework at the church fair, where everybody was showing off their skills at handicrafts, and I thought it would be fun to do, and to see what other people were doing with their hobbies. For two months, I worked on my embroidery, preparing for the fair. I put the pattern on an old tea cloth, which I covered with embroidery. This was easier for people who didn't draw their own patterns, and it showed that one could use something old and revamp the piece into something that looked like new. I was looking forward to the fair, but a few days before the show, I was called by someone who told me that there wouldn't be any room for my work after all. She suggested I could share a booth with somebody else, but nobody would help me. I asked one older lady if I could share a booth with her, and she was adamant that she had done this by herself for years, and wasn't interested in sharing. Needless to say, I felt hurt and left out. All my work was for nothing, but then the lady realized how disappointed I was, and she offered to show off my work herself. I thought about this for a while, and then accepted her offer, took my work to her house and explained how I had done the work, saying "It is for the church, after all". A few days later, this woman took my work to her table at the church fair. But I was so disgusted that I didn't even go to the fair at all.

The fair turned out to be a big success, and I was told that my work had drawn a lot of attention, and folks were asking why I wasn't at the fair and why somebody else was showing my work. This came to the attention of a church official, who asked if I had been ill. When I told her what had happened, she was shocked, and couldn't believe how I had been treated. It turned out that this woman was the president of the women's club of the church and was my foe. There had been space for me, but she didn't want me to know because she was jealous of my children and me. Our minister found out what happened, and he had a chat with her, I assume the talk was about Christian ethics, because she apologized to me, which was water under the bridge by then.

Each year our church had a Christmas fair, and I would help with the "White Elephant" table, where all kinds of miscellaneous items were sold. I remember one happy moment when an old lady came to my table, and she was looking for a particular pattern of china. She wanted to look through the huge stack of unmatched pieces. She said that she was only missing one piece from a set and she had been trying to fill in this one piece for years. Amazingly, she found the plate she was looking for, and I will never forget the happy look on her face when she found it. I was pleased that small miracles do happen, once in a while.

GROWING WITH CHILDREN

The children went through the normal stages that parents can expect from children and teenagers growing up. There was a short period where Ingrid became very difficult, even to the point that she told us that she hated us, and of course, we were hurt by this, even though we knew that she didn't really mean what she was saying. We knew we had to do something about it, so we told her that perhaps it would be better if we sent her to a boarding school for a while, where there would be strict rules and regulations. Bram asked around and found that there were four good boarding schools in Massachusetts. At first, Ingrid wasn't opposed to the idea of these schools. So Bram took her to visit one of the schools, where they were shown around and met with the principal. The weather was nasty, with freezing temperatures, and on the way back home, it started to snow, which made the trip quite unpleasant. Ingrid was very quiet during the trip, and the next day she asked if she could "please" stay home, because she didn't like that school, and she promised to behave better if we would let her stay. The change in her attitude was miraculous, and it was just as well, because Bram and I could never have afforded to send her to that expensive school anyway.

Years later, we found out that the school we had visited had a serious drug problem, and several of the students ruined their lives by succumbing to temptation. God was good to us, and prevented us from making a big mistake after all. We tried to keep the children busy in a practical way. We made sure that they didn't squander their time away in Sharon Square, where some of the young people would make a nuisance of themselves because they were bored. We took the children with us when we went on short vacations, and we really enjoyed their company.

For quite a while Ingrid had wanted to learn horseback riding. She pleaded with us, to buy and keep a horse. She reasoned that we had a three acre lot and a two car garage, so there was plenty of room for a horse, but Bram knew that there were a lot of expenses related to horses, which made the price of keeping one much higher than a young person realized. Not only was there the feeding and the grooming of the animal, but the veterinarian fees were high too. We didn't feel we were well enough off for such a luxury. But when we saw how serious Ingrid was and how much she longed to have a horse, we decided to do something about it. For several weeks, I looked around to see if there was anyone who needed help caring for their horse, and at the same time would allow Ingrid to learn how to ride. I knew a man, who went by the name of "Gardener Gaines". He had two horses, which he actively showed, and in between, he gave riding lessons, so I approached him and asked if it would be possible for Ingrid to help take care of his horses. At first, he said that he didn't need any help, but I kept asking him until he agreed to give her a chance, on a trial basis.

Ingrid was so delighted when we told her the arrangement, so for a long time I took her to the stables several times a week. Each time I picked her up from the stables, she reeked of pungent horse odors, which filled the car, but I didn't mind, as one look at her delighted face told me that she was very happy. Not only did she learn how to take care of horses, but later she participated in horse shows, as she learned how to ride better, and this sport took up a lot of her free time. I remembered wanting to learn how to ride when I was about her age, but the only opportunity I had was in Indonesia, for a very short while when I was about eighteen. Then we moved back to Holland, and riding was out of the question then, because in Europe, riding was only for the very rich. So I was very glad to see that my daughter had the chance to do what I hadn't.

During these years, I had to deal with a lot of pain from cystitis attacks, which usurped a lot of my strength. What irked me the most, was the fact that my bladder problems were caused by an error made by the specialist who had performed my hysterectomy. The large benign tumor had pushed my bladder out of position, and it wasn't until later that I had another operation to correct the reoccurring bladder trouble. I could have sued the original physician for his error, but I believed that with God's help, I would be able to cope with whatever happened to me.

When Ingrid graduated from high school in June 1966, I was so proud of her. There was one thing that had bothered me over the years, and that was the fact that Ingrid had needed to wear glasses since she was thirteen. She had the same near-sightedness that Bram and I had, and she felt the same way about wearing glasses that I had when I was her age, unattractive and plain. I felt so badly that she had to deal with this inherited gene deficiency. When there was a school dance, Ingrid was considered a "wallflower", and it was so sad when she came home and I could see the sadness on her lovely face. Her girlfriends didn't wear glasses, and the boys were fickle enough not to ask a girl that wore them to dance.

In later years this changed, as more and more people started wearing glasses and the frames became more attractive. It seemed so unfair that looks seemed so important in the growing up years. Kids can be so cruel to each other. But then something happened that brought luck our way, as contact lenses were invented and would soon be available to the public. As soon as I learned that the contact lenses were safe, I made sure that Ingrid got them. It wasn't long before Ingrid got used to them, and it made an amazing difference in her self esteem. As she felt better about herself, her beautiful green eyes sparkled and she felt more confident about her popularity with the boys.

We shopped around for the right college for Ingrid. She was accepted by a girls' college in New York State, Elmira College. She stayed there for two years, but then in 1968 she decided that she would rather go to a coed college, so she moved to the University of Massachusetts at Amherst, where she stayed for another two years. Bram, Eric and I would go up to Ingrid's University to see her from time to time. She was doing well and seemed to enjoy herself. There were some unpleasant times, like the time she and three other girls decided to rent a house off campus. She wanted to have more freedom, so she rented the house in her name, which made her responsible for everything, of course. At first, everything went well, but late the first night, something went wrong, when she went to her bedroom and found one of her roommates, also a student, busily engaged in taking some kind of drugs. She knew that if the police found out this was happening, she would be in a lot of trouble, so she ousted that person fast enough that nobody found out what had happened. Then another one of her roommates decided to use Ingrid's car, without permission, crashed into several parked cars, creating a sizable amount of damage. It was much later that the girl who had caused the damage was able to pay her back for all the costs incurred. Although these were all unpleasant experiences, I felt they taught Ingrid valuable life experiences that helped her to grow up. She really started to be able to take care of herself, and Bram and I were very proud of her.

The winter of 1969, I was in a lot of pain from more bladder problems. I stayed a week in Norwood hospital, and when I came home, I was only there a few days when I had to be rushed back to the hospital, hemorrhaging from complications. After another week in the hospital, I came home, and this time I recuperated quickly. The doctor had told me not to go out in the cold weather, and I didn't see any problem with this, as I was at home most of the time. But then Ingrid had to go back to the University after her vacation and I needed to drive her because Bram had already committed to take Eric and his friend Mike skiing in Vermont. By this time I felt good enough that I told Ingrid that I would be able to take her. It would only take two hours. The weather wasn't too bad, and so far there was only a little snow on the ground. The sun was shining, and it was a crispy cold day, as we started out, taking turns driving. But just as we were getting close to our destination, we were stopped by a grim looking highway patrol officer. Ingrid was driving, and she asked him what the trouble was, and he asked her "Where is your new sticker?". It was the first day for new registration stickers for the year, and they were stopping a lot of people, asking them to comply, or they would be in trouble.

The stickers were at home, and Bram was supposed to have put them on the cars, but he had forgotten. He had always taken care of this, so I didn't give it a thought. I told the officer that we had them, but my husband had forgotten to put them on the car. The officer was not empathetic, nor did he believe me, so he ordered Ingrid and me out of the car, into the freezing cold and all of a sudden I had a very bad feeling about the whole thing. It didn't help any when I told the officer that I had to be careful about catching a cold because I had been operated on recently. He still didn't believe us, and told us that we couldn't drive the car without stickers, and that we would have to call a garage and have the car towed. We were also told that we couldn't leave the car beside the highway, and adding insult to injury, he handed us a ticket, as he drove off, leaving us stranded.

We found a telephone nearby and called for a tow truck to come, and then returned to the car, where we waited in the snow and cold. It was getting late, and Ingrid had to be back for her classes, and I assured her that I would be all right until the tow truck came. So Ingrid called one of her friends to pick her up and she left. When the truck finally came, he took the car to his shop, and showed me where the bus stop was located. I had to wait an hour before it came, and then sat for several more hours before we reached Boston. By this time, it was late in the evening, and I still had to walk to the train that would take me home, only to find out, it wasn't scheduled to leave for Sharon for at least two hours. My energy was running out, and I wasn't feeling very well, so in my desperation, I took a taxi home. I was glad that I had enough money with me to pay for the ride.

When I got home, I realized that Bram could also get in trouble with his car, when I saw the stickers sitting on the bureau. Luckily, Bram had told me that he would be staying with our dear friend Madeleine in Vermont. At first I called the ski slope, but they had no way of contacting Bram, as there were so many people on the slopes, it would have to be a real emergency for them to go after him. Then I remembered that Mike's father was going up to the ski area the next day, and I might be able to catch him before he left. He was just heading out the door when I called and he said he would be glad to take the stickers to Madeleine's home. Bram would have them that evening, thank goodness. It all worked out very well, and Mike's Father was thanked profusely for being such a help. As for me, I got past my time outdoors without any more health repercussions with the help of some rest. The next week, Bram and I drove out to Amherst and picked up the car at the gas station where Ingrid and I had left it. We placed the stickers on the car, drive it back to Sharon, and thought we were done with this episode.

This, however, wasn't the end of the saga. Bram felt badly about forgetting the stickers, especially when Ingrid was summoned to appear in a courthouse in Northhampton, because she was the one who had been driving when we were stopped. When Ingrid went to court on the appointed day, she sat through a whole day of cases from burglary to misdemeanors. The judge never called her name, so she went up to ask what happened, and sure enough, her case was buried an the bottom of a large stack of cases. When the judge found out how old she was, he told her that she had wasted her time coming because she was under age to represent herself, and needed to come back with her parents in two weeks.

Two weeks later, Bram had to take a day off work for a one hundred mile trip to Northhampton at nine in the morning. They arrived at court just in time to sit for another whole session of listening to cases about store thefts and run away girls. Finally the judge asked what they were doing there. Ingrid told him the story of the missing sticker, and the judge asked if the car was insured, to which Ingrid replied that it was. The judge seemed confused about why the officer had made such a big deal about the situation. So Ingrid repeated that it was because the sticker was missing. At this point, the judge had heard enough, and said that the officer should have been more lenient and he dismissed the case. Our attorney lodged a complaint against the court for the barbaric treatment I had received, just having been released from the hospital, and I do believe that this helped the courts demeanor about our case.

Meanwhile, Eric was about to start his college experience, and decided to attend Colby College in Waterville, Maine. Like his father, his interests turned towards Chemistry, after trying out some other subjects that were of interest to him. The first year he lived on campus, like most freshman. During the second year he and his roommate house-sat for a family called Lambert and took care of their farmhouse for the winter. He told us that this place was so isolated that outside there was complete and total silence; so quiet that one's ears would ring trying to hear something. Often, if you looked into the night sky, you could see the northern lights. The third and fourth years he was happily ensconced in the cozy basement apartment of Bea Georgantis's home. Bea had owned a candy shop in town and was a very amicable woman. When Eric got his bachelor's degree in Chemistry in 1974, we were very proud of his efforts.

MRS. SULLIVAN

Before I write about my encounter with Mrs. Sullivan, I want to relate a story a I remember from my days in Indonesia and a family I knew there. When I was in high school in Malang, my history teacher had a remarkable experience. One afternoon, he was sitting on his porch when an old beggar approached him, saying "Tabe Toeani", which meant "Hello Mister, would you like to have your fortune told?". My teacher, Mr. Schweitzer, being in a happy frame of mind, told the beggar to continue, his curiosity having gotten the better of him. The beggar took his hand, and studied the lines of his palm, told him that he would have a winning lottery ticket and would soon be very rich. He also told him that one of his colleagues would marry one of his very young students. Then, as he rose to leave, he told the man that he wouldn't have to teach any more, and would return to his own country and be very happy. At first, the teacher was skeptical, but he went out and bought a lottery ticket anyway, and sure enough, everything the fortune teller had told him came true. Years later, when I was visiting Holland, I did go to visit him, and he was indeed, very happy. Meanwhile, many people had tried to find this beggar, but he had disappeared, never to be seen again.

The native Indonesian people are noted for having special clairvoyant capabilities, which they quite often use in their lives. The experience I just described convinced me that the human race has more than the five senses, and that most of us don't take the time in our lives to develop and use the other senses that are capable of taking us to a higher awareness.

When Ingrid graduated from the University of Massachusetts in1970, with a B.A in French Education, Bram and I went to the ceremony. It was very impressive and we were so proud of our daughter, who had grown into such a beautiful adult. Ingrid was very impressed with a young man that she had been dating while she was in college, and when we first met him, he seemed nice, but as we got to know him better, we had serious doubts. We were worried that Ingrid might be serious enough about him to think of marriage, but we didn't want to hurt her feelings. We did worry about her future, were she to choose the wrong mate with which to spend her life. As time went on I got increasingly desperate, and realized that to intervene directly into Ingrid's affairs would have estranged her, and caused her to rebel. I really did not know what to do. I discussed my concern with one of my Dutch friends, Marina, who had also lived in Indonesia. She told me that she had a friend that might be able to help us. This friend was working at New York University in research on Parapsychology. She was quite renowned for using her talents to help people by giving advice to those who sought her expertise. Her name was Mrs. Sullivan, and she lived in Rhode Island, close enough that I could make an appointment with her. Bram was not very happy about it because he thought she might be an impostor, but I convinced Bram that we should at least try to see if she could give us any insight to our dilemma.

So Marina and I made arrangements to pay Mrs. Sullivan a visit in the summer of 1972. My friend had her own problems to deal with, so off we went. Mrs. Sullivan was a remarkable woman, who was modest and sincere, and had a lasting effect on both of us. We were amazed how much she could tell us, which included some events that had happened in my past that even my parents weren't aware of. We estimated that about 85% of what she conveyed to us was accurate.

She told me that she had seen a woman with blue eyes and beautiful blonde hair, who loved me and wanted so much to help me. She had described my maternal grandmother perfectly, Then she described a beautiful farm with lots of cows and chickens all over, and then all of a sudden it was gone overnight. She seemed slightly puzzled, but I understood, as this was the farm that my paternal grandfather had lost in a gambling bet one night long ago, leaving his family poverty stricken for the rest of their lives. This was one reason why only two of his ten children survived to adulthood.

She also saw stormy weather, and a dike with large boulders, and an older man, also a relative, who was always out in the bad weather. I recalled that my maternal grandfather was always fighting the sea by keeping the dikes in order. Then she saw a lot of turmoil surrounding and upsetting me a lot, which was caused by a female blood tie, a daughter, who was involved in a friendship which would be harmful for her. The male of the couple had a roving eye, and wouldn't make my daughter happy, but she warned me not to interfere with the relationship because it would make things worse if I railed against the situation. She told me to back off and mind my own affairs, otherwise my daughter might make the mistake of her life. She said the girl was going towards the relationship out of anger and spite, and if we would back away, she would come to her senses and break off the relationship of her own volition. It would take a few years before she would find real happiness, and sure enough, all this came to pass.

Mrs. Sullivan also prophesied that my daughter would eventually marry before her twenty sixth year. Her husband would be in business and would have beautiful teeth, which made him very attractive, and they would be happily married. Meanwhile, she said that when my daughter broke up with her current boyfriend, she would decide to go to Europe, Paris to be exact, to study French. Ingrid would go with a girlfriend named Alice, according to Mrs. Sullivan, but that they would end up quarreling, and go their separate ways. Ingrid would have a very good time in Europe, but would end up having to come back quite suddenly, and she would continue her studies at a University, where she would meet her future husband. This also all came to pass, which amazed me.

She also saw a young man, a blood relative, surrounded by medical books. Somehow, in later years, he would be involved in medical research, and would work very hard to finish his studies in order to find a job which he would really like. He owned a station wagon right now, but something was wrong with the machinery, and that they were looking in the wrong place for the problem. They should not look at the back end of the car, but instead under the dash for the problem. Then she said that she saw a broken back, but it would work itself out. This boy wouldn't marry his current girlfriend, but later he would marry a nurse.

Then she saw a nun who first wore a white habit, and then a black one, and later yet, a white one again. This was a symbol of religious difference, but would do no harm to anybody. Eric later married a physical therapist, who was Catholic, so this also came true.

Then she told me that I had a blood relation that had a beautiful colorful bird, and that she should be careful about her health, because she had a throat condition, and that the problem with her husband could be solved by giving him a room of his own. And by the way, this woman needed to watch her blood pressure, because it was bad! This all described my sister and her life's condition.

She also predicted that Bram was under a lot of strain at his work, caused by pressures from a difficult boss and a colleague. It would get better later on, when his boss would be removed from his position, and Bram would end up happily in retirement, and we would travel several times. Looking back, she was very accurate.

A book that a friend had borrowed and was lost, would be found at a later date, in a place she hadn't looked, and the important dates in my life would be 1916, 1932, and 1974. Happy years would be 1977 and 1978. I was born in 1916, 1932 was the drama with the soldier friend, and Ingrid got married in 1974. In 1977 and 1978 I was very happy because my art classes were full and my family was doing very well.

She told me that I would suffer a big loss around Easter time and another around December. My Mother died in May, 1962, and my Father died in December of 1963. As for my health, she told me that I would have problems with my bladder, (how well I knew,) and my back and bones. She scolded me about working too hard, but said it would be better in later years.

We would buy some real estate which would turn out to be wrong, and we would be cheated. But within two years, after a lot of problems, we would sell the house, which would be the right thing to do. What we actually experienced was the loss of some land in New Hampshire, built a house on Cape Cod, sold it, and bought our home on Sanibel Island in Florida. So she was very close to the mark on this one.

And by all means, she told me that I should and would write a book that I had always wanted to write. After my death, my children and their children would benefit from it philosophically and economically, and that I could even have a chance to turn my work into something more commercial, like film rights, but she warned me to make sure that nobody stole the contents of my book. The last years of my life would be quite happy, and that I would reach a definite senior citizen status, but would not be too elderly. The house in Florida would be a source of much happiness with its view of a large body of water, which is definitely true.

When it was my friend's turn to speak to her, Mrs. Sullivan astounded her as well. She said there was a small boy who was playing in a garden, but once in a while he was very sad. He felt tears of sorrow for his Mother, whom he loved very much. This was preventing his soul from being really happy. This woman had lost her five year old son a few years before. Then she was told that she wouldn't get the divorce she was seeking, but in later years she thought the woman would remarry, but she wasn't positive about that. My friend was very surprised that the psychic would mention a divorce that wouldn't happen, but as it happened, soon after that, her husband died suddenly, so she didn't get a divorce, after all.

Mrs. Sullivan made such an impression on us that we wanted to know something about her too, and she told us that she had lost her husband and had two children. She was very calm because she was sure that their souls would all be together in another life. She believed that each person on earth goes through many different lives, and what we make of our lives while we are here is up to us, and that God places us here on earth for a purpose and sets a goal for each of us which will have an impact in our next life. She told me that I had gone through many lives. I wanted to believe this, but I wasn't sure, so I asked her what would happen in the next century. She said that she believed that there would only be small wars, especially in the middle east, but World War III wouldn't happen. There would be some conflict between Russia and China, but that it would be resolved. The next century would be more peaceful, and medical science would make great strides towards curing many types of illnesses. I hope so much that Mrs. Sullivan is correct about her predictions so the human race can unite to create a much more peaceful world than we have now.

The encounter with Mrs. Sullivan took place in 1972, and quite a few of the predictions that she made at the time had already come true. Then she told me that I was a clairvoyant like my Grandmother Kooreman, and that quite a few times in my life, I had foretold things before they had happened. I have a very strongly developed sense about people, and the vibes I get about people when I first meet them is usually correct. But the times when I had ignored my feelings for some reason or other, I had gotten hurt from not paying attention to my sense of truth. As I got older, I learned to be more careful about my associations with people in my life by listening to myself. Believing that my life has a purpose, I hope that when I am gone, I will have born some fruit from my existence in this world. Mrs. Sullivan's predictions were valuable to me, grounding my thinking, to be sensible, realistic, and still stay open to the fluctuations of truths concerning predictions. My Mother had deep faith, and she used to say that there were so many mysteries between heaven and earth. The human race still has a long way to go, and although the twentieth century accomplished amazing feats, hopefully the coming years will bring about a united understanding of how to resolve the negatives of life, so that all people, everywhere can be at peace on this wonderful planet.

INGRID'S WEDDING: JUNE 15, 1974

Mrs. Sullivan's predictions about Ingrid turned out to be uncannily accurate. After graduating from the University of Massachusetts in 1970, she got a job working as the assistant to the Dean of Students at Newton College of the Sacred Heart. I was not pleased at all of her choice of boyfriends; that was the reason that my girl friend went with me to see Mrs. Sullivan in the first place. But as soon as I stopped my opposition to Ingrid's boyfriend, a remarkable thing happened. Ingrid became suddenly less interested in this young man, and decided to change her job and her life drastically. Ingrid had worked hard, and had saved some money in the two years since she finished college. So in 1972, she came up with a plan to go to work and study in Europe for a few years. She planned to stay with my cousin, Fransje in Neuchatel, Switzerland, and look there for a job to sustain her for a time. Ingrid had a friend Alice who was to accompany her.

With the money Ingrid had saved, from the sale of her car, and with a little extra from Bram and I, we sent Ingrid off to Neuchatel to experience Europe first hand. To Brush up on her French, she studied intensive French, at the Alliance Francaise, in Paris for 6 months. By coincidence, this was the same school where Eric had studied for a month almost a year earlier.

Then Ingrid moved on to Neuchatel and stayed with my cousin's family, the Hartmann's. Fransje and Erich Hartmann had two sons and a daughter. Ingrid got along famously with them, and the experience changed Ingrid's life. Before going to Neuchatel, Ingrid had no clear direction. She was a hard worker, interested in French and in education, but she really did not know what she wanted to do with her life. But after her Europe experience, it was a different story. Ingrid chose to continue her education.

After her Neuchatel experience, Ingrid stayed with my cousin, Medi Bartelds in Rome. Medi had a job with the Dutch Consulate in Rome, and Ingrid greatly enjoyed meeting Medi's friends and experiencing Rome firsthand.

When Ingrid returned to the US, she wanted to pursue a master's degree and in the spring of 1973, she applied to various graduate programs throughout the country. When her acceptance to the University of Pennsylvania graduate school of Educational Administration was received, Ingrid was ecstatic. It was her dream come true!

Ingrid moved into the International House on the campus of the University of Pennsylvania at the Philadelphia campus. After only a few months, Ingrid began writing home about a new young man she had met there, Fernand.

When Ingrid graduated in May of 1974, she had already planned her wedding a month later in June, to Fernand, in the First Congregational Church of Sharon, Massachusetts, where she had been a regular attendee growing up, also participating actively in the Senior Fellowship youth group. It was a dream come true for Ingrid to return to her hometown for a storybook wedding. It was June 15, 1974.

Ingrid's wedding was a small, intimate affair with friends and family invited from both Fernand's and Ingrid's family. Uncle John, our eccentric travel agent from Chicago, was there; so was Aunt Meta who came all the way from Houston. There were students there from Fernand's school, the Wharton Business school at the University of Pennsylvania. Fernand's parents from El Salvador came. And Ingrid had a variety of best friends and International

A NEW LIFE IN AMERICA

House friends from all over the world.

The ceremony went off without any problems. Fernand's sister, Jackie, was a bridesmaid, and Eric was an usher. Ingrid's Maid of Honor was Trink Laxner, her best friend from the days at Elmira College. Fernand's best man was Fernand's classmate also studying at the time at Wharton. The reception would be held outdoors in my garden on Maskwonicut Street.

It seemed to me as if I had worked all those years in the garden to trim and refine it for just this one occasion. I had removed literally tons of rocks from the New England soil. I had planted ground cover on the hillsides, and pines along the top of the hill around the house. Flower banks circled the house, the driveway, and the edges to the woods. In June, everything was blooming, everything was trimmed and in its place. The garden was at its peak, finally. Eric and his friends helped to set up the music, to take care of all the little details, and help make it all run smoothly.

Fernand had taken a job at IBM in Philadelphia, and Ingrid was interviewing for jobs in elementary school administration in the Philadelphia suburbs. They had picked out an apartment in Philadelphia in Society Hill. Ingrid and Fernand were bright and optimistic and filled with hope for the future. It was a wonderful time for my daughter, and I relished watching Ingrid be the radiant and attractive bride that she had become. It was a very happy day too, for Bram and me.

ERIC GRADUATES COLBY: MAY 1974

After four years at Colby College, in Waterville, Maine, Eric graduated with a degree in Chemistry. During his years there, Eric was uncertain about his future, possibly medicine, definitely science, but Eric felt restless for not knowing what his specific direction should be. Bram took action in this regard, and set up a number of aptitude tests for Eric that might give Eric feedback about what career would fit. These tests showed great creativity and science aptitude, low aptitude for clerical type work. It did not help Eric very much to know that the tests showed good potential in a scientific or health care field. Eric already knew that.

When he graduated from Colby College, Eric decided to take a year off from school to work in the medical field of Endocrinology at Massachusetts General Hospital in Boston. The Bullfinch Building, where he worked, was famous for being the place where ether was first used on patients. During that year, he took some biochemical courses at Boston University. Eric realized early on that his job at Mass General had no long term future, and so he decided to get his Master's degree in Biomedical and Chemical Engineering from the University of Rochester in New York. He applied and got a full scholarship starting in the fall of 1975. Two years later, in August of 1977, Eric joined his first company, Mobay Corporation, in Pittsburgh, Pennsylvania. Later, this company was called Bayer.

BRAM RETIRES, ERIC STARTS WORKING, AUGUST 1977

Bram retired from his job at Cabot Corporation in 1977, just as Eric started his professional work career. There was a farewell party for Bram at Cabot, and I was very proud of him. It was clear from the comments of the people at this party that Bram was much loved and honored over the years that he had worked hard at Cabot. When Bram first retired, it was hard for him to make the adjustments in work and lifestyle. But after only a short while, Bram started to enjoy this "free life". Soon after Bram's retirement, we decided to spend more time in our new house on Sanibel Island, Florida. The construction had just been completed, and we started spending time there in the winter months.

A few years earlier, in 1973, our next door neighbor in Sharon, Massachusetts had purchased a small lot of land on a pond on Sanibel Island. She bought it with the expressed desire to have us as neighbors, and so she proceeded to convince us to buy this lot from her. We had spent some time with our friend on Sanibel, and had become interested in the Island. After some discussion, our friend convinced us to buy the empty lot from her. Bram established a payment schedule and in just a few short years the lot was paid off. We proceeded to build a "Michigan Home" style house on this lot overlooking a pond. The contractor performed well, and the house was completed the same year that Bram retired in 1977.

We owe it to our friend that we actually ended up living on Sanibel, and I am still grateful to her for nudging us in that direction.

OUR FIRST GRANDCHILD, MICHELLE

Our first grandchild, Michelle Suzanne Sarrat, was born September 13, 1978, but it was not easy. Fernand's mother, Irma, was already staying with Ingrid and Fernand in their house in Berwijn, to help with the birth. It was, after all, her first grandchild too. Michelle's birth turned out to be full of complications. They were, in fact, very similar to the problems I had had in delivering Ingrid. Once in labor, Ingrid's doctor discovered that her baby was in a breach position. After taking some X-Rays, it was decided that a C-section operation was necessary. So, Michelle came into this world upside-down and with completely loose hips, just like Ingrid had done so many years before. She had to wear leg braces, just as Ingrid did, for the first 6 months of her life. And, to make matters worse, the wrong needle had been used on Ingrid's spine in administering the spinal anesthesia, with the result that Ingrid had a period of severe spinal headaches. So, Ingrid had to stay a little longer in the hospital. It was under these circumstances that I arrived in Berwijn. I had to drive from Ingrid's house to the First Pennsylvania Hospital in Philadelphia with Fernand's mother, Irma. Fernand couldn't come with us because of his work. He gave me a slip of paper with directions to the hospital. I had a great deal of trouble finding the hospital in the first place, and then even more difficulty finding a parking space. So when I arrived, I just parked the car in an empty field, and hoped for the best. When I saw Ingrid, she was lying flat on her back and was in terrible pain. I knew exactly what she was going through, because I had had a very difficult delivery too. It was not until the next day that I got to see my grandchild, Michelle. She was beautiful! And, I was present when the head of neurology attempted to repair the spinal leak in Ingrid's spine. She was moaning in pain and I felt so helpless thing to help her. But it all ended happily, because Ingrid got instant relief from that procedure. The next day, Ingrid and the new baby came home. Irma and I stayed for a few weeks to help out and we had many interactions, both good and bad with each other. So the two grandmothers were there together to share in this happy event. I thought it was ironic that this birth was almost an exact repeat of my own delivery with Ingrid.

TROUBLE COMES IN BUNCHES

The year 1979 turned out to be one of the most difficult years of my life, or so it seemed at the time. It was right up there with the height of the war years. We had sold our home in Sharon and bought a piece of land overlooking a lake in Marsten's Mills on Cape Cod. It was a beautiful spot and we had high hopes of building a nice vacation home to escape to when the weather in Florida became too hot. We found a contractor to build a two story home for us, but then we had to go through all the machinations of red tape and decisions about building a new home, which took a lot of time and patience. In the beginning we didn't have too many problems, but as the house progressed, we suddenly were hit with several pressing impediments. The building code for Cape Cod was very strict and they informed us that our plans weren't acceptable. The plans they would approve entailed drastic changes to the original architecture. Our builder was upset, but managed to work with the plans to rebuild the house, but we were unhappy with it. The plan wasn't half as nice as the original, and it seemed so disconnected, that it even looked ugly in some places. Bram and I were renting a home in a nearby town during the building process, and almost every day we would go to the building site to watch how the builder was doing. Then we suddenly got a phone call from Florida that changed our lives drastically.

In October of 1979, Eric was in South Carolina on assignment, working as a project engineer for Mobay Corp. building a chemical plant there. Eric had recently learned to SCUBA dive on a vacation in 1978 in the Virgin Islands with two of his Colby College friends. Being the curious risk taker he was, Eric's intellect was fed by a great variety of outside adventures. He had a small mishap spelunking in a cave in West Virginia, having fallen onto a ledge, landing on the thoracic part of his back, resulting in a sharp pain that diminished over the next few months, so Eric thought nothing of it.

Eric commuted each day in his yellow VW Rabbit diesel and lived in a beach house on Isle of Palms in Charleston, South Carolina. Eric rose to the sounds of the ocean waves, and ran at the edge of the surf for several miles each morning. On one weekend in October, Eric had made plans to go scuba diving with friends in the limestone caverns near Lake City, Florida. He had rented the equipment, but then he decided to return his equipment to the dive shop because he was too tired and wanted to get some rest. His friends at the dive shop encouraged Eric to go with them anyway, saying how interesting and how exciting it would be, diving in limestone freshwater caves. Eric agreed to go, but later he came to a fork in the road, left to go back to town for a rest, and right to join his friends for the weekend of diving. After a twenty minute pause, he chose to turn right to meet his friends, one of whom was an EMT, another a navy trained diver. The weekend started out well, making two dives in caverns down to 150 feet. They were down long enough that they had to depressurize on the way up. Then, before the next dive, they had to stay on the surface for two hours, to blow off nitrogen, before they could dive again. They swam around in the shallows and swung from a rope into the water, to pass the time. One spot was about a forty feet in diameter, about 80 feet deep in the center, with a lip around the perimeter that was about three feet deep. Swinging on a rope from an overhanging tree, Eric decided, at the last minute, to dive instead of jumping, and overshot the deep middle, landing directly on top of his head on the shallow lip. The EMT kept him in the water, while help was sought, and the next thing he knew, he was in the hospital in Gainesville, where we were called.

The call we got told us that Eric had had a scuba diving accident. We knew right away that something drastic had happened, and it turned out to be worse than even I had imagined. Eric told us that he had a diving accident, that his back was broken and that his legs were paralyzed. I asked where he was and told him we were on our way to him without even knowing exactly where Gainesville was. Bram had to stay in Cape Cod to keep an eye on the builder, who was starting to show signs of not being reliable, I called Ingrid and we decided to meet halfway, and go together. Unfortunately, Bram had made a mistake with the airline schedules, so we didn't meet until we got to Florida. Eric's girlfriend Beebe met us at the airport, and as we drove, she warned us not to be too upset when we saw Eric because he was in a rotating bed. I will never forget the terrible pain we felt when we saw Eric so broken up. He seemed to have a good attitude and was demonstrating great courage for the position he was in. Later, I talked to the neurosurgeon, who was impressed with Eric's reaction when he was informed that he had a broken back, and that he would probably never walk normally again. Eric had retorted, "Okay, Doc, now tell me what I still can do, and we'll take it from there".

Ingrid stayed with me for several days in a motel, and Eric's girlfriend also joined us for a few days. Ingrid and Beebe drove Eric's bright yellow Volkswagen Rabbit Diesel back to Charleston, where Eric had rented a beach house, and then on to Pittsburgh. I stayed two weeks more with Eric. At that point, the Orthopedic surgeon agreed with us that it would be better if we transferred Eric to Massachusetts General Hospital in Boston. This Hospital could offer him the best neurological care possible, and to give Eric the emotional support that only Boston, where his friends and family lived, could provide. A close friend, who ran a travel agency, arranged for an air ambulance to transport us to Boston. For me the trip in the air ambulance was traumatic, I was very upset. Eric had gotten sick during the flight, and I realized how diminished in function Eric had really become from this accident. In Boston, we were met by Bram and our friend. Everyone felt so badly. We were all in tears.

Eric arrived at Mass General Hospital towards the end of October, I remember that there were Halloween decorations up everywhere. Eric was placed in the orthopedic ward with many other patients, in an older section of the hospital. For the first six weeks that Eric was in the hospital, he was strapped to a Stryker Frame. This device, designed to avoid pressure sores from lying too long in one position, was changed every two hours. First Eric would lie face up on his back looking at the ceiling. Then two hours later, Eric was flipped around so that he was lying on his stomach facing down, looking at the floor. Every two hours the Stryker Frame was switched, day and night, for six weeks.

One day we saw large cockroach running under Eric's Stryker Frame. We also noticed a very thick layer of dust under this contraption, just inches under Eric's face when the Stryker Frame was in the down position. This was inexcusable for a hospital, we felt, and so we complained. Also, although Mass General is an excellent hospital, the residents and attending physicians were very busy, overworked, and scarcely had time to spend with Eric. They would peek in for only one minute at 5:30 or 6:00 AM asking Eric how he felt, even though he was usually barely conscious from sleeping, and then would move on. This infuriated Eric, who had many questions for these physicians, and wanted to find out as much as he could about his injury. For the amount of money being charged to be there on the orthopedic ward, Eric felt he should have received more attention.

In addition, Eric had only a few possessions in the hospital, not even a full set of clothes since his transfer from Gainesville, FL. So when his swiss army knife turned up missing one day, he was again furious that even in a hospital setting there could be theft. Eric was living in a very small world at the time. He did not move out of his Stryker Frame for six weeks, never out of a small corner of a two -person room, not until the time came to move from the Stryker Frame to a normal bed. The shift from being horizontal for six weeks to just sitting up again was enough of a change to cause him to feel very lightheaded and dizzy. This change was a taste of the many adjustments that we all had to make in accepting that Eric had become a paraplegic.

Moving Eric to Boston for more family and friends' support turned out to be a very good thing for Eric. Many of his friends from grade school, high school, and from college, from Mass General Hospital itself, from Grad school, and even from Pittsburgh were able to visit on a regular basis. In fact, Eric received so many visitors, and so many calls in the first few weeks that he was in the hospital, that the hospital operator came by one day to see Eric. She wanted to meet this person who had caused so much traffic on the telephones. This support helped Eric to realize that he was still the same Eric, the same person, with the same interests and experiences, and friends,... just now changed in a way that made him move about differently.

Eric adapted amazingly well to all the changes, and to life in the hospital. The staff learned that Eric could speak some German, and so when a German couple came from Europe for special laser treatments for an inoperable brain tumor, Eric was there to translate. In fact, four years earlier, right out of college, Eric had been a research technician at Mass General Hospital, and he was still in their database for speaking French as well, so he also translated one time for a French Canadian man down from Montreal. It turned out that because Eric was able to help the hospital staff with his language skills, he got a feeling of being useful, something that Eric really needed badly. I remember feeling that it was as if God had opened another door for Eric and also for us to learn to cope with the heartbreak that Eric's accident had caused.

After nearly two months in the hospital, Eric started to feel better and to regain some strength. He had to accept the fact that he was now a paraplegic and had to learn to manipulate a wheelchair. Eric had a lot to learn in order to become independent again. Daily sessions at physical therapy were helping, and soon, Eric would need to be moved to a rehabilitation center to complete his transition back to "normal" life. He learned to get around in a wheelchair in record time. He had always been a sportsman and he had a will to survive. This helped him to start to build a future for himself. While Eric was in the hospital, Bram and I visited the hospital many times, almost every day. Eric arrived at Mass General Hospital in late October, in the fall, but the weather was getting colder and as time went by, Bram and I found ourselves driving up from Cape Cod in the winter through the snow and ice. Upon arriving at the hospital each day, we had to park our car quite far away, and it would take about 20 minutes of walking to reach Eric's hospital room. Before the snow started to fall, we would walk part of the way along s strip of grass with some clover in it, and each day I would look over at the grass and find four-leaf-clovers. As a child I loved to look for four-leaf-clovers because I believed that they brought the finder good luck. Even Bram found it remarkable that each day I seemed to find at least one four-leaf-clover, even finding one day a five-leaf-clover. It was as if God was sending me a message of good luck, a message of hope for Eric. Everyone, including me, was amazed at the number of four-leaf-clovers that I spotted during my walks along the strip of grass.

The fall and early winter of 1979 to 1980 was a terrible time for all of us. Not only did we have to deal with Eric's accident and its aftermath, but we were exposed to all of the suffering of all the patients in that hospital, on Eric's floor, and throughout the hospital. Sometimes when we were in the waiting room, we met people who had to deal with all sorts of sicknesses and death. It made us appreciate more than ever before how fragile life is, and how one's life can suddenly change drastically. This realization also hit home because of two close friends who happened to be in the hospital at the same time, fighting for their lives against cancer. One lady,

Mary Bell, was one of my closest friends in Sharon, Massachusetts. She was back for another battle with her long time cancer. The other was Gordon Hawes, a history teacher who had taught Ingrid in high school, and who had become a close personal friend as well. He suffered from leukemia. I spent my time each day at the hospital between three sick beds. On Eric's ward was a lady who kept crying out for help. She was disoriented and would cry constantly "Help me, Help me,...Help me, Help me...." This crying out would go on day in, day out, it seemed. As long as the patient was awake, she would cry out these words. Much to everyone's amazement, one afternoon she stopped this routine briefly, and instead said: "I can't find my shoe!" Everyone on the floor, patient, staff and visitors were amused at this sudden change in her pattern. Right after that (maybe she found her shoe), she continued with her repeated cries for help. Thinking back on these times now, it amazes me that we made it through as well as we did. Maybe the time during World War II prepared us already.

After eight weeks in the Mass General Hospital, in Boston, Eric was moved to the New England Rehabilitation Center in Woburn, Mass., north of Boston. Rehabilitation focused on training Eric to live on his own and to function independently. We had never before realized how complicated life becomes when one cannot use the lower part of your body anymore. At the same time it amazed us how Eric adapted to a different way of living. Eric worked hard to become independent and progressed well according to his therapists. Eric's girlfriend came over a few times more to see Eric, but it was difficult for both of them.

When Christmas time came, Eric had moved into the rehabilitation hospital in Waltham, Mass., but we had all decided as a family that we would like to spend Christmas together. By this time, Eric had been moving around in a wheelchair for two weeks, and with much negotiating with hospital physicians, therapists, and staff, we managed to arrange for Eric to visit his sister in Berwyn, PA for the holidays. Ingrid and Fernand had purchased their first house there late in 1977. Bram and I were worried about Eric's safety so soon after the accident, but his specialists gave him permission to travel. It took some doing to get him to the airport and into the airplane to fly to Philadelphia, and then on by car to Berwyn, PA. But with the help of Alexander Bock, our travel agent friend, it was all organized, and all went smoothly.

Eric was very happy to be out of the hospital after two months. Ingrid had extended the sofa-bed in her living room where there was more room for Eric to maneuver his wheelchair. Eric's girl-friend, Beebe, came over to see Eric; she was a big help. It was clear, though that Eric was still a hospital patient. He had to be turned every two hours during the night to avoid bedsores, and we had to help him with his daily routines. All of us pitched in to help, but it was a difficult time for all of us to see Eric in this condition. At the same time, it was a very special Christmas for us. We were grateful that Eric was still alive and still with us. I myself would have given anything to trade places with him, to give him my legs which still worked, and to take his place as the paraplegic. It's one of the most heartbreaking things for parents when one of their children is hurt.

In the days right after Christmas, Bram was not feeling so well. He thought he was coming down with the flu or that it was just tension and nerves. Early in the morning, he took a walk outside, thinking it would help him to feel better. But after this walk, he still did not feel well.

Eric's girlfriend, Beebe, was a nurse and she advised Bram to see a doctor as soon as possible. She suspected some trouble with Bram's heart. Because we were all so very busy taking care of Eric, we all thought that Bram was not feeling well because of the strain he had been going through. We returned to Boston several days later. The trip went smoothly, and I drove with Bram to Boston to pay his company doctor a visit. Eric was now back in the rehabilita-tion center in Woburn.

I was still convinced that Bram just had a case of the flu, or some bad indigestion. But after Bram's doctor examined him he told me that Bram had suffered a heart attack several days earlier. Then he said "We have to keep Bram in intensive care for a while for monitoring". I could not believe what was happening to us, after all that we had gone through in the past few months. I knew that we had to just try to make the best of things, no matter what. Of course, Eric was also upset when he heard of his father's heart trouble. We had hope though, because Bram had always been very healthy, and he was still relatively young.

That evening, with Bram staying in intensive care and Eric in the rehabilitation center, I had to drive alone back to the rental house on Cape Cod. I remember praying as I drove, asking God to help me and guide me, because I felt I could not do it all myself. I was leaving the two most important men in my life behind in their respective hospitals, and whatever befell us now would fall on my shoulders alone. To add to my feeling of hollowness, the drive to our rented house was terrible. There was a snowstorm in full force just outside my car. It was dark, and there was a menacing, howling wind driving giant snowflakes on to the windshield, faster than the wipers could take them away. I prayed silently that I would make it back. Struggling through the weather reminded me of wartime in Holland.

The next day I drove to the spot where our new home was being built. There I met the builder, who told me that he was not going to finish building the house unless I paid him in advance the remaining construction fee. Bram had told me already to pay the builder if he asked, so I wrote out a check for a large sum of money and gave it to him.

Afterwards, I drove back to the hospital and I went straight to the intensive care unit where Bram was. Just before entering Bram's room in the intensive care unit, I met a nurse who stopped me and told me that I had the most impossible husband. When I asked why she said that she had found Bram early in the morning doing his daily exercises next to his bed. The nurse said that she herself nearly had a heart attack when she saw Bram exercising. The physician's instructions had been for Bram to take it very easy and to rest. I started to laugh and agreed with the nurse that Bram was impossible, but also that I knew now that he would be all right after all. This turned out to be true, and Bram told me that he felt fine. He wanted to get up and leave to go home. It took a few days, but finally his doctor allowed him to go home.

In the meantime, I noticed when I went to check up on the building process for the new house on Cape Cod, that the builder was nowhere to be found and only a few workers were still there. It gave me an unpleasant feeling that something was wrong. It turned out that after I paid the builder the day before, I never saw him again. He just disappeared, taking our money with him and never finishing the house. When Bram returned home, he found out that the builder had used our money to pay for bills he had from previous building projects. Because several sections of the house were not finished, Bram had to arrange with another construction crew to complete the job, all at extra expense. We were paying double for this completion work, since the original contractor disappeared with our money.

Someone told Bram that the builder had paid off all of his previous debts with money that he collected from about 10 other families, all of whom had uncompleted construction projects. I felt especially bad for one of his victims – a lady who had given him her entire savings for payment on a small house she wanted built. Later I heard that she was bankrupt, and never did get the house she had dreamt of having. I do hope that his conscience caught up with him though, and of course, I had to tell Bram our bad luck. He has always been a very strong man, and sloughed the whole matter off as just a material thing, which could be replaced. What had happened to Eric was much more important.

It was quite a shock for Bram and me when it dawned on us that we had dealt with a crook, who had stolen a large sum of our money. The local police told us that there was a warrant out for his arrest, but as far as I know, he was never caught or punished. We heard a rumor a year later that he was working in a bar in Florida, but who knows...

Every other day we traveled to see Eric, while the new construction crew completed the house on Cape Cod. These two activities kept us very busy for the next two months. Eric progressed very well in the rehabilitation hospital and this pleased us, but we all still had difficulty accepting the fact that Eric had become a paraplegic. I had then, and still have now, a strong feeling though, that somehow in the future there will be a cure for him. Science was, and is still, making big steps forward and I would not be surprised if in the year 2020 there will be cures for many illnesses.

I was so proud of Eric, and how he handled the challenges before him. He was courageous to deal with this ordeal, and there wasn't a day that he didn't have visitors stop by. They helped him tremendously during his rehabilitation. The other patients on Eric's ward in the rehabilitation hospital broke our hearts with their stories and situations. Most of them were far more impaired than Eric, with higher levels of spinal cord injuries, and therefore less function. One older man, married with children, had fallen out of his hammock one afternoon and suffered a spinal cord injury when he fell on his back. Another young man, twenty years old, had been in a motorcycle accident, and had a spinal cord injury with extensive nerve damage. One side of his face was frequently very cold, while the other side would be hot and drenched in sweat. Another patient, a young lady of twenty, had been four-wheeling in a Bronco when it over-turned. She hit her head and broke her neck, sustaining a spinal cord injury high in her neck so that she became a quadriplegic. She was a beautiful girl and after her accident only had limited use of her arms, and very little use of her hands. Eric stayed in touch with her and told us later that she became involved in social services and that she adapted quite well, even finding a companion to live with her and help her in her daily functions.

One day, the whole group of spinal cord injured patients went out by van to a restaurant to socialize and to try to function in a public restaurant. I happened to sit next to a handsome young man who had been a marine. Now a quadriplegic, he hardly could move his arms, and with great difficulty he tried to feed himself. He spilled his food all over the table, and I felt terrible for him. Seeing how these patients struggled at that restaurant to be normal made me realize how much suffering there is, and how few people see these struggles. I admired these patients and their caretakers tremendously for their courage and their perseverance. I felt that faith had a great deal to do with their courage. As long as you know that you are never alone, that you are God's child, you can endure more than you realize.

At last, the house on Cape Cod was nearly finished, allowing Bram and me to move all our belongings from the rental house to our new home. But we were not at all happy with our new home. It was badly planned due to a last minute change to comply with some local building ordinances about the locations of the front door and of the garage. The living room did not look right, and when you entered the house, you were right in the kitchen, which was a nuisance in many ways. The basement was supposed to have been finished, but it was only half done. The workmanship left something to be desired, so that the whole house looked cheap. The unfinished driveway caused lots of dirt to be tracked in. Bram and I had planned to spend the rest of the winter in Florida, but of course, we had to stay with Eric, and we had to finish the construction of our new home. It was a stormy winter, and very often the winds howled across the lake and against our new home. I had a forlorn and desolate feeling living in that new house during this time. We realized that this house was too isolated with a lake in the back and fields all around. To top off our problems flocks of Canadian Geese bothered us because of their voluminous droppings on the edge of the lake. But for the time being, we had to make the best of it living in this new house.

Eric stayed with us for several weeks after he was released from the rehabilitation hospital. To cheer him up, I decided to have a dinner for all the people that visited Eric and that helped Eric over the past four months of his recovery. They all came to feast on an Indonesian Rice Table, which I had prepared for them. They all spent the afternoon at our new house. It was very cold and the lake was frozen over with a thick sheet of ice. Everyone went out on the ice, including Eric sliding along in his wheelchair. Bram and I worried that Eric's wheelchair would fall through the ice, but Eric's friends assured us that it was safe and that they would keep an eye on him. The afternoon passed quickly and we all enjoyed seeing Eric with his friends out on the ice. It gave Eric quite a boost to know that he could still go out and have fun with his friends and family.

Shortly after this party, Eric decided that it was time for him to get on with his life, and to return to work. He left us to spend a week with his girlfriend, Beebe, who was studying to be a nurse midwife in Washington, DC. This week with Beebe was a difficult one for Eric. It was the first time he realized how different life had really become, and what mainstream life would really be like. Several months later Beebe and Eric decided after much thought to cut off their relationship. I was relieved that Eric took it quite calmly. I understood why Beebe could not cope with Eric being in a wheelchair, because her own mother had contracted polio the year that Beebe was born. Beebe had known her mother only as sitting in a wheelchair, and to add an additional wheelchair to her life was more than she could bear. When she explained these reasons to me, I understood very well, and did not blame her for ending the relationship. Although Bram and I never saw Beebe again, we heard later through Eric that she never did get married, but continued to work as a nurse/midwife.

Eric had agreed to meet Bram and I in Pittsburgh, at his town home there. We would get there a few days early while Eric was in Washington, DC. Bram and I stayed in a hotel near the airport in Pittsburgh. Bram had to travel to Detroit for some consulting work, leaving me alone to find Eric's townhouse north of Pittsburgh. On the day that I was to go to Eric's house it was snowing very hard. The snow made the roads slippery and dangerous. Somehow, I lost the sketch that Eric gave me with directions, so I tried to use a map of Pittsburgh, although I am not very good at reading maps. This trip to find Eric's house turned out to be one of the worst trips I ever had to make, being all alone in a snowstorm in a strange city, trying to find my way to a house I had only visited once before. On top of all that, the roads in Pittsburgh are unbelievably difficult, going steeply up and down, winding around all the hills, and not being very well labeled. All of these things did not give me any peace of mind. Although the distance from my hotel to Eric's house should have taken about 25 minutes, it actually took me over two hours. I stopped several times at gasoline stations before I finally reached the area called "Hemlocks", where Eric lived. When I could not find Eric's street address anywhere I stopped at someone's house to ask for directions, only to find that there was another Hemlock's a short distance away from the one that I found. I started to feel really desperate and lonely, I was wet from the snow, and I started to pray that I could please find Eric's house soon. By some miracle, just after that prayer, I found the right Hemlocks, the right street, and Eric's house.

Eric had told me that there had been renters in his house since he was working in Charleston, SC., but that they would be out by the time that I got there. The renters had been informed of when Eric would move back in, as stipulated in the original rental contract that Eric had with them. The neighbors were supposed to have a key, but when I got there, the renters were still in the house. I saw some activity in the townhouse, so I rang the doorbell and a woman came to the door. She let me in and said that she knew that I was coming. She told me that she, her husband, and her five-year-old son were just about to leave. I looked around inside the house and was appalled to see an unbelievable mess everywhere. Obviously the house had not been cleaned for a very long time.

I talked with the renters for a short while before they left. They told me that they were writers and hated house work, which explained why the house was so filthy. When they left I looked around and could not believe the mess that I saw. How people could live in such a condition was beyond my understanding. I opened a kitchen cabinet and saw a jar of molasses which had fallen down from the highest shelf, leaving a stream of sticky substance all over the lower shelves, gluing and sticking together everything. Under the kitchen sink I found a bag with rotting onions, filling the surrounding air with an incredible stench. All over the kitchen and in some other rooms as well, I found thick globs of dried-up oatmeal porridge, mostly about a yard up from the floor on the walls and cabinets. I wondered if the five-year-old had just played with his porridge, or if there had been some great family food fight resulting in all these porridge gobs. It seemed to me that the best way to make Eric's townhouse habitable again was to simply start cleaning. I chose the kitchen as the best starting point, since it was by far the worst. The kitchen took two days of hard scrubbing to make it clean again.

When Bram came back from his trip to Detroit, most of the cleaning was completed. Eric returned to his townhouse after a week and we were glad to see him again. The following Monday, we drove Eric to his work, reporting first to the company physician who examined Eric for fitness to return to work. His first day back, after nearly 6 months away, was both traumatic and very touching for Eric. His colleagues met him at the door with a large sign saying "Welcome Back" and he spent the day getting re-acquainted with his work place. Eric arranged a car pool, and soon he was going to work each day, getting used to his new routines. Eric had taken driving lessons at the rehabilitation center, and in one week Eric had purchased a car and had it outfitted with hand controls. Being able to drive again meant a great deal to him.

During this time, the weather was just miserable, with snow and ice everywhere. Altogether, it was a very difficult time for all of us, although Bram and I were grateful to be able to help wherever we could. But we also felt that Eric resented us, because he was sliding backwards, in a way of speaking, to the time he was a child, and we as parents cared for his every need. Emotionally, it helped Bram and me to work hard to clean Eric's house from top to bottom, which took a while.

Eric started more and more to be able to take care of himself. Driving a car again made Eric feel more independent, and Eric tried more and more to do things by himself. When he would carry heavy things on his lap in his wheelchair, I would worry. One time, we went to restaurant with a step in the entry to get in. Eric tried to get over this step with me pushing from behind, but could not make it and started to tip over backwards in his wheelchair. I started to panic, because I could not hold him by myself, but fortunately two men standing near the entrance quickly pitched in and pulled Eric into the restaurant. I still worry about Eric when I think about him almost falling over backwards.

Eric made arrangements at a local Rehabilitation Center called Harmarville to continue physical therapy. Harmarville was very new, and very well equipped with both personnel and equipment. Over the period of a month, Eric gradually really started to be able to take care of himself and the day came when Eric told us that although he greatly appreciated our help, he wanted to live his own life independently again. Bram and I realized that this was very important for Eric, although he had to adapt to many changes. So Bram and I decided to leave him. I did talk with his neighbors, giving them my telephone number. They said that they would keep an eye on Eric, and to help him, and to let me know of anything untoward happening. So with a heavy heart, in April of 1980, Bram and I left Eric on a cold snowy day in Pittsburgh, and returned to put the finishing touches on our house on Cape Cod.

Back on Cape Cod, we worked for several weeks to finish the landscaping around the house. There was a lot of poison ivy on the shores of this lake, and we were told that we were not permitted by the township to remove the poison ivy because it was such good ground cover. The fact that I am extremely allergic to poison ivy did not matter to the township officials. It took us two months to completely finish the house. We wanted some of our friends to see the place, so we arranged for a dinner at our home one night. Some of the guests came from far away, so they would stay with us overnight. Shortly before the guests arrived, and just before I was cooking the main part of the meal, the power went out. This left us in the dark, with an unfinished meal. Bram fired up the wood-burning stove in the basement and used it to finish the cooking. We ate the meal with our guests by candlelight, and in the end everyone enjoyed themselves, having pitched in anyway they could to make the evening a success. This evening reminded me of the war years, of many similar dinners where we cooked over an even smaller wood stove. Thinking back on this years later, it was one of the few good memories this new house offered us.

Ultimately, we decided to sell this house for many reasons. Real estate doesn't move at all in the winters at the Cape, so we got the house ready for sale in the spring. As the good weather returned to come back, and the house started to look attractive, the coup de grace, which reminded us that we really did want to sell, took place around Thanksgiving of 1980. Eric had driven his car from Pittsburgh to visit us for the Holidays in Marston's Mills in the new house. Directly next door, a house was being rented to a single man. Bram had helped him to start his car in the winter, and as a result, this man was very nice to us.

Then one day he called us to tell us that he was planning to have a large party with lots of friends, and hoped that this party would not disturb us. Bram turned down his invitation to attend, and said that we would not mind the noise. So the next day many cars pulled up to this neighbor's house, and we started to worry about the large number of these cars. There were two live rock and roll bands playing at this party and it was very loud. We closed all the windows in our house to keep out the racket, but even that was not enough. Another neighbor from down the street called and asked us if we knew what was going on. We told this second neighbor that we knew about the party, but he said that he was getting so worried that he was thinking about calling the police. Soon afterwards, the police did come, and the noise quickly subsided. But as soon as the police left, the loud music and noise started right up again. Many more people came, and groups of them moved to our neighbor's back yard by the shore of the lake. We suspected that the sweet smelling cigarettes that they were smoking was marijuana. The situation got more and more noisy and raucous, and soon two men had stood up, confronting each other and started to fight with each other. Some of the people started to scream, and soon the police came by again. After the second visit of the police, the music stopped for a brief time, but again, after the police left, the music started all over again. All this happened in a relatively short period of time, and we were quite surprised when, quite suddenly, at around midnight, the music stopped and everyone left the party. We found out later, that the police had been summoned a third time, and this time they broke the party up, and told everyone to go home. But that was not the end of our troubles.

We thought we had gotten through this with no real problems, until the next morning when we looked out to see that our mailbox had been demolished, and three cars parked in our driveway had been vandalized. One car had a hose hanging out of the gas tank, with the water still running, so the mixture of gas and water was overflowing. The second car was even in worse shape. It had been filled with water, and when we opened the door, water cascaded out of the vehicle, like we had just pulled it out of the lake. Eric's outside mirrors and his CB antenna were broken off. We thought it must have been revenge on the part of some of the party attendees. They must have thought that we caused the police to show up. Our young neighbor wasn't sorry enough to do much about the damage his friends had caused, and was asked by the owners of the house to move shortly thereafter. We felt that this house wasn't meant to be for us, and that we could pay for the children to visit us in Florida whenever they were able to get away.

Another reason we decided to sell the Marston's Mills house was that it was financially unfeasible for us to have houses in both Florida and Cape Cod. We were disappointed about the hoards of tourists during the high season, and the city had a water quality problem in that area, which was getting worse every year. We thought we would rent the Cape house while we were in Sanibel, but it turned out to be a real headache. The renters were sporadic, and some were irresponsible about the care of the house, leaving more than minor problems for us to fix. The city of Marston's Mills wasn't thrilled that one of the renters of our house had dumped their garbage in the pond, and they had left the water faucet running for two weeks at a time, leaving us with a tremendous water bill. Fortunately, one of our neighbors told us what was happening, but we still had to pay the bill.

Christmas of 1980 was good. Eric was settled in Pittsburgh, and Ingrid was happy with her second child, a little girl, named Jennifer. Jennifer was born on November 18, 1980, during a snowstorm when Ingrid and Fernand were living in Danbury, CT. They had moved there from Berwyn, PA earlier that year. Fernand had been transferred to a new position in IBM. Bram and I had anticipated being there for the birth of our second grandchild. This time, there were no complications, although Jennifer was also delivered by C-Section. We all spent the Thanksgiving holiday together, which was quite nice, and then we knew that we had made the right decision sell the house on the Cape. We didn't miss having to deal with the lonely feeling of winds howling around the house, and snow piling up everywhere outside.

Early in 1981, our real estate agent finally found a buyer for the house on the Cape, but the buyers wanted to pay much less than we had been asking. In addition, they wanted us to leave an heirloom candelabra that was not included in the sale, so we had to negotiate to pay them to buy another chandelier instead. All this went against the grain for us and then it got down to what was attached to the house, and what wasn't, in order for us to keep some of our sentimental mementos that they claimed should go with the house. Eric had brought us some beautiful driftwood from his hikes at Flagstaff Lake in Maine. There were some cast iron plaques of birds, both of which we could prove were personal items, but an old closet that Bram had built to keep his tools in, wasn't as significant to us, so we let them have that.

Finally, Bram and I were so desperate to get the sale over with, that we agreed to sell the house for less than we wanted. The real estate person turned out to be incompetent in her dealings, not having asked for a large enough deposit. It should have been about 10% of the total price, but she made a mistake. So it ended up costing us, but we were so sick of dealing with bargaining, that we just wanted to get on with our lives, and we let it go. I did have some bad feelings about these greedy folks who bought the house.

Later, I was talking with one of my previous students, who worked for a lawyer, and this man just happened to be the attorney for the people who had bought our house, and he said that these people had a reputation for being the worst clients with whom they had ever dealt. Our bad luck seemed to be coming in bunches, as the old belief goes, and we hoped that we were at the end of our misfortunes. Hectic days followed; we emptied the house, getting ready for garage sales, and there were some special plants that I thought I would sell, when a lady came by who was very enamored with my plants, even though she had a limited budget. I found myself happy letting her have them for a lesser price. When I saw the joy in her eyes at inheriting the responsibility for these special friends of mine, I didn't even feel badly about thinning out the landscaping a little bit.

SETTLING IN SANIBEL 1981

In August of 1981, we moved to Florida for good. We sold both cars, and bought a new one, as Bram was retired now, and we didn't need two. The day we arrived in Sanibel Island, it was very hot, and it was even hotter when the movers arrived two days later. One of the movers asked if we were really going to stay because he couldn't understand how anybody could put up with the heat in Florida. For a few seconds, I tended to agree with him, but then I remembered how nice it was to live here in the winter, when there were blizzards up north, not to mention the aches and pains one experiences in the cold climates of New England.

There was so much to do, juggling the furniture around, deciding that we preferred the furniture from the north to replace the Sanibel interiors. After several months of garage sales and donations, we felt comfortable with our surroundings inside, and had laid the sod that we hoped to develop into a really beautiful garden.

We made new friends in the Sanibel area. Bram joined the Rotary Club and with the help of our minister, we became charter members of the new Congregational Church, which didn't even have a building when we joined. They were meeting at another church, but eventually a new church building was built, and the membership grew, much to our delight. There were several people in our neighborhood who we befriended too, and we discovered that most of the people were from the northern states, like ourselves. A few of them still had properties up north, and others, who had financial setbacks, like ourselves, had decided on one residence. Once a year, our development, called the Gumbo Limbo Association, held a picnic, and everyone was welcome. Houses were built all around the lake, and there were lots of new people to befriend. The development was named after the Gumbo Limbo tree, a beautiful shade tree that grew in our area. The word itself means "peeled skin", and the tree was named appropriately because its bark peeled in layers, like someone who had been sunbathing too long.

The summers in Sanibel were hot, so most Florida homes have air conditioning. Since Bram and I had hobbies and projects in progress, we didn't mind being closed in the house during the scorching summer season. It did take some time though, to get used to the different lifestyle. Because Bram was retired, we could choose what we wanted to do, one day at a time. We worked on our garden and took a lot of walks early in the morning, when the birds congregated. The animals in our area seem to sense that they were protected, so they allowed us to get closer than usual. I couldn't resist painting again, and collected a few students, too, teaching art to them.

I was grateful to be able to see my children every summer. We would stay with them for a few weeks and then Ingrid would come with her children during their winter school vacation in February, and visit us. Our grandchildren really enjoyed the beaches, which were considered to be the best shell beaches in North America.

INDONESIAN DEJA VUE 1981

About this time, Bram and I decided to take a trip back to Indonesia. I had always wanted to see the land I considered to be "my country". We decided to go via Holland, to see Bram's sister, and other friends we hadn't seen in a long time. We'd had this idea for quite some time, but kept postponing the trip because we were so busy, but we felt we should go before age prevented us from traveling. We made arrangements with the travel bureau, and two days before we were to leave, we got a call from Bram's niece, telling us that Bram's sister had died suddenly from a heart attack. This was a shock because his sister had always been so healthy. We couldn't change our flight plans because they were non-refundable, and we had already missed his sister's funeral. Since we had planned on staying with her, we had to call other friends, who offered their home for our lodgings.

A few days later we met with a group of Dutch people at the Schiphol airport to leave for Indonesia. There were thirty of us, and we were the only couple from America. Everybody was curious to meet us, although they knew we were Dutch because the "Boonstra" name was very Dutch, indeed. We had received a list of the names of the people in our group in advance, and I noticed that one of the passengers were friends of my parents. When I inquired, I was pleased to find out that this person was the son of my parents' friends. We had many conversations about our mutual connections during the twenty one-hour-flight to Singapore. From there we flew to Djakarta, better known to me in my youth, as Batavia.

As I stepped off the plane, I was moved to tears because I hadn't seen Indonesia in forty-five years. All those years fell away, and it was like I had returned to my childhood again. The sounds, smells, and even the language suddenly came back to me, like there was no time in-between, so I guess our childhood leaves a stronger impression in our minds than we know.

After a while, I was even able to help some of the group with bargaining when we went shopping. Most everyone in the group was amenable and we got along well as we traveled to the other islands of Java and Sumatra. I saw a house in Bandoeng where I had lived when I was sixteen years old. I saw the high school in Malang. These places seemed miniaturized in my view, because I was smaller at the time, and because the Banyan trees had grown so enormous that they dwarfed everything around them.

We also went to Bali, which had a beguiling beauty of its own. Unfortunately, the tourists had spoiled some of the native responsiveness. One group of Australians, in particular, were very inappropriate about their dress, noise, and politeness towards the local people, and I could see expressions of disgust from a race of people who were graceful and handsome, and apparently quite a bit more civilized than their visitors.

I was sad to see that the country had been neglected since the Dutch had left. The roads were in quite a state of disrepair, and the trains were dirty and falling apart; not what we were used to, and it was disappointing to have to deal with the discomfort that it caused travelers. When I spoke to some of the older natives about this, they said that they would be very happy if the Dutch were back, with its order and protection keeping the country in order as it had years ago. The younger Indonesians' attitude was less polite towards the Dutch. They wanted to rule their country themselves, but they weren't doing such a good job. It was still a country of diverse races, languages, and religions, but they didn't seem to have the cohesiveness needed to create a more peaceful place. I realized that I could never live there again because the Indonesia that I knew as a child did not exist any more. With some nostalgia, the Dutch speak of the times in Indonesia as "tempo doeloe", or "times gone by", times that will never come back again.

After Bali, we flew to Sumatra, where we saw the so-called Charm of Hazau. The Dutch people called it the "water buffalo hole", probably because there were so many of that species living there. The buffalo were used for turning the soil of the rice fields in a place where the landscape had been created by an earthquake long before. When I was five, my parents had taken me for walks through these fields, surrounded by high cliffs, like the Grand Canyon. Later, we took a bus to the famous Toba Lake, considered to be one of the most beautiful lakes in the world. It was formed by an earthquake, is very deep with crystal clear water, and high hills surround it. The climate is temperate, making it a famous tourist attraction. In the middle of the lake lies a small island called "Samosir", where old graves lie. I was glad to be able to show Bram the splendor of this typical Indonesian attraction, especially since his Mother had spent part of her childhood there, and had also loved the environment.

Bram's grandfather became a sea captain in Indonesia and married a Chinese woman. He placed his family in Soerabaja, on the northern coast of Java. Bram's mother spent her childhood there, up to her teenage years. She always told stories of her youth in Indonesia; so Bram had some ideas of what to expect in Indonesia. Bram could speak some Indonesian words, because his Mother had spoken some of the language at home and had sung him songs as a child. These songs contained both Dutch and Malayan words – which only the people of Indonesia could have understood. White people weren't as welcome in Indonesia anymore. They called us "Blanda's" now, and as we flew back to Holland, I felt sad that the place I had loved so much, had changed so.

BACK IN SANIBEL

We had a busy and exhausting time when we returned to Sanibel. Before we left, we had decided to add an annex to the house so that I could have a studio for working and teaching, and Bram wanted to have a room where he could keep all his books and records.

The builder who had constructed the original part of our home was very good and we wanted him to do the addition for us, but he was reluctant because he wasn't working on Sanibel Island anymore. Despite this, we managed to reason with him until he agreed to do it. We were lucky, because he was one of the best in the area, and when his people came, they had to remove a small forest of Australian pines to make room for the new annex, creating a marvelous view of the lake. Where they had dug for the foundation, there was a hug pile of dirt, which Bram and I decided to use to fill in a swampy area near the lake, resulting in more land on our property.

As soon as the new addition was finished, we brought the stored furniture and many boxes to our new rooms, but before we had time to get everything arranged, some guests arrived. First Eric and his old girlfriend and then Fernand's parents, and finally Ingrid and her family. There was enough room for all of them, after we fixed up my studio with extra beds, even though there were still boxes piled everywhere. Eric and his girlfriend left, and then Ingrid and Fernand and her family went to visit Disney World for a few days. Ingrid left the baby Jennifer with us, and by the time they all returned, I was so exhausted that I could hardly cope.

After they left, my sister Meta, called and was concerned about our working too much. She asked us if we would like to visit her in Austin, Texas, for a few weeks. We gratefully accepted, did some clean-up, and then drove for three days to Texas. Meta was shocked at how tired we looked. So relaxed for a few days, and then went to visit Laredo, Texas and Nuevo Laredo, Mexico, which lies right across the border. When we finally drove back to Sanibel, we were rested, happy and ready to tackle the unpacking.

Meanwhile, Eric had sold his house and moved to a place that was easier for him to get around in with his wheelchair. He was working at his job full time again, but he still had to have therapy. He met a lovely therapy nurse, and they soon became friends, and as they saw each other more frequently, their relationship grew and they fell in love. Bram and I were happy for them because we knew that this would make Eric's life much richer, give his ego a boost, and give him new purpose in his challenging life style.

To help with the payments of his new rented house, Eric found room-mate to share the costs, and Bram and I came over to see if we could help Eric settle in. When we met the young man who would be in the house with him, he seemed to be rather strange. He was degreed and seemed educated enough, but I had trouble coping with his habits. He was untidy, and had an unhealthy manner of living and thinking. He took great pleasure in going out on weekends with the objective of getting drunk, then coming home and throwing up; the noises of which made everyone queasy. One morning I was cleaning, when he came down to the living room, dressed only in his underwear, and plopped himself down on the sofa. He moaned about how terrible he felt, for which I had no empathy, so I politely asked him to recuperate in his bedroom, where we wouldn't have to put up with his nonsense.

Later, he told me that he had a brother who was mentally retarded, which was probably one of the reasons why his behavior was sometimes peculiar. He told me that he had trouble keeping a girlfriend, so I asked him how he treated these girls and what he did with them on a date. "Well" he said, "I take the girl out for dinner, and then we go to her place or mine and have sex ". He felt that he was entitled to sex because he had paid for the meal, so I pointed out to him that no girl that was really viable would accept that behavior. He asked me how he could win a girl's favor, and I told him that he should slowly wine and dine the girl, and talk to her a lot, court her, and then gradually get closer with her consent.

I always had the suspicion that he was in love with Eric's girlfriend, and couldn't seem to understand how a beautiful girl like that could possibly be in love with a man in Eric's position, especially when he was there, available, good looking, and whole. So I told him that what really mattered was the personality of the person, and what he is like as a human being, not what he looked like on the surface. I only saw him once more, about two years later, when Eric had moved into his own home and this fellow had offered to help him transplant some trees on the property. I had been right about him; he had grown in some areas like keeping the rented house up better, although when he had left, there was still some machinery of his in the yard, and it took Eric ages to get him to remove it.

Gradually, Eric and Regina were together more and more, and it became clear to Bram and I that they had a serious relationship. Eric had saved some money over the years, and he found and bought a piece of land on which to build in a suburb of Pittsburgh, Oakdale, PA. The property was located on top of a small mountain with a beautiful view of the valley below. It took some time for Eric to find a builder who was willing to construct the house to Eric's specifications, but we were all very proud of Eric's courage to undertake such a large project. Four months after the house was finished, Bayer relocated Eric and Regina to Germany for an assignment in reaction engineering. This meant that they wouldn't be returning to their new home for two years.

ONE MORE TIME TO INDONESIA 1984

Bram and I decided to make another trip to Indonesia in 1984 with the new friends we had made on the first trip. After visiting the familiar places on Java and Bali, we went on to new places, like the Celebes. This place was quite interesting in that it was still primitive. We were traveling by bus over dirt roads with big potholes, so the driver couldn't go very fast. The jostling we got was very tiring and unpleasant, but it was worth the effort, because the scenery was splendid, with its high mountains, deep valleys, dense jungles, and fantastic views from the mountain tops. Happily, it reminded me more of what the area had been like when I had lived there as a child. Our group was very nice, but the leader wasn't as good as the man on the first trip.

One day, walking alone in a park near Malang in East-Java, two young Indonesian men started to bother me, pushing me to give them money for food and drink. They were so persistent that I was starting to get frightened, and since I wasn't close to the rest of our group, I started to walk faster, luckily managing to reach the group leader. The funny part was that the men were talking to each other, saying that they thought I would give in, if they persisted long enough, not knowing that I could understand everything they were saying. When I complained to the group leader, he was very angry, and wanted me to point out the pests. We found them nearby, and he started to curse and yell at them, asking them if they were crazy to be frightening the tourist trade. He told them that if they continued their bad behavior, it could ruin the tourist trade business, and the money they brought to the country because travelers wouldn't come anymore. They apologized, and were afraid of his outburst, but I was glad they were gone.

When we were in Jakarta, a couple from our group went shopping on their own, and as they passed under a bridge, two hoodlums jumped at them, trying to take their cameras. In the middle of the scuffle, the woman yelled, while she was bashing her attacker with her purse. Luckily, a policeman was nearby, and came running to the couple's rescue. He took the thieves into custody and marched them off to jail. At the station they appeared to have been pretty badly bruised from the couple, and the police wanted to keep the cameras as evidence in the case, but our guide convinced them that it would be bad publicity for the country if the cameras had to be left behind.

Bram and I enjoyed ourselves tremendously at a museum in Jakarta. In one of the rooms there was a showcase with coins from all over the world. All the denominations of the American coins were there except the half dollar. We asked the docent why there wasn't such a coin in the collection, and he said he didn't know there was one. For two years, I had been carrying around a half dollar, for good luck, and then I got the idea that it would be nice to offer the coin to add to their collection. They were excited and happy to add my contribution to their collection. I asked him to open the showcase, to add the half dollar, and at first he hesitated, but then he decided to unlock the case, and I moved other coins over a little, and placed the new coin beside the others. Everyone around us cheered and they all thanked us profusely, with big smiles on their faces, and ours too! Now I knew why I had been carrying that coin around with me.

ERIC'S WEDDING: SEPTEMBER 29, 1984

No sooner had Bram and I returned from Indonesia, than it was time to attend the very special occasion of Eric and Regina's wedding. They had decided to get married in September of that year, and Regina had made all the arrangements, which turned out to be very special and moving. There were many guests; Regina's family, Ingrid and Fernand with their two daughters all came. We weren't sure that Ingrid would make it because she was pregnant with her third child, and due to deliver at any time. Eric had even arranged, through a physician friend of his, to have a physician on hand at the hospital, just in case the baby decided to arrive during the time they were with us, which made everyone feel more secure.

Meanwhile, Eric had ordered a stand which enabled him to stand up from his wheelchair during the ceremony. As they were married, everyone was in tears, because Eric, with a lot of effort, got up from his chair and stood next to his bride, for the first time since his accident, five years before. Later, Regina remarked that she was surprised how tall Eric was when he stood. After the ceremony, everyone went to a nearby reception, the band played, and the guests danced. Amidst the dancers was Eric, wheeling around the floor with his bride, having a grand time. Ingrid danced slowly with her husband, who was concerned about her condition, but everyone had a great time, and Ingrid thought the baby probably enjoyed the swaying back and forth, and she kidded us about how funny it would be if the motion shook the baby right out of her.

Eric's wedding was out of the ordinary, and showed, clearly, that no matter what happens in life, it's important to turn it around, making something positive and happy out of one's circumstances.

After the wedding, most of the guests went to a nearby motel to stay overnight. In the middle of the night Ingrid went into labor, was rushed to the hospital, and another baby girl, Emily, was born early the next morning. Everything went well with the delivery, and as the guests were having their breakfast that morning, the word was passed about Ingrid's "feat", and it just added to the celebration, with happy joking and laughter. Bram, Fernand, his girls, and I all stayed at Eric's that night and went to visit Ingrid for the next few days Then Fernand took the children back to Westport. Ingrid stayed in the hospital for a week. Then Bram and I drove her to the airport for her flight back home with her new baby. Now we had three grand-daughters.

Back in Sanibel, Bram and I gradually settled in, and as time passed, more and more tourists came to visit Sanibel. It was delightful to encounter people from all over, especially when they were Dutch. One little boy excitedly told his mother, in Dutch, that he had just been to the post office and a man there had given him some beautiful stamps. So I turned around and told him that I was happy that he was so glad about his present, and he acknowledged my comment, started out the door, and stopped suddenly when he realized that I had responded in his language. We both had a nice laugh, and went our separate ways. I felt good about hearing my own language again, and do miss it at times, but that's the price of moving on in life.

In 1985, our son-in-law, Fernand, was transferred to Minnesota. The family had been living in Westport, Connecticut, and the move had to be made quickly; so Ingrid and the girls came to stay with us, while Fernand arranged for their new home, and had their entire household moved to Minnesota. I had a good time with Ingrid and the children. The oldest daughter, Michelle, temporarily went to school in Sanibel. It wasn't as academic as she was used to, but it didn't really matter, for such a short time.

Fernand had quite a time coping with getting a new home and dealing with his work at the same time, but he was very efficient, and we admired him for his efforts. The new house was the prettiest home they had ever had. It was "Tudor" architecture on the outside, had lots of spacious rooms inside, and was located on a beautiful tree lined street. When Ingrid went to see the new house, she was pleased, and asked if we would come the next summer to enjoy it with her. At the same time, Eric was transferred to Germany for two years, so both the children were on the move.

In 1986, Bram and I took a plane to Holland. We stayed there with friends for a week, and then they drove us to place near the German border where we met up with Eric and Regina. We stayed with them for two weeks, and we were really amazed that Regina, with some lessons, had picked up the German language so quickly. Eric insisted that we visit my cousin and her family in Switzerland, so we drove to visit them for a few days. The traffic was unbelievably congested, and the drivers seemed so rude, compared to America's commuters.

We were astounded that the Germans had been able to recuperate from the war so quickly, considering the tremendous damage from all the bombings. Our stay was enjoyable, but I still get an eerie feeling when I hear the German language spoken. As time passes, I'm hoping that the memory of it all dims, though I think I shall never totally forget the war era.

Eric and Regina enjoyed their two years in Germany, and used their weekends to travel all over Europe. Despite Eric's handicap, they managed to see a lot of it. After our stay with them, we were driven back to Holland, where we met and had some good times with some people we had met on the previous trip to Indonesia. Finally, we said good-bye to our Dutch friends and family, and flew back to the United States.

We were glad when Eric told us that they wouldn't be staying in Europe for good. He missed the American culture; the German attitude and lifestyle were very different from what they were used to, and we were glad too, because we preferred that our children live close enough that we could visit from Sanibel, if we were so inclined. In 1987, Eric and Regina moved back to the United States.

MOVING AGAIN!

When we left Holland after the visit to Eric and Regina, we flew directly to Minnesota to see Ingrid's family and their new home. It was a lovely place, only needing a few repairs, which had been done by the time we arrived. Ingrid and Fernand had moved several times over the years, and each time they had bought houses which needed something done to them, allowing them to buy at a lower price. Then they would remodel, and having very good taste, were able to sell the houses for a good profit. Bram and I were proud of their efforts. While we were with them in Minnesota, they were told they would be moving yet again in 1987.

There were a few things Ingrid thought could be done to make the house more appealing, so we volunteered to help. The work included cleaning and painting the basement till it looked like new. I went with Fernand to the nursery, where we bought plants for the garden, and two potted plants for the front door. It all looked so attractive that Ingrid said she didn't want to move. Real Estate people were contacted, and an open house was planned, which turned out to be very crowded. Fernand had set the price just a little high, thinking he might have to come down just a little bit. As it turned out, there were multiple parties interested. When the first party accepted paying the whole price, the real estate person accepted it, but then something happened to make her change her mind. A bidding war started among four parties who wanted the house. By this time, the second party had also offered to pay full price in cash, and their offer was accepted. Of course, the first people were angry, but that first party had signed no papers, so they were out of luck, and had to accept their disappointment. Ingrid and Fernand made a handy profit on the house.

Fernand had to work while all this was happening, so when Ingrid got the word about what the house had sold for, she called Fernand at work. He was so astounded, that we could hear his reaction right through the phone lines. It was a good feeling of accomplishment. But now Fernand had to find another house in Connecticut, because he would be working in New York again. They decided to return to Westport, if possible.

Years ago Ingrid had gone to Mrs. Sullivan, and she had told Ingrid that eventually she would have the house of her dreams, with white pillars in the front. Fernand knew what style house he would be looking for, but that also eliminated a lot of the market because most homes wouldn't suit their tastes. He finally found the house to fit the bill, but it was in rough condition, having been neglected because of an inheritance war between the wife and her stepsons. All this legal mess lasted two years, during which time the house had stood vacant.

The house itself was basically viable, with large rooms to accommodate a large family. When Ingrid and Fernand moved into the house in October, 1987, they hired some men to cut some of the trees and clean up the yard, and meanwhile, they had people working on the house, rebuilding parts of it. Bram and I came to visit during this time. The previous owners had left a lot of surprises, goods that they hadn't bothered to get rid of, so we took some of it to the Goodwill, and with the rest we decided to sell.

In the attic there were piles of amazing things left behind, some of which we decided would be fun to sell at a garage sale. Even though it was a lot of work getting ready, you did make some money, and it was fun to watch folks browsing and buying. I had done this several times before, so I knew how to set it up. We did make one mistake with some frames we thought would bring about eight dollars a piece. A few days after the garage sale, Ingrid and I were in an antique shop, where you could bring things in on consignment. Ingrid talked to the owner, while I wandered around and came across a case that had some frames in it, exactly like the ones we had sold at the garage sale, only they were priced much higher. Needless to say, I was unhappy with myself, that I hadn't known more about the price of antiques. We brought the rest of the frames to that store to get a better price.

As we drove back to Sanibel, the traffic was congested. More and more people were escaping to the southern states to avoid harsh winters. We were very happy in Sanibel in the winter, not missing the snow shovel detail we had up north. Shortly after we got back, however, something very unpleasant happened to me.

ACCIDENT PRONE IN 1987

One afternoon, not long before Christmas in 1987, I had an accident. Bram and I were bicycling around our development, when I decided to stop to watch an anthill. The hill was covered with thousands of red ants, which are a menace in the South, causing a lot of discomfort, if they bite. I made a wrong move as I tried to get off my bike. I was wearing some shoes with too high a heel, instead of sneakers, and the heel of my left shoe got caught in the pedal, making me lose my balance. Down I went, onto the hard pavement, the bike falling on top of me, pinning me down with my left leg stuck in an upward position. I realized that something was terribly wrong right away, but as I tried to get out from under the bike, I couldn't move. My leg felt paralyzed, and my thoughts immediately flew to Eric.

Bram was standing next to me, wondering why I wasn't getting up, and when he tried to lift the bike off of me, he couldn't, because my leg was wound around the metal of the bike, and I couldn't budge. I asked him to go for help because I thought I had broken something, and at first, he didn't want to leave, but soon realized he had to go for help. Bram called a neighbor who had always been a lot of help and knew a lot about medicine. He also called for an ambulance and then hurried back.

While I was lying there, something rather funny happened. A couple came by, walked up to me and asked why I was lying there, not trying to get up. They were incredulous that I just lay there, but I told them that help was on the way. About this time, Bram returned, our neighbor came over with cold towels for my head, and the ambulance arrived. It took two men to disengage me from the bike. They were asking me if I could move my toes. At first they felt numb, and then I did feel my toes, and as the shock started to wear off, the pain started up my leg to my hip. The good news was that I wasn't paralyzed, but when the police asked me what had happened, I had to tell them that I had made a silly error in judgment and was paying for it.

I was driven to a small airstrip nearby, where a helicopter was waiting. My stretcher was placed outside the helicopter. I felt as if I were floating in the air, all by myself. I wasn't afraid, just grateful for the help I was getting. Landing in Fort Myers, I was transported by ambulance to the local hospital. Meanwhile, Bram drove our car and met us at the hospital. X-rays were taken, and then I ended up in a hospital bed, where the Doctor told me that I had a broken hip. The next day they operated. About ten days later I left the hospital, and was transferred to a rehab unit, where they gave me therapy which was very painful, as I exercised to get back to normal. There were several other hip fracture cases in the hospital at the same time I was there, so I guess this is one of the things that people have to put up with as they get older.

I felt guilty about leaving Bram on his own, but he was being spoiled by our neighbors on the Island, so he was all right. Eric and Ingrid wanted to come down, but we told them not to because this was something we had to cope with on our own.

When I returned home, I managed to maintain my daily routine with the help of my walker, and then later with a walking stick. I made up my mind to heal myself as quickly as possible. It took six months before I could walk normally, and then I could walk faster than Bram. The stainless steel pin they had put in my hip didn't bother me a bit, although when I had time to think about it, I felt like a robot, with metal pins holding me together.

The specialist told me that I had better be more careful, as my bones were brittle and could break easily, so I took special care, especially when I was working in the garden. Even though I was careful, a year later I stepped on a coconut, slipped and fell in the yard. When I fell, I heard a cracking noise, like a branch breaking, and when I got up, I noticed that I had broken my wrist this time. Bram had gone to a Rotary club meeting, so I was alone. Therefore, I decided to go in and have a shower, since my wrist didn't hurt that much and I didn't want to go to the hospital looking like a tramp. I called Bram at the Rotary Club when I was clean, and he drove me to Fort Myers again where an X-ray told them that I had broken the small bones in my wrist. It wasn't too bad, so they put me in a sling, and sent us home. We were surprised that they didn't do more, and a couple of weeks later, my fingers started to feel numb, which alarmed me, so we went back to the hospital, where they operated to relieve the pressure on a nerve that was causing the problem. My wrist was distorted, but once I got over the pain, I didn't mind, as long as I had full use of my wrist and hand.

AT HOME IN SANIBEL

Bram and I felt blessed that we were able to enjoy our children and grandchildren as we grew old together. I also thanked God for my ability to paint, garden, and for the friendships we had. In 1988, I showed my garden in Sanibel to the public for a few hours for a fundraiser for the Sanibel Historical Museum. Some of the other special gardens in the area also participated in this fundraiser. We even had people come from the Florida mainland to see our efforts.

My garden is landscaped with plants, shrubs, and trees indigenous to the climate and the soil, which is sandy and salty. Rows of these plantings made a nice display, and then I made some Bonsai trees, which were sold for this good purpose. Some people were encouraged to improve their own yards, when they could see what it was possible to do with their surroundings.

Ever since my childhood, I have been interested in chameleons. It was always a mystery to me how they could change color, depending on their surroundings. Soon after we moved to Sanibel, I noticed that we had a lot of them in our yard. They came in brown and green. The Florida version are called anoles. They are a sub species, and different from the larger chameleons that I was used to seeing in Indonesia. The brown version are much more aggressive, originating from Cuba, and they seem to be taking over in SW Florida. I favored the green ones, however, and wanted to catch a few of them; a hard task since they were very quick and their eye-sight was perfect. I have a screened-in porch which is perfect for raising several special tropical plants, and I wanted to put green chameleons in them. My granddaughters and friends really enjoyed my "pets" when they came to visit. I was a little concerned that some people would think that I was a little strange, raising reptiles, so I was always grateful when someone showed an interest in my hobby. Friends of friends called me to see if they could visit to see my collection of anoles, which made it fun to compare notes with other people.

Sanibel Creatures

Herons and Ibis Feeding on the Pond at Our Sanibel House

My Sanibel Garden

KEEPING A STIFF UPPER LIP

At four A.M. one morning, in March 1988, our phone rang. I woke up with a start, thinking it would be a wrong number, but when I picked up the phone, it was Fernand's voice, telling me that he had bad news. Ingrid was ill. I told him that we would be able to be there in two days, but he said his parents had been visiting his sister Jackie, who lived in Indiana, and they had already arrived to help with the girls. I said we would come soon, and when I put the phone down, I felt as if a truck had run over me. I didn't want to wake Bram, and give him a sleepless night, so the news would wait till morning. Bram was upset too, and it wasn't until several days later, that we heard more about Ingrid's condition. She had gone to a scout meeting, when she suddenly developed a very severe headache. She excused herself from the meeting, and drove home alone. Nobody realized how sick she was, but when she got home, she was violently ill. Fernand took her to the hospital, thinking she might have had a stroke.

Later, after all the test results came back, the doctors told us that she had an A.V.M. (Arterio-Vascular-Malformation) on her brainstem, which was life threatening. She had been born with this malformation, and she might have lived her entire life without ever having known that she had this problem, but if bleeding occurs, as in Ingrid's case, it was very dangerous. There was an operation for this, but it was very delicate, and there were very few surgeons who could perform it. Luckily, the bleeding was on top of the brainstem, instead of being imbedded in the middle. The whole family was on the phone, trying to find the best surgeon to perform the operation. There were five physicians capable of this, and they chose a doctor from Boston, transferred Ingrid to Mass General Hospital, and prayed that this man would be successful in his efforts. Bram and I couldn't believe that both of our children had been hit with major health problems, but God was with us, as Ingrid came through with flying colors. It took a long time and a lot of effort, and exercises on Ingrid's part, before she was normal again. After two months, Bram and I went to Westport to take over helping with Ingrid and her household.

We were grateful to Fernand's parents for their help. Fernand had needed them for moral support at the beginning. They had arranged for a Salvadorian woman to come for some months to help manage the household duties. This helped ease Ingrid's mind, so she could conjcentrate more on recuperating. Ingrid's survival of her ordeal had been a miracle, and her daughters were very re- lieved too, to get their Mother back home, assuring them that they weren't going to lose her.

Bram and I stayed longer that summer, and were happy to help. The Salvadorian woman was still there, and since she didn't speak English, and we didn't speak Spanish, we did a lot of gesticulating, and drawing little pictures on paper to communicate. It worked most of the time, and we had some very amusing times getting through to each other. We often laughed about it, but it was easier when Fernand was home and could translate for us. When Ingrid was able to live normally again, we left her and went to visit Eric and Regina for a few weeks.

Shortly thereafter, it was Bram's turn for problems. This time he was troubled with his prostate. After a period of indecision about either having surgery or radiation treatments Bram decided on the radiation. At Lee Memorial Hospital, he went in for 28 radiation treatments in the spring of 1992, and was declared cured, which made us all breath a deep sigh of relief.

Meta wanted us to visit her again, before we were too old to travel. She had the idea of driving through part of western America. Bram and I took three days to drive to Austin Texas where Meta lived with Theo, her husband. The three of us drove thousands of miles through Arizona, New Mexico, Utah, and Texas. It was a marvelous trip. We never realized how diverse this area was from other parts of North America, and we saw that this was the area where most of the western movies had been filmed.

Some of the very high cacti, the Sugaros, were quite impressive. They were so old that it made us feel young by comparison. It was fun to imagine what the very first travelers to the west must have thought of these giants when they first saw them, and it was so much better to see these places in real life, instead of in pictures.

Returning back to Florida, I realized how different our Island was from other parts of the country. There are drawbacks to every place one chooses to live, so I think it's important to appreciate the good things about the places we live. I loved New England with it's variety of seasons, wildlife, and beautiful landscapes, especially in the fall, but I don't miss the winters, and there was never going to be anything that compared with the scenery of my childhood.

If you had a good childhood, you long for those years later on. But we forget that everything changes, and happily we tend to let the bad times dim from our mind. I was happy that my children had a good childhood experience, even with the natural ups and downs that everyone experiences.

On the drive back to Austin, I realized that something was wrong with my eyesight. I made an appointment with the optometrist when I got back to Sanibel. Bram took me to the optometrist who told me that I had cataracts in both eyes, and needed an operation. He tried to convince me that these days the operation was an easy matter to take care of, that my eyesight would be so clear after the cataracts were gone and that I would be startled how well I could see. I was upset about my eyes because sight was so important to me, but I have always had a philosophy of facing problems right away, instead of wasting time worrying about them, which often doubled the trouble itself. I made plans to have the operation as soon as possible. The cataract operations on my eyes were a success, and it amazed me how much more colorful the world became. I had a new appreciation for the color and beauty of the world!

In the meantime, I had managed to have another accident, and I couldn't believe my bad luck. One morning I fell on a stepping stone in the yard. I knew right after the fall, that something was wrong with my left arm below the elbow because it was dangling at an awkward angle. I found it difficult to get up because I was supporting the hurt arm with the other one. Bram came running when I called him, and was shocked to see my predicament, but I was calm, knowing it could be fixed.

Bram drove me to the emergency room. I had my arm in a sling, and told the nurse I had a broken arm. She was skeptical until I took my arm out of the towel, and she concurred that I definitely had broken it. This time I was in the hospital for two days, and I could take care of myself, but driving was too difficult. I hoped my string of accidents was over, and gradually our lives started to get back to normal. We were always busy, between keeping up the house and the yard, walking on the beach, talking with friends, going to church, and visiting with our family in the summertime. I had a few students, and painted a lot for myself. I felt contented.

In June, 1992, Ingrid arranged a very nice 80th birthday party for Bram. Ingrid made it a very special occasion. Bram did not know anything about it until we went to a restaurant close to Ingrid's house, in Westport, CT. Supposedly Bram and I were just going to eat out one night, but when we got there, there was a loud chorus of familiar voices: "Surprise!!!".

The party was a great success. Many of Bram's friends and colleagues from Boston were present, and Bram was dumbfounded to see them. That was the time I realized, though, that all of us were getting older. We all have our dear memories and it was great to talk about our shared days gone by.

NOTES ABOUT MY SISTER

About my sister, Meta, I feel the need to relate some more details of her life. She wasn't an easy person to know, as the circumstances of her life were difficult, and often tragic. She had so much bad luck, it seemed almost too much for one person to have to cope with. Her childhood in the Indies wasn't too bad, but her teenage years were very difficult. It was hard to tell if she was born with, or just naturally developed stubbornness and bad temper. As we say in Holland, "stubborn as a mule". Our Father, as years progressed, wasn't easy to get along with, and he picked on my sister more than on me. Leaving Indonesia was traumatic for her, since she had so much freedom there and loved the animals not available to us in Holland, not to mention she had to leave all her friends behind. She became lonely and bitter, as being at home wasn't a happy situation for her, and I was too busy growing up myself to be of much help to her.

When our parents moved from Bloemendaal, it gave Meta more freedom. She found a job in Amsterdam, so she wasn't around much, and soon after she left, she met a young man. She fell head over heels in love with him, and soon he asked her to move in with him, which she did. My parents knew nothing of this situation as they would have greatly disapproved. Meta lived with him for nearly a year during the war, and was very happy, saying in later years that this was one of the best times of her life. I've already written about her wartime adventures, during which she showed great courage. I disagreed with her living with someone out of wedlock. I liked her friend, but there was something about him that I didn't trust, and sure enough, their relationship came to an abrupt halt when Meta discovered that he was cheating on her. He even tried to pawn her off on one of his friends, which was a sure sign that he was a cad.

Meta came back home, which made her unhappy and she felt confined. She went through several jobs that she hated, and then finally found a job with the Colonial Institute of Amsterdam, where she was a secretary. She liked that job very much and worked there for nearly five years. About this time she had a nervous breakdown, and got some time off to rest, and get well again. Meanwhile, Bram and I had been in Denmark, so we arranged for her to work in Denmark when we returned to Holland. We thought it would be good for her to be out of the country, but it turned out to be a disaster.

The Danish family she was staying with abused her presence, using her as a maid without pay. She was forced to stay longer than she was supposed to. Finally, with the help of one of the family's cousins, she was able to gather her belongings, and fly back to Holland. And to top all that, she had been gone long enough that the job she had at the Institute was given to someone else. Then her luck seemed to change, and she got a chance to apply for the test to become an airline stewardess with KLM Royal Dutch Airlines. She was very smart and was accepted for the position, which she held for about two years. Once she became ill, and was stationed for a short while in Jakarta, Indonesia, to recuperate. Meta had time to think and came to the conclusion that she didn't want to be a stewardess for the rest of her life, although she was at a loss about her future.

During this time, she befriended quite a few young men, but she didn't want a serious relationship with any of them. There was one young man though, that she began to care for, and then someone told her that he was married and had children, so she confronted him with it. She was crushed to hear his patronizing retort, that she was a naive girl that didn't know the rules of relationships. Meta spit at him, and, very angry with herself for letting him get so close, swore she would never allow herself to be cheated again. About this time, Meta was introduced to an older man, through friends, who had known this man from a Japanese prisoner of war camp. They knew him to be a good man from this ordeal they had been through together, and felt she would be lucky to have him. Meta was lonely, and when the man proposed, she trusted him, and accepted him, and went to live in America, where he worked.

Her husband was intelligent, good looking, and financially secure, but on their wedding night, it turned out that her groom had been tortured in the prison camp, and that had caused him to have many physical problems. He worked for an oil company, and after the war, this company wanted to send him back to Indonesia, but he was still too weak. He refused to go, and in the disagreements that followed, he was stubborn enough to sue the company. Theo won the court case, but because he had sued, he felt that his name was put on a blacklist, and for years, he found it difficult finding a good job. Two of his fortunes were confiscated, businesses he had in Guatemala and Indonesia. So while they were married, they had hard times financially, but Meta stayed with him because she felt sorry for him. Although the first few years they were together were fine, and they had some good times on trips to South America, the remainder of their forty three years together were difficult. She never told any of her family about these marital difficulties.

Meta loved cats. They were her children. Meta also had an artistic streak, and would paint pastels of her cats. She was also quite handy with carpentry. She made some beautiful refurbished furniture by herself, but she was very bitter about life. I had come to the states too, but we would get together only rarely. We had such different views on life that most times it caused a clash of personalities.

Theo Vreugde, my sister's husband suffered from heart disease, and received a new heart valve through open heart surgery. But he never really recovered from the surgery. Meta struggled to take care of him for a year, as she watched him deteriorate both mentally and physically. She found a nursing home for him but he proved to be a difficult patient and she had to move him from one home to another for several months. Finally Theo was brought home under 24 hour nursing care, where he died a few weeks later. I was proud of Meta during this time for the way she stood by Theo, cared for him, and fought for him through the medical system. She accepted Theo's death as a merciful end to his suffering, and moved on, alone, with her life.

Things went better though, especially after my children were grown and married. Eric, especially, did a good job of befriending Meta. He saw what a good person she was, under all the bitterness of her life. Bram and I did have some good times with her and her husband, and I was glad about that, because her husband died two years before Bram's life ended. Her husband had nightmares from the war, which we know now to be post traumatic stress syndrome. Consequently, he had some problems with his blood. At least Meta and I had the memories of the happy Indonesian years; simple, but enjoyable and that counts for a lot. Meta now has a weak heart, so we keep in touch by telephone, talking about the past, mostly. I will miss her when she's gone, but we made a date that our souls would meet on the beach in Lhoknga in Sumatra, where life had been so good.

BRAM'S ILLNESS

Starting in 1993, our lives became more difficult. One always wishes that a happy retirement can last forever, but that's not the way it worked. Bram started having trouble with his heart about the time I had my broken arm episode. One evening his heart was acting up, so I drove him into the local hospital, where they told me that he had congestive heart failure. He stayed in the hospital for several days while they ran tests, so they could give the best advice on our course of action.

Bram had been very supportive through all the physical problems I had, even though his body was starting to give him some problems too. His heart had a defect, a calcified heart valve, and the doctor told us that he could have a very serious heart valve replacement operation. No heart surgeon in Florida would touch Bram, the risk factors were too high. The good news was that if Bram came through it okay, he would be in much better shape. All the heart specialists in Florida said that Bram was not a good candidate for heart valve replacement surgery. Eric and his physician friends investigated this further and did find a hospital in Cleveland where they were willing to do it. After much deliberation, and after an initial evaluation at the Cleveland Clinic Foundation, in December of 1994, Bram decided to go ahead, despite the risks. A date for the operation was set for the spring of 1995.

With the help of several medical advisors, we took Bram to the famous Cleveland Clinic Foundation in Ohio for the operation. The heart valve and bypass operations were successful, but when Bram became conscious it was clear to us that he had undergone some changes. The operation lasted for eight hours and also included de-clogging of the carotid artery on Bram's right side. It soon became clear that Bram's mind wasn't as sharp as it had been. We were told that he had experienced some small strokes, which had effected some of his brain function. This was very upsetting to all of us, but soon Bram started to feel better, which allayed some of our fears.

Eric and Regina took us to their home in Pennsylvania, not too far from the Cleveland Clinic Foundation where we stayed for a while. At first, it seemed that Bram was really feeling better, but then one morning he couldn't get up from his bed, and was very confused. With difficulty, we put Bram in his wheelchair, and drove him to the hospital in Pittsburgh, and they told us that it would be better if we took him to the hospital in Cleveland, where his medical records were. We took a three hour ambulance drive back to Ohio. That was a traumatic trip, and when we finally arrived, it was three A.M. in the morning. At first, the hospital had trouble finding a room for Bram. Meanwhile, I had decided to take a small walk round the hospital to a nearby hotel but a security guard was kind enough to stop me, saying that this was a dangerous neighborhood for a woman to be walking alone. I was put in a police car and escorted back to the safety of the hotel. For the first time I felt a little more relaxed. I stayed at the hotel, and each day I visited Bram. Each day he seemed a little better.

There were some interesting folks in the hospital. There was a whole group from Saudi Arabia, and it was fascinating to watch their children play, and see the women walking behind their husbands. One morning I was having breakfast in the cafeteria at the hotel, and an Arabian man passes by. He glanced at my dish, pointed to it, and yelled at the waitress, telling her that he wanted what I had, RIGHT NOW! He ignored me totally, which was extremely rude. The waitress told me later that she was used to being treated like that by the Arab customers because she was a woman. I thanked God that I lived in America, where women weren't normally treated like that.

I stayed at the hotel for ten days, visiting Bram most of the time. I was grateful that he was getting such good care, but the specialist told me that the strokes he had were causing his body to deteriorate rapidly. We decided that Bram should go home again. At first we stayed with Eric, and then we flew back to Sanibel when Bram was feeling better. It soon became apparent that Bram needed more care than I, alone, could provide, so we had the health care center send health care aides over to give us a hand. This proved to be a God-send, as it was difficult for me to do it all.

Gradually Bram became more and more demented, and I had to accept the fact that I was losing the Bram I had always known and loved. Especially at night, when we were alone, I had to get up several times a night to tend to his needs. One night he fell out of bed, and when I lifted him back up, I noticed that he had a large cut on the top of his head. I bandaged his head to stop the bleeding, and called 911. It was amazing how fast they arrived. They took Bram to Lee Memorial Hospital in Fort Myers, and I drove our car, to meet them there. This turned out to be a challenge because the roads weren't marked very well. I got lost, but finally I found the hospital. Only it was the wrong entrance, so I was redirected to the emergency room entrance, and as I drove up, I started to laugh because there was a whole crowd of people who were happy to see me, especially when they found out that I was Mrs. Boonstra. Bram had been giving them quite a difficult time, so they all chimed "Hallelujah!, Mrs. Boonstra is here". Bram was sitting in a wheelchair nearby, and with a big frown on his face, asked me why I had brought him to such a miserable place.

In April of 1996 we celebrated my 80th birthday party, also arranged by Ingrid, with all of our friends in Sanibel. Bram was quite ill by this time, and we were not sure how he would handle the party. Many of our Sanibel friends gathered at a local restaurant, and we enjoyed a nice lunch. Gifts were exchanged, and at one point Bram quietly stood up and walked the length of the room to the far end of the lunch table. Everyone watched in anxious anticipation, not knowing if Bram was lucid or confused. When he got there, he asked for everyone's attention, and he gave a very moving speech about how he was happy to celebrate my birthday, and grateful to have had the privilege of being married to me all of those years. It was one of Bram's lucid moments during his illness; a moment that gave me the reassurance that even though it seemed to me that I was losing Bram a little more each day, his love for me remained strong and very much present. I will never forget that moment, it reminded me that I would never lose Bram.

Some time later in 1996, I had to call 911 again, when Bram got his head caught under the bathroom faucet. Don't ask me how he managed to do this. He wasn't hurt, but he was stuck, and the emergency people had a good laugh about it. A short while later Bram managed to fall out of his bed again, and this time he cut his arm. Luckily, his arm wasn't broken, only bruised, but I was mentally and physically worn out by this time. And so the children and I reluctantly decided that it would be best if we placed Bram in a nursing home where he could get the care he needed. In November of 1996, we found one place that looked satisfactory, and we arranged for Bram to stay there. But Bram was only there ten days when we discovered that he was being abused and traumatized. His body was covered with bruises, and he was afraid of the large health helper, who treated him roughly.

When I picked Bram up from the nursing home, he was sitting in his wheelchair, with one hand resting in his lap. There was a large cut on his hand, and it was still bleeding. I was appalled. When I asked one of the personnel how he gotten the cut, and why someone hadn't done something about it, they said that they didn't even know that he was wounded. Later on, I found out that the home was in financial trouble. I took Bram home, but knew that I couldn't keep him there for long.

With the help of several health care advisors, we found another nursing home that was closer to our Sanibel house than the first one. It was heartbreaking for me to take Bram away from his home again. The nursing home, called Shell Point, had much older facilities, and did not look as new and expensive as the first nursing home. But the personnel at Shell Point were much nicer. Several hours a day, I would keep Bram company, pushing him around the beautiful grounds. I had long talks with the nurses and caretakers, which Bram enjoyed initially, but later on, he really didn't understand what we were talking about. There were about forty patients in the Alzheimers section of the home, and they were all in various stages of this insidious disease.

Each person in the nursing home had his own symptoms, and some of them, who had been prominent citizens, didn't even know who they were anymore. It was so sad and angering to know that nothing could be done to help them. There was one funny moment though, when I was visiting one morning. Bram was sitting quietly in his wheelchair, and several of the patients were making all kinds of noises. Some were screaming, two were tapping on a table, one was singing hymns in the corner, and one woman next to Bram started yelling, "Shut Up!", followed by very dirty words. Several other patients added to the chorus by cursing and complaining loudly. The head nurse came in, and asked everyone to be quiet. They ignored her.

Bram, who had been quiet through all this, suddenly sat bolt upright in his chair, and asked in a very loud tone, "Everyone could please be quiet, because it bothers me and some of the others, so please be quiet!" All of a sudden there was silence, and Bram said to me, "I did it, I stopped them all". Bram had not said anything for days, so they were startled by his input, and a few even laughed. I was so proud of Bram. He'd had one of those bright moments that reminded me of the Bram that I loved and knew so well.

Visiting Bram each day meant driving twenty miles, but I didn't mind. We could speak in Dutch, when he was able, and for a while I had one of the helpers pay him an extra visit in the afternoons, until I found out that Bram didn't like that person at all. Bram's lucid moments became more and more infrequent, and for those of us who loved him, his deterioration was hard to watch. He was slipping into another world, a little more distant each day. When Ingrid and Eric came to see him, we were happily surprised that he recognized them.

Shortly after that, he became worse, so he was transferred to the hospice area of the building, where they placed people who were about to die. Everybody was wonderful to Bram, and he received round the clock care from very supportive people. Eric and I talked, and decided that Bram was hanging on, as best he could, because he feared for the welfare of his family if he weren't there. Eric came up with the thought that we needed to give Bram permission to move on, to let go of his life. If we were to assure him that the family would be all right without him, and that he could go on ahead, and I would join him a little later, then he might be able to let go and have peace. I promised Eric that I would discuss this idea with the medical staff at the hospice where Bram was.

On January 11, 1998. I discussed Eric's idea with a specialist to help Bram pass over, and to leave life, as he knew it, because I was convinced that Bram was hanging on because he didn't want to leave his loved ones. Talk to Bram, he said, and tell him that it's all right for him to go, because his family will be all right, and he didn't have to worry about them anymore. So I sat with Bram for several hours, and looked at the face I knew so well. I talked to him, telling him that we were going on a wonderful vacation. He was going to see his mother, his sister, and some of his old friends again, and that they were all waiting for him. I would join him a bit later, because I had a few things I needed to finish up. Before I left, I looked at his face once more, and I thought he had a smile on his lips, and on his face, a vision of peacefulness.

I drove home feeling more lonely than I had for a long time, praying that God would take him back. A bit later, after 6:30 in the evening, I got a call from Bram's specialist, telling me that Bram had passed away quietly at 5:11 PM. Bram's doctor added that Bram had a smile on his face just as he died. I called Eric and Ingrid, and of course, they were upset, but they had expected the sad news.

The doctor who had been treating Bram told me after Bram's death that Bram did not die from Alzheimer's Disease, but from multi-infarct dementia, caused by blood damage from his open heart surgery three years earlier.

The was no reason for me to go back to the hospice except to collect Bram's personal belongings. Several years before, Bram and I had decided that we both wanted to be cremated, and we had arranged for the home to take care of all that. When I showed up at Shell Point again a week later, everyone was so nice. They all tried to console me. One gentleman, whose wife had been ill with Alzheimer's for years, told me that he wished his wife would pass on, because it was so hard on both of them. "At least you will have some peace now" he said to me, and somehow it did console me, although I felt sorry for him. All this made realize the inevitability of death, like it or not, and the hope that the best of what our souls got from this world would go on to the next.

One of the health caretakers had taken a picture of Bram and me a few months before. The picture showed very clearly that Bram was dying, and that I should be grateful that his suffering was over. When I saw Bram's wedding ring amongst his belongings, I put it on, next to my wedding ring. It gave me a feeling of peace to be wearing something that was a part of Bram for so many years. Except for some tools that I gave to Eric, and some other items I gave to Ingrid, I donated the rest of Bram's possessions to various organizations and friends, because they were too much of a reminder that he was gone. Besides, Bram was a believer in helping others, so donating many of his belongings was consistent with his wishes. Accepting Bram's death was much harder on me than I thought it would be. When he was so sick, I mistakenly had the idea that I could help him somehow. A bit selfish, but a common thread of thinking, and I was glad that I was able to make him feel comfortable about leaving us in the end.

The children and their families were wonderful to me in so many ways, as we all arranged a memorial service at my church on February 20, 1998. The whole family contributed, in their own precious ways, to honor Bram's life. The service was a great success, and very moving as the minister gave a sermon, and our friends had gathered, as well as family, to show us what they thought of the courageous man named Bram.

MEMORIAL SERVICE FOR BRAM B. BOONSTRA

Here is what I said at Bram's memorial service on Sanibel, on February 20, 1998:

It is not easy to say something about Bram's life, which covered 85 years. What I liked so much about Bram's life was his deep faith. He loved to help someone whenever he could. He had a brilliant mind and spoke 4 languages fluently, But he always said that many people knew more than he did. Bram's life was quite a full one with many ups and downs, yet somehow he always managed to cope with it. His honesty did get him in to trouble sometimes, because not everyone wants to hear the truth.

In his early childhood, he did not have it very easy. His father died when Bram was 5 years old, so he never really knew how it would have been to have a father. But his Mother was a wonderful woman, who managed to give him and his sister quite a peaceful and even happy childhood after all. There never was enough money available though, since Bram came from a very poor family due to his father's death. Bram, for instance, never got a new present. A small rusty pocketknife, or a broken down bicycle which had to be repaired were the only type of presents he ever received. But Bram learned to accept these presents without complaints. When Bram graduated from high school and was about to go to the University in Amsterdam, his mother had a major stroke and became paralyzed on her whole left side. At first, Bram wanted to find a job to earn some much needed money. But his mother insisted that he should go on to study chemistry. Some money Bram had saved when he still was in high school, by tutoring high school kids in chemistry, made it possible for him to pay his tuition at the University. For 4 years Bram studied very hard. At night he took care of his mother, together with his sister, Cobi. There was not enough money for a private nurse. Somehow Bram managed to finish his study successfully. He received his PhD degree when he was only 23 years old. He always felt bad that his mother passed away 4 months before his graduation. She had been so proud of him over the years.

I met Bram at a friend's home. We discovered that we both belonged to a rowing club, and Bram invited me to go sailing with him afterwards. At first I was not interested in him because I thought he was too young for me. He had told me that he loved chemistry in high school where he went, so I thought he was still a high school student, maybe a senior. But sometime later in relating this to a friend, I found out that Bram was not sitting as a student in a high school class, but that he was standing at the front of the class teaching. This was a great surprise to me, and suddenly I became much more interested in him and started to get to know him better.

During the war years, we experienced some terrible times. We had very little food to eat, and one time I had prepared for him a meal made from sugar beets. I had spent a lot of time preparing the meal and when Bram complained about the taste, I got so mad that I hit him over the head with a pot for his lack of gratitude. Later, I found out that this was the decisive moment for Bram, because up until then, he had thought I was too sweet and not forceful or determined enough for him. The moment I hit him over the head with that pot was the moment he decided he would ask me to marry him! We were married after the war in 1945.

We moved to America in 1951, and it was a difficult transition for us, coming into a strange land. After renting a house for several years we finally decided to build a house in the same town of Sharon, Massachusetts. Building the house was an adventure; the contractor went broke, the house foundation broke, and we spent hours and hours weeding the lawn and establishing a garden. Bram and I had chosen to build the house in a rocky area. The boulders were everywhere. Bram took up the hobby of using all of these boulders to build a 300 foot long wall along the bottom of the hill. One time he had hooked up a system of pulleys with block and tackle and used our 1952 Chevrolet to move a large boulder about twice the size of a passenger car. Well, move it he did, and it rolled out right into the road where the police department only shook their heads and asked Bram how he was planning to roll this boulder off the road again. Somehow, he managed to do so.

Bram and I had a lot of adventures, too many to mention here, but together we always made the best of things with God's help. I was very lucky to have loved Bram and I could not have chosen a better father for our children, Ingrid and Eric. Bram made many friends in his life, he had many accomplishments, and yet he was a very humble man. With his poor and difficult youth, he had learned to make do with very little. It taught him to be creative and resourceful, yet appreciative for every new day. When the choice came to have heart surgery or not, he labored over the decision for some months, and then chose to take the chance at still a longer life, his zest for life was that strong. I am glad for him that he is at peace now after his long illness.

LIFE GOES ON

The rest of 1998 was difficult for me. The children went back to their lives with their families, and I visited my sister, as well as the children, for the first time in several years. I was doing the best I could to give myself some strength, with the feelings of Bram's passing, always on my mind. I wanted to live my life the best way I could, and I needed to develop a reason to stay alive. My family, of course, was the most important reason, and I also tried to help some friends, who also had to deal with Alzheimer's patients in their families, by attending weekly support meetings. This is a very cruel and long lasting disease. Gradually, I learned to cope with being alone in my beautiful house. I tried to be thankful for each day, and the blessing bestowed upon me by so many good friends.

Just when I was starting to enjoy life again, something happened to test my will to live. In mid year of 1999, I took a fall in my front room. I made a sudden turn on a loose rug, slipped, and fell. It was a very bad fall, and when I tried to get up, I realized that I had broken my arm. I also couldn't stand up because there was something wrong with my left leg. It turned out that I had cracked my pelvis as well. Thank goodness, I was expecting a friend, who was bringing lunch for both of us, right about the time I fell and hurt myself. I dragged myself to the front door, unlocked it and waited. In a short while, my friend came, opened the door and looked at me sitting on the floor of the entrance, a wry smile on my face.

"What did you do now?" she asked with a puzzled look. She arranged to have a friend drive me to the hospital. Due to a mix-up in the emergency room, the physician in charge decided to send me home for the weekend, even though I had a broken left elbow, and a cracked pelvis. It was during the weekend, and the attending physician decided to wait until Monday for further treatment, so they sent me home. It was a painful two days of waiting at home until the orthopedic surgeon could see me on Monday. When he found out that they had sent an 83 year old woman home alone with a broken elbow and a cracked pelvis, he was furious. I can honestly say that I was not very happy about the situation either. The surgeon admitted me to the hospital immediately, apologized profusely, and scheduled a surgery to place fixation pins in my left elbow.

So, it was back to the hospital for me. This time I was there for five weeks and then I went home to recuperate. Eric came to help with the transition back home, and we spent some time together again working on this book, in fact.

THE FIRE AND FLOOD: JUNE 2000

About a year later, Meta asked if I would like to visit her in Texas for a few weeks. Meta liked to go shopping in Laredo and especially Nuevo Laredo because in some ways the place reminded us of Indonesia, and also we wanted to do some early Christmas shopping. So I flew to Austin where Meta picked me up at the airport. We two ladies then headed for Laredo which involved a very long drive through the desert. We had a good time, but Nuevo Laredo had fallen onto hard times. The shops were in worse condition than we remembered from years before, and we although we stayed in the same hotel as in previous years, we did not feel safe there anymore.

I was dealing with a new frustration, though. My eyes were giving me a bad time. The Doctor told me that I had a disease called macular degeneration, which is a progressive loss of eyesight, and as an artist, I can tell you that this was very hard to accept. I prayed that there was something they could do, but I was told that my eyesight would continue to disintegrate until I was blind. I really started to notice everything I could, and hoped that the progression would be slow, that I would pass on before becoming completely blind. It was getting close to the time when I would fly home, and I was ready. I missed my friends on Sanibel, and the young woman, Lavonne, who came to my house, at least three times a week, to help me with whatever I needed.

But Lavonne called one morning, to tell me that she had gotten a call from Harry Gleitz, our next door neighbor, telling her that he had to call 911, after he noticed that water was coming out of my garage and front door. Lavonne immediately went to the house, joining hoards of police, firemen, and the water company representatives, not to mention everyone who lived nearby. The house had been cordoned off, until the investigators could figure out what had happened.

Before I had left, I had given permission to the Gumbo Limbo Association to install a drainage pipe from the road, through my property, to the lake in back, which would alleviate a flood line on the street in front of the house. A landscape firm had been contracted to do the work, and in the process of digging, some wires were cut. The ground fault caused by this, caused a hot spot back in the house, and started a fire in the attic. The fire in the attic burned through a PVC water pipe that was close by, releasing a deluge of water. The water put out the fire, but then it kept flowing, until it saturated that whole section of the house, and started pouring out of the entrance and garage, at which point Harry Gleitz, noticed it, and came to our rescue.

The good news was that the water pipe had put out the fire, or else I wouldn't have any house at all, but I wasn't able to come back to my house. So I stayed with Ingrid in California until some kind of temporary living arrangements could be made. Eric arranged with one of my realtor neighbors for me to stay in a small cottage at the other end of our street, about ¼ mile away. After the initial clean-up effort, intense efforts began to repair the house. It took many months of inspections and reports and the insurance companies had to approve contractor estimates; so it took about three months before any reconstruction work could begin. We chose a contractor after Eric checked his references from four possible contractors. Finally in August, the reconstruction work began. Several truckloads of additional debris were removed from the house. The trusses for the roof reconstruction were the hardest to get. It seemed that all of the truss companies were backordered due to a tremendous building boom in southwest Florida. Most every day I would walk over to the house and report back to Eric by telephone each night on whatever progress was being made.

Finally, serious construction work started in late September. Very soon though, there were additional delays. We had already paid the contractor over 50% of the agreed upon estimate, and already there were problems about delivery dates and work schedules. Eric had even begun to seek the help of an attorney to try and motivate the contractor to finish the work. Meanwhile, from my little cottage I lived in limbo, without my belongings around me and I worried about the damage that had been done to my house. I wondered if it would ever get repaired again, I even thought about selling the place. More importantly, I had too much time on my hands to think about my eyes, which were getting worse with the macular degeneration as time passed. I was having a hard time adjusting, mentally and physically, to the reality of living without my eyesight.

To compensate for this concern, I decided to paint some more. Lavonne and I went out one afternoon and bought supplies: canvases, paints, brushes, thinner, and rags. We set up a whole art studio in the living room of the small cottage, and I started to paint skies – Florida skies. There was one dark thunderous and gloomy sky. And there was a hazy doubtful one. One sky was glorious and hopeful, and another showed a night-time beach under a full moon with the sea turtles hatching and crawling out to sea. Altogether I painted eight skies, all quite different from each other. These sky paintings were a great release for me. At last there was a way to express my feeling of frustration and fear, but also of hope, that in the end, all would be whole again.

In November of 1999, I was aghast to find that one of the two brothers who had been repairing the electrical wiring in my house, had disappeared. He was a nice young man, and we were startled to find out that he had gone into Fort Myers one evening, and was found a few days later, murdered in his truck by an alleged thief. They never found the assailant. Another electrical contractor was hired to finish fixing my home.

The goal became to finish the work by the first of November, and Eric came down at the end of October to supervise the completion of the work. Even with Eric there on a daily basis, the work was not completed by November first. Plans had been made for Ingrid's entire family to come down over Thanksgiving, airline tickets had been purchased, and they were definitely coming. This finally did work to get the contractor to complete his work. Ingrid's family came and stayed in the house, while I stayed in my little cottage for just those few days more to have less congestion. It was wonderful to be back in my home for Thanksgiving dinner. Ingrid's family was very active and under a lot of stress from Silicon Valley, but I really enjoyed having them all home with me in Florida. They all pitched in to help me move back into my house during the Thanksgiving holidays.

Close to the Christmas holidays, I went to California to visit Ingrid's family. Ingrid insisted that I needed a break from all of the stress in Florida, and she wanted me to participate in her 2000 Millenium party. They had moved to Silicon Valley two years before, and bought a beautiful English Tudor home on the top of a hill, which had a barn and stables next door, where Ingrid's daughter, Emily, could keep her horse, "Morgan". Eric always called him "Morbid" or "Mordred". In this house too, they had gutted the inside to rearrange the rooms. They finished that just in time to find out that they had a water drainage problem that ran from the front of the house, down a slope towards the back, and had to tear the whole yard apart to put new drainage pipes through their property.

By the time I arrived, this was all taken care of, and with the beautiful landscaping, nobody would ever have known that they'd had a problem. Ingrid had friends over for a cookie exchange and tea, and before we knew it, Christmas was upon us. Fernand's parents and nephew arrived for New Years, and Ingrid had planned a spectacular Millennium 2000 celebration party. My beautiful daughter, dressed as the fairy godmother, tapped the shoulder of each guest, granting them a wish for a happy New Year.

NEW MILLENIUM

Finally. I am back in my home, thank goodness, and it's freshly painted and revamped. I am so thankful to be back in my familiar surroundings, because my eyes are getting worse, and my back is starting to be painful due to the deterioration from Osteoporosis pressing on my nerves.

So, I will try to relax, and live each day as it comes, as I have so much to be thankful for. In times of trouble, I've found that it's wise to live each day as if it were your last. This attitude kept me going during the war, when we never knew if we would see the next day or not, and yet hoping the next day would bring better times.

As my years are piling up, I realize more and more that my generation is vanishing. So many relatives and friends are already gone. I start to wonder again what is left of you that goes on; what is it that gives you the feeling that you have not lived for nothing?

At last I am ending my written memories. I am glad that I wrote them down, not for myself, but also for my family. Hopefully they will not make the same mistakes I made. Life is a mystery for every living creature on this earth. What is important is that you don't live only for yourself, and to make the best of whatever comes your way.

I hope so much that there won't be any war in the future. We have come a long way already and, who knows, maybe we will achieve building a wonderful existence for everybody. I am so grateful for all the good things I experienced and also for the courage God gave me to make the best of all the problems we had to face.

I will end my writings with a prayer. When I was a little girl, I made up my own prayer which went as follows:

> "Dear God: The person who prays to you is just a little girl who makes mistakes and has to learn still so much. Please forgive me my sins and teach me to become a better person. Thank you so much for everything You gave me. Amen."

That little girl became a sister, a woman, a bride, a mother, and a grandmother. That little girl lived through the end of the Dutch colonial days in Indonesia, the Second World War in Holland, and she came to America to start a new life. When I think back on the life of that little girl, it amazes me that she is now eighty eight years old. In one sense very much the same little girl she always was, and yet in so many ways different. But one thing has remained the same:

I still use the same prayer today that I made up so long ago, only inserting the words "old woman" for the "little girl" part.

MY PHILOSOPHY

As I think back on the accuracy of Mrs. Sullivan's predictions, I wonder what it would have been like to have had her insight from the time I was born. Would it have changed the course of our lives? I doubt it, and if it had, I might have missed some of the wonderful loves of my life in the process.

I do have good insight of my own, and I really know society will try to be at peace in the future. Is it too much to expect that the peoples of the world will not war with each other, but instead work with each other towards solving the unanswered riddles of the universe? I don't think so.

I always wished that my children could remain young and innocent for as long as possible; the years go by so quickly, and the harshness of the world comes soon enough. A happy childhood is so important for a child. In the sixties, crime and drugs weren't a big problem in Sharon, and for this, I was very thankful. Relations with other people are a little trickier, but I believe it is up to us what we make of it. I realize that often there is a good reason why people behave badly, so I would try to break the cycle of unpleasantness from downright mean people by not treating them the same way. With kindness, you can help those people rethink their ways and feel good about yourself at the same time. There is trouble enough in the world, and when you can avoid trouble in your own little circle of life, one can feel that they are doing their part towards peace on the earth.

I see around me so many people, who are good and who try to make life better for everybody. When you try, in your own small circle of existence, to live for others, and try not just to help yourself, but to help others towards a better world, the circles will come together to form a large one that is bound to have an impact on the whole.

One thing I know for sure is that I never would have been able to cope with living my life, if I didn't have faith in God; a God that is called by many other names in other beliefs. The efforts by so many people, all trying to reach a higher level of meaning in their earthly existence, all these efforts can only result in a peaceful world, I am so sure of this.

I have called my writing "Threads" because of the Dutch custom of saving threads from all kinds of clothes and places and times and winding them together in a ball. When you then need a certain thread, you can go the ball and pull out the thread that seems to match the current need. These threads remind me that a life is a ball of threads, a collection of experiences, all interwoven, all related to a specific time and a place.

Every human life is decided by many threads of influence, by many possible paths. Which thread we follow and which one we live, which thread we remember, and which thread pulls us along is not for us alone to decide. Now that I am older I can pull out these threads, untangle them gradually, remember those places and times, and ponder on what each of them has meant to me. Each of these stories I have tried to pass on to my own children and to my granddaughters. In some small way I hope and pray that these stories will help them find their own "niche" in life. I hope it helps them to live at some higher level of existence. If they will learn from my stories how their parents and grandparents coped with their lives maybe that will help them, maybe it will help whoever reads them. I hope so.

My Images of Sanibel Poster

POSTLUDE FOR
JOHANNA CORNELIA BOONSTRA

My mother, Johanna Cornelia Boonstra, continued living in her Sanibel home after returning from the millennium celebration in California with Ingrid and Fernand. She continued to teach art to a few select friends in her studio, overlooking a peaceful pond filled with wildlife, including alligators. Ingrid, my sister, and I visited as often as we could, typically 2 to 3 times per year each. Mother's eyesight seemed to stabilize, the frequent visits to the eye doctor confirmed that her vision was at least not getting worse. But she gave up driving, because she was afraid that she might not see something in the road, and might end up injuring someone. She donated her car to a friend's daughter who was in desperate need, and was happy to be able to do something good for someone.

In August 2004, Mother evacuated to a Fort Myers hotel as Hurricane Charlie approached. She stayed there with a next door neighbor for the better part of 6 weeks as slowly the Sanibel infrastructure recovered. Fortunately her Sanibel home suffered only very minor damage – a credit to the Sanibel building codes. In 2005 she evacuated again for Hurricane Wilma, this time with Sandy, up to Tampa, Florida for a week.

In 2003 and 2004 mother struggled with dizziness and nausea, made many visits to various specialist and doctors in the Fort Myers region. We discovered that she had developed late onset type II diabetes. Managing this disease added another layer of complexity to mother's routine. With the help of three wonderful home health aides, Lavonne Carolyn, and Sandy, mother was able to stay in her home, living still very independently.

Mother had a hip replacement in 2004 just before Christmas, and spent the holiday in the Hospital. Her enthusiasm and positive spirit carried her through rehab and by her Birthday on April 8th, she was walking normally again. She still held art lessons for some good friends, and took great joy in the visits with close Sanibel friends. The fruits of her green thumb were evident throughout the yard, and she took great delight in working with her aides in the house and yard to "complete" her gardening. Often I would call and hear her say one more time that now, finally, the garden was completely finished, only one smaller corner left to neaten up.

Thanksgivings, Ingrid would come with her family, and for Christmas I would come with Regina to spend the holidays with Mom. Sitting on the back sun porch for morning coffee, looking out over the pond early in the morning were special times with my mother. One time she complained that her eyesight seemed to be deteriorating. She said "It's getting so bad; I have a very hard time seeing that osprey at the top of the Norwegian Pine tree over there." I looked at the tops of two Norwegian Pines and saw only branches, unaware of any osprey. No sooner had I said that she had to be making it up, that there was no bird in the tree top, I looked again to see a large bird take off from that very same tree top!

I visited Mother a few days over Thanksgiving in 2005; she had high spirits, but was still struggling to balance out her meals and blood sugar. We enjoyed each other's company, sitting on the sun porch, drinking coffee in the morning as another Sanibel day started. Each time recently that I would leave her, seeing her standing in the driveway and waving, the thought struck me that this might actually be the last time.

Ingrid and I were pleased when Mother agreed to go to California for the Christmas Holidays in December of 2005. She flew first for a weekend to Houston, Texas, where I worked, and enjoyed seeing how I lived there. Mother truly enjoyed her stay in Santa Barbara with Ingrid and her family, she had a wonderful Holiday. On her return flight, this time accompanied by Ingrid, she would stop again in Houston for a few days, and then proceed home to Sanibel.

My Aunt Meta, mother's sister, had passed away on Pearl Harbor Day, December 7, 2005. She had left many family belongings to Mother, and to Ingrid and me. So when Mother returned from Santa Barbara, we took the opportunity to drive to Austin, Texas, where Meta had lived, to spend a day sorting through her house, to help organize Meta's estate. This visit gave my mother closure, but it was difficult for her, bringing up many memories of the war, and of her frequent quarrels with Meta. But mother was in good spirits on the way back to Houston. The next day, I drove Ingrid and Mother to the Houston International Airport, and they flew back to Sanibel. It was to be Mother's last trip.

The trip to California and back had exhausted my Mother, and she slept quite a bit for the entire first day that she was back. When she did rise the following morning, she had a dizzy spell, and fell in the shower, hitting her head and lower back. Ingrid found her sitting on the living room sofa, with a worried look on her face. "I have had a bad fall this morning, and I think this might be it." Ingrid questioned her about what that meant, and Mother answered that she was worried that she might have broken something. Mother walked to the car and Ingrid took her to the Emergency Room at Health Park Hospital. The X-rays showed a badly fracture T-12 vertebra. Mother was admitted to the hospital, given a clamshell cast, and pain killers since the pain had become very intense.

Complications with pneumonia, a blood infection, a urinary tract infection all set in requiring many different drugs and lots of pain medication. After two weeks, Mother was admitted to the Hope Hospice. Three days later, surrounded by her family and some close friends, Johanna Cornelia Boonstra took her last breath and passed on.

Mrs. Sullivan predicted that Mom would not see the actual publishing of her book, but that it would be published posthumously. She encouraged Mom to write it, saying that some good would come of it. In the past ten years, the family has helped Mother with her book, all the while hesitant to actually finish it. Maybe we created a self-fulfilling prophecy out of Mrs. Sullivan's predictions, or maybe it just took us all that long to savor the stories, repeating them over again to get them right in time and place.

So here it is; the collected stories of Johanna Cornelia Leeksma Boonstra, published in her book, Threads. It was Mother's wish that some good would come of this book, and maybe she will be right. I certainly hope so....

Eric F. Boonstra

MOM'S MEMORIAL CELEBRATION OF LIFE: APRIL 8, 2006

DESIDERATA AND HANNY April 8, 2006

Ingrid M. Boonstra-Sarrat

I always knew I was in trouble with my mom when I would ask her opinion about something, and she would ask me sweetly, "Do you want an honest answer or a diplomatic one"? Usually, if you got that question, it meant that she did not really like what you were doing, or how you were doing it! Actually I'm sure some of you have had a similar experience with her. We would surely get a very honest and thoughtful answer, presented in a wise and loving way. And, that's how she lived – every day of her 89 years!

She lived a long and colorful life. When our kids were little, whenever Oma came to visit, they would ask her to tell stories of her many adventures in Indonesia, Holland and America. And I think she delighted in telling them as much as they enjoyed listening! Our kids never tired of the stories, even if they had heard them 20 times before! There were so many lessons and uplifting messages in them; she had so much experience to share.

After many years of this, her grandchildren repeatedly said to her: "Oma, you should write a book." So she finally did! All her stories are in her soon-to-be-published autobiography 'threads'. While reading the book's drafts, it struck me how my mother lived three remarkable lives: in Indonesia, Holland and America. One of the book's recurring themes is that while living in many places, she was still very Dutch, with characteristic stubbornness and determination. After all, the Dutch decided their country was too small and pushed the ocean back with dams!

She just didn't give up! And with a great sense of humor to boot! No matter what the circumstances, she was determined to make the best of things and move on.

Right after mama passed, we held a farewell dinner party. My brother Eric, his wife Regina, my husband Fernand and I, our eldest daughter, Michelle, and my mother's 3 'earth angels' – Lavonnne, Sandy, Carolyn and her husband Andy, gathered at trader's, her favorite restaurant. She always ordered the crab cakes. So, we ordered a plate of them in her honor and passed it around so we could each take a bite. I decided we should each come came up with a word to describe my mother, to everyone's initial horror. This was going to be very difficult, for she was, after all, quite a character, and coming up with just one word seemed next to impossible. But as we began to go around the table, the words started to come easily. In fact, we went around the table twice! It was a good process for us to go through, for we managed to turn a sad occasion into one that provided us with laughter and great memories. Above all, and we felt a deep appreciation for having had her in our lives. (of course, Eric and I wouldn't be here if she hadn't been in our lives!)

Here are some of the words that came up: inspirational, honest, determined, uplifting, sweet, loving, wise, spiritual and Dutch. These words remind me of a poem very dear to me—Desiderata. It starts out: "go placidly among the noise and haste, and remember what peace there may be in silence. As far as possible, be on good terms with all persons." It goes on to say "speak your truth quietly and clearly; and listen to others, even the dull and ignorant, they too have their story." I'm not going to read the whole thing, but it's full of wonderful phrases on how one should try to live life, and

I think a very accurate description of the way in which my mother lived hers.

It is easy to weave our crab cake words with Desideratas' message. Having grown up in the jungles of Indonesia, my mother did not really have any established religion. Yet, she was very spiritual. She had a deep faith that carried her through many difficult times.

She shared the strength of her spirituality; she spread cheerfulness and hope, and where she saw sadness she brought consolation and wisdom. She shared her creative talents with those eager to learn. For all this she was considered a precious "friend" by many.

She was a terrific artist, gardener and sewing arts expert and knowledgeable about so many things... and yet, she was humble and down to earth about it all.

Her generosity, in fact, could be a real problem: if you admired something in her presence, she would want you to have it, and even though you would protest, you would somehow end up with it anyway.

So, more of these words came up at this dinner: creative, sunshine, friend, humble, precious, special; reminding me even more of Desideratas' many words of wisdom. My mother and I often talked about our souls, and how she felt that hers was very old. She had a tremendous talent for living in the moment and appreciating even the most simple things.

But the word that brought a big smile to all our faces was 'nut'! Life with my mother was always an adventure, from as far back as I can remember...some of her stories from Indonesia, in fact, are about her love of animals and nature, and some of the crazy things she did as a result! I think she drove her parents a little crazy... when you read her book, you'll see what I mean!

Anyway, she transferred that kookiness to her family and friends, and she was much loved for it. As kids, she had Eric and I running around with butterfly nets catching butterflies; adopting

all kinds of wild animals that had fallen out of nests, or had somehow found us. We used to have an iguana for which my mother
knit a red sweater. We would take it for walks on the beach – needless to say, it caused quite a stir!

When we were campers at a nature camp, she ordered some
tarantulas from Mexico, which arrived in the mail, so that we could
see them firsthand! Even the mailman couldn't believe it – he was
quite traumatized. We used to go to the Mohawk trail up in the
Berkshires in Massachusetts, and collect all kinds of rocks and
driftwood to bring back to her very beautiful garden – and salamanders too!

One of our favorite crab cake words is intrepid; my mother was
fearless. When Fernand and I were living in Minnesota we had a
bat living in our attic when she came to visit. One day she just went
up there, put on a heavy glove, and grabbed the bat. She then released it outside, but not before showing it to us, declaring that it
was really beautiful!

here on Sanibel, she had a porch full of chameleons that had
become her pets. They would come and eat out of her hand! She
had some iguanas too, but they, well…they escaped! The only creature that she did seem a little wary of were the alligators…

She saw everything with a unique eye…and about being a nut
– well, she would say "I'm a nut. But because I know I'm a nut, I'm
not really a nut'…

Our last crab cake word is grateful. My mother appreciated
even the smallest things and saw beauty in everything: rocks, driftwood, moth cocoons, flowers, frogs, people's smiles, butterflies,
tarantulas, herons, bats, lizards, and twinkling lights. She loved
people and thoroughly enjoyed their company. One of her favorite
activities was drinking coffee on the porch and swapping stories
with friends and family.

Mother spread her gratefulness out to all she touched. I have
her gratefulness now for teaching me about all life's wondrous
treasures, grateful for the life she gave me, grateful for my family,

grateful for her constant love and support over 57 years. And I am hopeful, hopeful that I can pass on her legacy of gratitude, wonder and joy in how I live the rest of my life.

The last words of desiderata are "with all its sham, drudgery, and broken dreams, it is still a beautiful world. Be careful. Strive to be happy." As my mother used to say to me on the phone every whenever we spoke, "Geniet van je leven," enjoy your life. And that's what she taught me to do every day.

Thank you all for coming.

April 8, 2006

Letting Go, Again Eric F. Boonstra

Here we are hello again, we are letting go again, to celebrate a life again, to celebrate Mom's life.

Johanna was a friend to me, Johanna was my Mom to me, Johanna was a friend to you, and you and you.

Fifty four years a Mom to me, the soul mate to her friends was she, a teacher to the young and free, devoted to the core.

"Enjoy your life" she said each night, "grab hold, make something of your life, take this, make something, make it nice, create a thing of beauty.

"There's beauty in this butterfly, beauty in the setting sky and beauty within you or me, there's beauty in us all.

"I can draw this you can too, I can make this so can you, come with me now and yes we two will make a thing of beauty.

"Come look at this, a tiny fish, a seashell fine, a frog shaped dish, this dragonfly come look at its great wings so fine and lacey.

"Come walk with me down memory lane, remember with me all the pain and joy and laughter all the same walk with me through the decades.

"Indonesia's where it started, Mother and Father from Holland parted just after they were married, I was born in old Djakarta.

"Fort de Coq father's assignment, far from home out in the rimboe, I grew up among the natives, speaking just Malayan.

"Eight years later Meta's born, a sister now for me to care for, Mother has her busy schedule, I have a cockatiel, happy in my home – Sumatra.

"Djakarta, Kota Radja, Fort de Coq and Java, Bandoeng, Malang, Magelang Sumatra, Toba Meer, Boeloe Blang Ara, places where I prospered, I had to let them go.

"Back to Holland, back to family, now for me a foreign country, snow and ice, and grandparents, no longer in the army, father's work on wharves is offered, his army let him go.

"Bloemendal, and Harlem, Amersfoort and Arnhem, bicycling through snow and ice, the train to Amsterdam, and then Germans came.

"We had no food, had no wood, we feared the Germans, feared their mood, feared the bombings, feared the night, we feared all days and nights.

"Five years long, then, joyously, the war was over, hunger gone, with Bram my lover, start a new life, we'll start over, sweet Ingrid born in Delft.

"America, a job comes knocking, Bram and I start talking, of leaving Holland, and of walking down a new road, in a new land.

"We leave for Boston, God, its lonely, Americans brash, if only, I could go back to family friends and home again, Oh I'd be so grateful, so hard to let that go.

"Eric's born; a son, he's ugly, but kind of cute and kind of cuddly, moving out to Sharon smugly, its looking like we're staying.

"We rent a house, unfriendly neighbors, save our money, simple pleasures, loving children, walks in the woods, the Moose Hill Sanctuary.

"Weekends to the Berkshires, picking all the blueberries, salamanders, Whitcomb Summit, Falls by the Tannery, North Pond picnics; warm familiar memories.

"Ingrid and Eric, growing faster, amid the joys the tears the laughter, my mother dies and one year later, a broken man, God also takes my father.

"Art classes, down in our basement, the students love my special treatment, colors, charcoal, aquarelles, and in secret - they love my accent.

"College years, Vermont ski trips, getting older, painting bolder, hoping one day to leave the snow and ice and cold behind.

"'Florida's warm,' some friends have told me, trees and birds and beaches call me, plan to move one day to lovely Sanibel the island.

"The dream comes true when Bram retires, moving south this all requires changing, packing, selling, inquiries and letting go, again.

"The weather's hot like Indonesia, flowers grow like in Djakarta, in the backyard pick bananas, reminds me of my true home – Sumatra.

"We travel north, visit our children, once each year, then back in winter, Christmas eve on clean white beaches, singing ancient carols.

"Once more we travel with some Dutchman to Djakarta, to those places long let go; some 45 years since I walked in Magelang.

"I've let it go, its gone my childhood, gone the homes of Kota Radja, gone my friends, Baboe, my parents, all lives on now only, daily in my heart.

"Sanibel is home now, in my garden, warmth and family, we go north to see our, children's children, once or twice each year.

"Bram's heart is failing, operation, convalescence, home care failing too, it's time for Bram to move to Shell Point nursing care.

"Towards the end we talked, I told him, we'll be fine, it's time, your time to go, I held him, told him one more time I loved him, and then I let him go.

"I wore his ring each day thereafter, life went on, and each day laughter came back through my friends and family, I was at peace again.

"Art and beauty, friends in classes, we can draw things, we share stories, come and visit, have some rum cake, we'll share in our memories.

"Each day struggling, body aging, no more driving, careful eating, aides are helping me to stay in balance, it's all so complicated.

"One last fling, one last adventure, one trip more to California, one more Christmas with my children. Oh I loved this time.

"My book it's done it has my memories, all my tales and all my stories, and now at last my time has come, one last time, let go." And that's my Mother's story.

And now we must let go, the body, not the spirit, not the memory, not the great times with our lady, these we won't let go.

"Enjoy your life," she said each night, "grab hold, make something of your life, take this, make something, make it nice, create a thing of beauty."

Happy Birthday Mom!

ACKNOWLEDGMENT

For all the help typing and coordinating, discussing and remembering, editing, reading and re-reading, I would like to thank the following people.

Lore Katzenberger
Jack Ewing
Linda Hammens
Meta Leeksma Vreugde
Ingrid Boonstra Sarrat
Eric Boonstra

FOREFATHERS TABLE

Family Tree of Johanna Cornelia Leeksma Boonstra

Early Family History: (by Medi Bartelds-Kooreman)

Jiles Jariss Cooremans	(5 children)	1607 – ????
Pieter Jilles Cooremans	(? Children)	1627 – ????
Jilles Kooreman	(? children)	1660 – ????
Pieter Gillisse Kooreman	(5 children)	1696 – ????
Johannes Piterse Kooreman	(4 children)	1729 – ????
Jilles Johannes Kooreman	(8 children)	1768 – ????

Great-Great Grandparents:

a. Johannes Kooreman	(9 children)	1788 – ????
b. Maria van Espel (1st Wife)	(6 children)	????
c. Naaltje Bakker (2nd wife, m.1788, 6 children)		????

Great Grand Parents:

a. Jilles Kooreman	(6 children)	1830 – 1908
b. Cornelia van den Schijs (m.1851)		1829 – 1866

Maternal Grandparents:

a. Johannes (Leo) Kooreman	1858-1935
b. Cornelia van Rees	1854-1927

One son from earlier marriage: Wife died at childbirth

1. Jilles   18??- 1938
   Became an Engineer, much liked by family
   Two daughters and two sons from second marriage:

2. Cornelia Johanna   1889- 1962
   Mother of Johanna Cornelia Leeksma Boonstra
   Mother of Meta Louise Leeksma-Vreugde

3. Ploon   1890- 1974
   Married Max Bartelds: Lived for 20 years in Indonesia
   with another woman, died in ~ 1938
   Three daughters by Ploon:

Hetty	1917 – present
Lives in New Zealand	
Madelaine	1919 – 2002
Frans	1924 – 1996

4. Jaap: Married his cousin, Cornelia Kooreman
   Two Children:
   a.   Leo Kooreman
   b.   Elisabeth Kooreman

5. Johan: No children

Parents:

a. Koen Willem Karel Leeksma	1891-1963
b. Cornelia Johanna Kooreman-van Rees	1889-1962

Two Daughters:

Johanna Cornelia Leeksma – Boonstra:	1916 – 2006
Meta Louise Leeksma – Vreugde:	1924 – 2005

Paternal Grandparents:

a. Tine de Boer   1850 – 1946
b. Willem Leeksma   1851 – 1927
    Three children:
    1. Louise Leeksma   18?? – 1942
        Married cousin Bert van den As
        As had 4 children from a previous marriage:
        a. Annie – 5 children, Canada
        b. Aidee – adopted 2 children
        c. Jaap – Pilot, shot down by Germans
        d. Wim – died in German concentration camp
        Bert and Louise had a deformed child named
        e. Koenrad, who died in a swing set accident.
    2. Henk Leeksma
        Married Annie
        Two children:
        a. Henk
        b. Willy
    3. Koen Willen Leeksma   1891 – 1963
        Married Cornelia Johanna Kooreman   1889 – 1962
        Two daughters
        a. Johanna Cornelius   1916 – 2006
        b. Meta Louise   1923 – 2005

ISBN 141206929-7